Covering McKellen

An Understudy's Tale

by David Weston

Covering McKellen

An Understudy's Tale

by David Weston

RICKSHAW
PUBLISHING

A Rickshaw paperback
www.rickshawpublishing.co.uk

Published in Great Britain in 2011 by Rickshaw Publishing Ltd,
102 Fulham Palace Road, London W6 9PL

Copyright © David Weston 2011

The right of David Weston to be identified as the author of this
work has been asserted by him in accordance with the
Copyright, Designs and Patents Act 1988

A CIP catalogue record for this book is available from the British
Library

ISBN 978–0–9565368–0–8

*All events are presented in good faith as observed by the author at the
time. All opinions expressed are those of the author alone*

Original cover photo by Ben Delfont
Cover design by Michic

Printed and bound in Great Britain for Rickshaw Publishing Ltd
by CPI Group (UK) Ltd, Croydon, CR0 4YY

RICKSHAW
PUBLISHING

To all actors, past, present and future
Good, bad and ugly
Not forgetting the understudies
They also serve who only stand and wait

"What do you want to be when you're a grown-up?"
"An actor."
"You can't be both."

Preface

Why should anyone be interested in the meanderings of a relatively unknown old actor, when so many memoirs and biographies of the famous go unread?

Throughout 2007, I was part of a company of extraordinary characters in Shakespeare's greatest play, on an incredible journey that took our bodies around the world and our emotions even further. To add flavour to the mix, we threw in one of Chekhov's greatest plays as well. In Shakespeare's day, strolling players were treated as rogues and vagabonds; in some places we discovered that things have not changed too much, whilst in others we were cosseted like Lords of the Earth.

At the beginning of the year an old friend, Davina Belling suggested that I keep a diary; it seemed like a good idea at the time and, being an increasingly curmudgeonly old codger, I have left nothing out. This is my view, as seen from the trenches and I have attempted to be completely frank and honest. I have set down my feelings and observations day by day and have not changed them with hindsight when events have proved me wrong, therefore my opinions of the talents and characters of the people I meet and work with are not necessarily my final judgement. In many cases my personal opinions are contrary to those of leading dramatic critics and if they are too congenial in January they may well be too acerbic by December.

There are, as always, two sides to every story and I have only set down mine. I have yet to discover the moral but, as in *King Lear,* the young seem to turn against the old. Authority and wisdom are questioned whilst the world applauds. We had fun, shed tears; there was drama aplenty offstage as well as on. In fact, we behaved as actors have always behaved, since Shakespeare's pen first set it down.

The Players

Cast

Sir Ian McKellen	*King Lear / Sorin*
Frances Barber	*Goneril / Arkadina*
Romola Garai	*Cordelia / Nina*
William Gaunt	*Gloucester / Sorin*
Monica Dolan	*Regan / Masha*
Sylvester McCoy	*Lear's Fool*
Jonathan Hyde	*Kent / Dorn*
Guy Williams	*Cornwall / Shamrayev*
Melanie Jessop	*Gloucester's Servant / Polina*
Ben Meyjes	*Edgar / Medvedenko*
Seymour Matthews	*Curan / House Servant*
Julian Harries	*Albany / Estate Worker*
Gerald Kyd	*Soldier / Trigorin*
Ben Addis	*King of France / House Servant*
Peter Hinton	*Duke of Burgundy / Yakov*
David Weston	*Gentleman / Butler*
Richard Goulding	*Messenger / Konstantin*
Philip Winchester	*Edmund / Estate Worker*
John Heffernan	*Oswald / Estate Worker*
Zoë Boyle	*Lady-in-Waiting / Arkadina's Maid*
Adam Booth	*Servant / Estate Worker*
Russell Byrne	*Doctor / House Servant*
Naomi Capron	*Maid / Cook*

Artistic Staff

Sir Trevor Nunn	*Director*
Gemma Fairlie	*Assistant Director*
Christopher Oram	*Designer*
Neil Austin	*Lighting Designer*
Steven Edis	*Composer*
Fergus O'Hare	*Sound Designer*
Malcolm Ranson	*Fights Coordinator*
Morgan Large	*Associate Designer*
Lyn Darnley	*Voice Coach*
Simon Ash	*Production Manager*
Richard Clayton	*Company Manager*
Ben Delfont	*Stage Manager*
Klare Roger	*Deputy Stage Manager*
Harry Niland	*Assistant Stage Manager*
Rhiannon Harper	*Assistant Stage Manager*
Rachel Seal	*Wigs & Make-Up*
Claire-Louise Hardie	*Wardrobe*
Craig Almond	*Senior Props Technician*

Musicians

Adam Cross	*Clarinet / Saxophone*
Steve Walton	*Trumpet / Flugelhorn / Keyboard*
John Gibson	*Percussion / Keyboard*
Jeff Moore	*Keyboard / Violin / Accordion*

London, 2007

Monday January 1ˢᵗ

Today I start a new year, knowing that I'll be in permanent employment for the entire 12 months – a gratifying and unusual prospect for an actor (particularly one of my age). Tomorrow I begin rehearsing Shakespeare's *King Lear*, directed by Sir Trevor Nunn and starring Sir Ian McKellen which, after a season at Stratford along with Chekhov's *The Seagull*, will embark on a world tour to places my wife, Dora, and I have always intended to visit but never got around to. Now we'll both go for free and on top of that I'll be getting paid. We are both very excited, even though my part is small. Apart from major films, jobs don't come much more prestigious than this: Shakespeare's greatest play, directed by the most experienced and acclaimed director in the land, starring one of our finest actors at the very peak of his powers.

Speak to my old RADA chum, Bill Gaunt, who is playing Gloucester (I must admit I would have loved to be playing that part myself. Still, I'm glad he's in the play). He fills me in on some of the other cast members. I was at Chichester with Frances Barber, who is giving her Goneril – things are always lively whenever she's around. I don't think I know anyone else, although I admire the work of Jonathan Hyde (a very smooth actor who had a very good part in the film *Titanic*), and the lovely young Romola Garai, who I first saw in the film *I Capture the Castle* and was immediately convinced would be a star. And, of course, there's Sylvester McCoy of *Dr Who*.

Practically the first thing an actor thinks about once he's got a job outside London is his 'digs'. On my previous sojourns with the RSC I have stayed in the countryside outside Stratford but as the congestion charge has forced us to one car which will remain with Dora in London, this time I've decided to live near the theatre in official RSC-owned accommodation. I know the best locations will go first, so I ring Suzanne Harris, the head of the property department and leave a message on her answer phone, requesting a one bedroom flat with river view.

Have tickets to see Judi Dench in *Merry Wives* musical at Stratford tonight but decide not to go so that I will be fresh for tomorrow. I think Dora is disappointed and I feel a bit guilty. Later read in the *Daily Mail* that Sir Ian has attended a very glamorous New Year's Eve party in Cape Town, wearing a pair of extremely low-cut jeans. How fresh will he be I wonder? Or, indeed, how fresh was he?

We take a New Year's Day walk along the King's Road and then watch Trevor Nunn's Glyndebourne production of *Porgy and Bess* on Sky. I realise how much was missing from his new version at the Savoy. Afterwards, we watch one of the films I have been sent to judge for BAFTA: *Snow Cake* – surprisingly good. Alan Rickman, who is not a particular favourite of mine, (I sometimes think he looks as if he has a very unpleasant smell under his nose and cannot understand why some women go crazy about him) is excellent, as is Sigourney Weaver. My voting preferences have already gone in but if I have chance I will vote for it in the second round.

Tuesday January 2nd

It was 40 years ago to the day that I began my first Stratford Season – playing Benvolio to Sir Ian Holm's Romeo. Now I am playing the Gentleman and understudying Sir Ian McKellen as Lear. I'm 68; like every actor, even the young ones, I wonder if this will be my last job.

Go to Clapham on the 137 bus. The first day of a new production is always the best time. Richard Burton once said, when asked by a presumptuous young female interviewer why he made so many bad films, "It's good to have somewhere to go in the morning." The bus passes smart streets which were shabby when I was a boy. Get off and walk along Clapham High Street. It's full of restaurants of every ethnic variety but not one that really appeals – there's something sad and tacky about most of them. I feel strangely at home in this part of the capital. I am, after all, a 'Sarf' London boy, from a long-defunct fish and chip shop in the middle of Brixton Market.

Enter the depressing red brick building at the far end of the High Street, where the RSC has been rehearsing for the past 20 years or so. It was originally a Methodist Church, built in 1907 (I know this because the date is on the top), which the RSC converted into three floors of rehearsal rooms. It still has the air of charity and good works about it. It is not the most convenient place to get to, especially when the RSC were based at the Barbican on the other side of London. I suppose it must have been cheap.

The RSC head, Michael Boyd, is rehearsing *Richard III* on the ground floor. Pass some of his actors looking tired and ashen. The poor devils are working their way through all Shakespeare's history plays – they've been at it a year and have another year and a half to go.

A sign reads '*Lear Coffee Meet and Greet on Top Floor*'. Climb three flights of stairs, passing countless old RSC posters (but not one of any production I've been in) to large, empty room in need of a fresh coat of paint in the middle of which tables are stacked with unappetising croissants and waffles. Old sound panels hang from the ceiling – not much glamour here, but when were rehearsal rooms ever glamorous?

I've always had a phobia of being late and am one of the first to arrive. I nibble on a flaky croissant as the others begin to drift in. It's a bit like the first day at school for the younger ones. I remember when I was nervous, scared of being found wanting.

Most of them have never worked with Trevor or even been a member of the RSC. Not surprisingly I feel completely at ease. This is my seventh production with Trevor; he's about the only director that still employs me – nearly all the others I've worked with are dead. I've also been in the play four times, playing Albany to Sir Anthony Quayle, Burgundy to Sir Michael Hordern on TV, Kent to James Bolam at the Young Vic and Edgar at Westcliffe in the distant days of fortnightly rep – though, rather worryingly, I don't seem to recall the Gentleman doing very much in any of them.

At last, a familiar face comes in: Naomi Capron, who was in Trevor's *Richard II* with me last year at the Old Vic, understudying the Duchess of York. She's very keen. I and the other two cynical old occupants of my dressing room used to listen to her staunchly doing her vocal warm-ups every night without fail over the Tannoy even though she didn't have a single line. Nevertheless she's a good egg, a capable actress, and I like her. Glad to see Seymour Matthews as well, who will be playing the small part of Curan and understudy Bill as Gloucester. The only time I've ever worked with him was in my first season at the RSC in 1967. Seymour is a survivor like me – most of the young actors of that season are no longer in the business, although a few of them; such as Sir Ben Kingsley, Patrick Stewart and Dame Helen Mirren have gone on to be megastars.

Sylvester McCoy comes up and is very friendly – I like him at once. He tells me he only got the Fool because he met Trevor for the first time in a dressing room last week, and suggested himself for the part. I always admire honest humility in an actor; so many put on airs and graces, trying to give the impression that they are doing the world a favour by accepting a part. Jonathan Hyde, who is playing Kent, introduces himself. Discover we have a mutual friend in the charming actor, Rupert Fraser. The Gentleman has two nice little scenes with Kent – we both hope they will not be cut. There is a loud shriek as Frances Barber makes her entrance, looking very glamorous in a cloth cap. We kiss like the 'luvvies' I suppose we are. I ask her what she is doing playing Goneril to Sir Ian McKellen when she is such a bosom pal of Sir Derek Jacobi. She laughs and says that Derek is planning to give his Lear in the future, but she has come with his full permission. Derek and Ian have had almost parallel careers; from student productions at Cambridge and the early days of Laurence Olivier's National Theatre, they went on to be the most acclaimed Hamlets and Richard IIs of their generation, and were both knighted within a few years of each other: Ian in 1991 and Derek in 1994. It is only in the last few years that Ian has enjoyed his worldwide fame, thanks largely to films like the *X-Men* and *Lord of the Rings*.

Trevor enters wearing, as ever, a faded blue denim shirt, old trainers and jeans. He gives me his trademark hug, or 'Trev', as it is commonly called, and I thank him for thinking of me. He says how happy he is I'm able to do it. I first met him in Stratford in 1967 – he was then the bright young lad that Peter Hall had just discovered in the nearby theatre at Coventry. I've always regretted that I never worked with him then, but we often sat around a table sipping half pints in that perennial Stratford staple, the "Dirty Duck".

Bill Gaunt arrives late and anxious, having been stuck on the tube. Every actor has someone whom he blames for getting the parts he considers he should have played. Julian Fellowes once told me he firmly believed that Simon Callow had stolen his career. That is, of course, before Julian won his Oscar for writing *Gosford Park.* In my case it was Bill, as far as television was concerned. People always said we looked alike and should play brothers – and I remember a small triumph in the very distant past, when one of his girlfriends told me she thought I was better-looking. But rivalry, together with so many things, diminishes with age. I suddenly see that McKellen has slipped into the room. He looks very tired. He also hugs me and says how pleased he is I am in the company. Michael Boyd then comes up from his rehearsal below and gives a long talk standing on chair. He tells us the *Complete Works* has been a huge success and that *Lear* is expected to be the triumphant climax. Boyd Finishes at last and I can see that Trevor is itching to start, but first calls for a pee break. Stand next to him in urinal. Our ageing bladders seem to work at the same time – we often used to meet in similar circumstances at the Old Vic.

Back in the rehearsal room Trevor begins by talking about his early days with the RSC. Peter Hall, the veritable founder of the RSC, chose Trevor to be his successor when Trevor was only 28. He was a boy wonder; some called him the fifth Beatle. Throughout the late sixties and seventies, the RSC enjoyed its greatest days under the joint stewardship of Trevor and Terry Hands. Trevor tells us how he instigated doing small productions at the Donmar Warehouse (which he discovered) and the move into the Barbican. Does Trevor, like Lear, regret having given up his kingdom? I suppose many of these young actors have no idea what he has achieved. He and Ian have worked together since their student days at Cambridge and Trevor has directed Ian in two of his most acclaimed Shakespearean roles: Macbeth and Iago.

Trevor echoes my own thoughts, saying that *Lear* is the greatest play by the world's greatest playwright and we are performing it for the Royal Shakespeare Company, which has reclaimed its position as the premier Shakespeare-acting company in the world. No small task. We have a great challenge and we will become a true ensemble: everyone dependent on and supporting each other. We will never stop discovering things in these plays – that is the excitement of playing Shakespeare and if we are very lucky there may be one occasion, one night, when we will come close to getting it right. He considers Chekhov second greatest after Shakespeare. I've heard a rumour that he is working on his own version of *The Seagull*. With the responsibility of Lear on my shoulders, I won't be expected to understudy anyone in it. Hopefully, I will have those evenings off.

Go for a quiet lunch to read football in *The Times*. As I walk back to rehearsal rooms I pass the younger members of the company in various restaurants – getting to know each other. How many affairs will blossom and wither over the course of the year? Or have things really quietened down since the sixties? Does Hamlet sleep with Ophelia? Only in the provinces. Having an affair with one's leading lady used to be a sort of '*droit de seigneur*'. A close friend of mine once played Romeo in Sunderland and was mortified when his Juliet decided to sleep with Mercutio instead of him.

Ben Delfont, the brisk and businesslike stage manager, gives us a long talk on RSC procedure. I wonder if he's related to Bernard Delfont and is therefore a member of the illustrious Grade family. He warns us that if we have any criminal record we must inform him as soon as possible, as it is very difficult to get working visas in U.S. Should I mention the six speeding points on my licence? We are informed that there will be warm-ups every morning at 9.45. I catch Bill Gaunt's eye. As elderly actors, we both studiously avoided them when we were at the National. We are given masses of forms to fill in. It is all very pc and 'Health and Safety'. Can you push and pull? Can you kneel? Do you have difficulty standing or sitting for a long time? Why become an actor if you do? I have a word with Richard Clayton, the company manager, and tell him I will be bringing my wife on the foreign stages of the tour. He says it will be no problem; I will only have to pay for her air fares, which will be at the reduced company rate, and there will be no extra charge for accommodation. Several of the others are bringing partners for some parts of the tour.

All in all, it is a very pleasant and satisfying first day. Watch *Pan's Labyrinth* with Dora – too violent and the special effects seem nauseating. Turn off half way through. Switch to Sky Sports and find that my team, Chelsea, whom I have followed religiously since 1957, have only managed a draw against Aston Villa. The complete satisfaction of the day disappears rather abruptly.

Wednesday January 3rd

Today the tables form a large square. We sit around and are given a list of extracts, from early drama through to Shakespeare. Trevor does this to show how Shakespeare's verse evolved – it is also a chance for all members of the company, even the ones with hardly anything to say, to read aloud and gain confidence. We start with the mediaeval *Noah Play* and, naturally, Ian reads God.

Trevor is in top form and begins to talk about the verse – as in all his direction he keeps it simple and easy to understand, unlike some others I could mention. Bill Gaunt, a Yorkshireman, reads a speech in dialect from the Shepherd's play in the *Wakefield Cycle*. Then we move on to *Gorboduc* – the earliest Elizabethan play. American students would pay a fortune for one morning with Trevor. He explains the use of blank verse – the iambic pentameter which Marlowe invented, five beats to the line: the natural beat of the human heart, demonstrating how Marlowe uses verse to express extremely complex ideas. We finally arrive at Shakespeare. Trevor asks Seymour Matthews and me to read speeches from the opening scene from *Henry VI Part One*, which he thinks is the first stuff Shakespeare ever wrote. We go through all three parts of *Henry VI*. Trevor points out examples of antithesis: on one hand this, on the other hand that – Shakespeare was fascinated by opposites. Metaphors, similes – all the while Trevor continues to make it simple to comprehend. I am careful not to make too many comments – some directors don't like an actor to know too much.

I notice that there seems to be something going on between Trevor and Ian. Trevor, like me, is a Stratfordian; he firmly believes that Shakespeare wrote the plays, but he appears to hint that Ian is a follower of the heresy that Edward de Vere, Earl of Oxford, was the author. I've read that Sir Derek Jacobi, Kenneth Branagh, Mark Rylance, and even my old friend Michael York, who I always thought was a sensible chap, are supposed to hold this view. Ian looks bemused. I think in this instance Trevor has got him confused with Sir Derek.

Getting to know more of the company. Some of the younger ones; Ben Addis, John Heffernan (who looks a bit like Scooby-Doo's pal Shaggy), Peter Hinton and Ben Meyjes read very well. I cannot help but feel a bit sorry for them; old actors are always nostalgic and our lot has never been easy, but I really believe it was better in the sixties. We still had repertory theatres all over the country and although some of them were pretty tatty, nearly all the people who left RADA with me ended up getting some sort of job. Plus without the challenge of soaps and reality TV, there was far more opportunity for theatre actors to get involved in TV.

Back in the urinals again, Trevor surprises me by stating that Sir Walter Raleigh was executed by Queen Elizabeth. He doesn't seem to believe me when I tell him that Raleigh outlived Shakespeare by several years. Don't know if it's wise to push the argument.

Have lunch with Bill in a nearby greasy spoon under a railway arch. We decide to conserve our energy and not go to the warm-ups. We reflect on our long careers. Bill remembers the first time he was in the West End: a four-handed comedy on Shaftesbury Avenue. He came out of the tube at Piccadilly and looked up, expecting to see his name in lights for the first time. He saw: Amanda Grinling, Barbara Murray, Ronald Lewis and William Gunt. For a terrible moment he thought the 'G' was a 'C'. He stormed into the theatre and demanded that his name should be spelled correctly. He was told they had run out of 'A's, and he would have to wait until the electrician could find another. So for an entire week, 'Gunt' shone out on Shaftesbury

Avenue.

My friend, the actor and director Christopher Luscombe rings. He went to see *Merry Wives* on Monday and thought it was dreadful. I no longer feel guilty.

Thursday January 4th

Give Trevor some old notes I made on Raleigh when I was contemplating devising a one-man show based on him. Trevor takes it up as a gag that I mistakenly believe Raleigh wrote Shakespeare. I play along. Trevor continues his lucid explanation of Shakespeare's use of verse. He believes there are no strict rules as his style is constantly changing. So very unlike the verse sessions we had with John Barton and Peter Hall forty years ago. Back then, they believed that the end of every line of verse should be marked by a slight pause or stress. Trevor rightly says to follow the sense and the verse takes care of itself. He gives us many examples how Shakespeare uses the verse to show characterisation.

Some leading actors worry about their understudies watching them – I've heard the renowned director, Katie Mitchell, won't even allow understudies into rehearsals as she feels they break up the atmosphere. How on earth can the poor buggers be expected to learn how to do it if they can't even watch? Decide to tell Ian that I have no great desire to play Lear – am more than happy with what I've got. Do I really mean it? I think I do: for the moment. Although we've been acquainted for more than 30 years, I find I like Ian much more than I thought I would. I've only acted with him once on radio around 1970, when I played Benvolio (again) to his Romeo. I was stuck with Benvolio for quite a time. I even dubbed him in Zefferelli's film. Ian's voice was also tested, but for some reason Zefferelli chose mine. Must be the only time I got a job ahead of McKellen:

For never was a story of more woe,

Whatever happened to Benvolio?

Ian has a very dry sense of humour and genuinely listens and seems interested in what you say. He puts a sympathetic hand on my shoulder and tells me that he will not be off. I remember Derek Jacobi saying the same thing at Chichester in 1995 and then having appendicitis on the opening night. Decide to start learning Lear as soon as possible.

I have no illusions about being an understudy. Over the years I've covered some of the finest actors in England; Derek Jacobi, Alan Bates, Ian Richardson, Roger Allam, Corin Redgrave, Frank Finlay, Denis Quilley, Michael Bryant and Alec McCowen, and it's a thankless task. Christopher Robbie understudied Robert Stephens as Lear at Stratford in 1993. A few days before the first preview, Stephens had to go into hospital. Robbie knew the part and played it terribly well, with hardly any rehearsal, for about a week until Stephens recovered. No performances were cancelled. Christopher saved the RSC thousands of pounds. When the production reached the Barbican the following year Stephens was ill again and Christopher played the last two months of the run. A couple of years later, when his agent put him up for a line of parts at the RSC, a new casting director was in place and asked to be sent his CV – he'd never even heard of him! I prefer to say I'm 'covering', as it somehow sounds less subservient. It's not so bad when you are playing a part in the production, no matter how small you are part of the team, but being a so-called 'walking understudy', doing nothing but sit in the dressing room all evening is soul destroying. (How did the term 'walking' understudy come about? Maybe in the days of the strolling players there was only so much room in the cart, and the unfortunate understudies had to walk behind it.)

I will enjoy learning and rehearsing Lear with Gemma, the pretty assistant director, but I'm there as a very distant long stop, that's all. Can you imagine the groans of disappointment from the Gandalf fans in New Zealand if it were announced the old wizard wouldn't be appearing?

Another good day. Tomorrow Trevor will give us our scripts with his cuts. How many of the Gentleman's 87 lines will be left? Watch *Flag of our Fathers* with Dora. Surprised to discover that it is actually a very good film. Vote for second round of BAFTA awards. *Snow Cake* didn't get through.

Friday January 5th

Pick up discarded copy of *Independent* on the bus. *Lear* is listed as one of the things to see in 2007. Inside, Peter Taylor says he hopes that Trevor and Ian: *'will disprove his theory that university-trained intellects are at a disadvantage when playing this hero who rarely involves his brain in his gut reactions.'* It seems as if he has decided on his review already. It's not true of course; I have always found Trevor to be the simplest of directors – he only strives to tell the truth and make sense.

Before Trevor hands out his scripts, he explains that there are two distinct versions of *King Lear*: the Quarto, published in 1608, and the Folio, the official version published in 1623 – eight years after Shakespeare's death. There are approximately 300 lines in the Quarto that are not in the Folio and about 100 in the Folio that are not in the Quarto. He has mingled the two to make the plot easier to follow. He hands out the scripts and I am very relieved to see that the Gentleman's two scenes with Kent are still in. We spend the rest of the day reading and pondering over the text of the first three scenes, silently and dutifully, like well-behaved children at school. I have to say I'm surprised at the youth and relative lack of experience in the company. Apart from Ian, only Bill, me, Seymour, and Naomi have worked with Trevor before. At pee break, I tell Trevor I have never seen him in such fine form now he has got rid of the responsibilities of running the National and dealing with Kevin Spacey at the Old Vic. He laughs.

Ian is looking more like Lear every day as his beard grows. I am very surprised to learn he is addicted to watching *Celebrity Big Brother*. He has quickly formed a bond with his leading lady, Frances Barber. I am already quite fond of several of the young actors; such as Ben Addis, a Welshman with a face like a young eagle, John Heffernan, who looks more like Shaggy each day, and Richard Goulding, a public-school type, Oxford graduate and headmaster's son. They seem quite impressed that I have lasted in the business so long – I'm often impressed myself. I look back on so many companies that I've been in, full of bright young actors and actresses, and wonder what has happened to them? Most of them must have left the profession and, hopefully, are happy in secure and well-paid jobs. I've often thought that perhaps I should have got out, but then, apart from teaching, what else could I do? I have no head for business and am useless with my hands. Besides, I still love it. I love it even more when we're given the schedule and dates of the tour abroad: Singapore – Melbourne – Wellington – Auckland – New York – Minneapolis – L.A.!

Watch DVD of Royal Ballet's *Romeo and Juliet* with Dora. Her friend Wayne Eagling, who is now artistic director of the ENB, is wonderful as Romeo. I think it works better as a ballet; notwithstanding the loss of Shakespeare's poetry. Prokofiev's music, the superb grace of the dancers – more dedicated and skilful than mere actors – and the sheer spectacle make it so exciting and terribly moving.

Speak to David Warner on phone. A couple of years ago at Chichester he was the best Lear I've yet seen. He wants to know how things are going as he quite naturally considers Lear to still be his part. The irony is that he is about to play my favourite part, Falstaff, at Stratford; I tell him to put on some weight. He is his normal anxious, uncertain self – he hasn't changed since RADA.

Monday January 8th

Get up early to go to the dentist before rehearsals. I have a gap in my lower front teeth that needs a bridge. Use my senior citizen's Oyster card to get through the barrier at Victoria – am perturbed when the barrier won't open at Oxford Circus. The ticket collector accuses me of jumping over the barrier. I ask him if I look as if I could jump over anything. He has no sense of humour and refuses to believe that the barrier at Victoria would have opened for a senior citizen before 9.00 a.m. I eventually have to pay the maximum fare of £4. Not a good start to the week. With dentist for one hour but still manage to get to Clapham by 10.30.

An uneventful day. We continue reading and discussing the text. Ian already has the voice and characterisation. Some of the cast are very uncertain by comparison. Trevor will have to do a lot of work on the American, Philip Winchester, whom he has cast in the showy role of Edmund, and Sylvester McCoy, who has not had much experience of playing Shakespeare and has not been with us since the first day. Sylvester is still in demand for being *Dr Who* all those years ago, and has been doing a pantomime in Woking with matinees every day. He has finished the engagement and is now with us full time. Ian queries whether 'Your Grace' is a lower term of address than 'Your Highness'. Even Trevor doesn't seem to know. Later I phone the one person who certainly would. Julian Fellowes is delighted to tell me there was no distinction in Tudor times; Henry VIII was often referred to as 'Your Grace', but nowadays it refers only to a Duke. I'm sure this piece of information will prove vital to the production.

Starting to learn Lear. Nearly know the first scene.

Watch *The Prestige* with Dora – don't really understand it. Like Christian Bale though – reminds me of Frank Lampard.

Tuesday January 9th

Have to go in early at 9.45 for voice warm-up. Can't really get out of it as Ian and Bill are called as well. Ian would go in any case – he still goes in for all sorts of voice and movement classes. We have been informed that movement classes are voluntary, but as far as I can see there is only one day a week when they do movement without voice so we will have to go in early every day, even if we are not called to rehearse. Bill and I decide to get our agents involved and let them earn a little of the 12.5% they will get from us for doing nothing throughout the coming year. Although Ian and many other actors swear by them, I've always found voice exercises tiresome. At least I like Lynn Darnley, the chirpy little South African voice coach, she's much less precious than some I've suffered under. I've always had a strong voice – perhaps it's the only asset I have left – and the one thing I don't need is voice production. We do face-relaxing exercises and I struggle to prevent my top dental plate falling out.

Another day around the tables. Philip Winchester, the young American playing Edmund, doesn't seem to have read the text before. He stumbles over certain words. Hopefully he's one of those actors who are just bad readers but will be brilliant in performance. He must be good as he's played major roles in several action films, such as *Thunderbirds* and *Flyboys*. I'm not entirely convinced by his profile, but perhaps the camera loves him. In contrast Ben Meyjes, who plays Edgar, reads well; even making some sense of the Mad Tom scenes, which I know from personal experience to be bloody difficult. Playing a madman is hard enough, but playing a man pretending to be mad is even harder, especially if you're only wearing a haystack and are very concerned about showing your arse, as I was when I attempted the role at Westcliffe. It was in the days before *Oh! Calcutta!* and nudity on stage was practically unknown, especially in the provinces. Nowadays it is commonplace and Trevor and Ian have decided that Lear will literally follow the meaning of 'unaccommodated man' and strip naked in the storm. Ian Holm did it at the National and so did David Warner at Chichester.

David, I remember, was remarkably well-endowed. I suppose I'll have to show my all in the understudy rehearsals – but they can't expect that much from an old man.

When we get to the blinding of Gloucester, we pause to discuss how it might be done. Guy Williams, a tall, balding, roguish Kenyan, who is playing Cornwall, casually announces that he spent the weekend on a farm experimenting, and found that sheep's eyes were very hard to get out. There is a shocked silence. I am sitting next to him and edge my chair away. He senses our disquiet and adds, "It was a dead sheep." Trevor, perhaps suspecting that his instinct in casting was more accurate than he'd imagined, says he is very relieved for the sheep.

We have been sitting a long time now and Frances Barber looks as if she is beginning to wilt. We still have ten pages of the play unread, which we will do in the morning, and then Trevor will begin blocking: giving us our positions and moves. Ben Delfont, our efficient stage manager, tells me that he is indeed an offspring of the Grade family – I like him.

At the end of rehearsal, Russell Byrne, who plays the small part of the Doctor and looks a bit like Danny Kaye with muscles, announces that it is his birthday and brings out some cakes he has made. It is our first social event and everyone chats excitedly with one other about the tour to come. Richard Clayton, our company manager, announces he has made a list of everyone's birthdays and will ensure that we all get cakes throughout the year.

Wednesday January 10ᵗʰ

We plough on, reading through to the end of the last act. Trevor is like a Rabbi with his scholars: poring over his holy scriptures again and again, forever seeking the ultimate truth.

Have liver and bacon with Bill, who tells me Ian is getting restive because we haven't started blocking yet. We've used up nearly two weeks' rehearsal and with the two plays there's so

much to do. Am a little surprised when he tells me that Ian thinks
Trevor's style has changed – he now insists on being right all the
time, which he never used to. Is it because of the unwarranted
criticism he got whilst he was running the National? Bill wonders
why Trevor, with all his money, chooses to spend ten weeks of
his life rehearsing plays in such a dreary place as Clapham. He'd
heard another director once say that Trevor only accepted jobs
because he didn't want anyone else to get them. I don't agree. I
believe he keeps going because he is a true artist, and artists never
tire of creating.

After lunch, we finally get to the end of the play and then go
down to the big room below where Christopher Oram – who
designed *Summerfolk,* which I was in at the National a few years
ago, and is also currently engaged with the stage version of *Lord
of the Rings* – has a model of the set and drawings of our
costumes. We crowd eagerly around them. Christopher and
Trevor have decided to set the play in a non-specific period and
style, somewhat reminiscent of the end of the Romanov dynasty.
The set will be opulent at the beginning, like the interior of a
grand theatre with red velvet curtains and colonnades – then
slowly descend into chaos as Lear falls. The nobles will be
dressed in Tsarist uniforms; Lear in scarlet, Albany, Cornwall,
Kent and Gloucester in black and silver. The lower orders, such
as the Gentleman, will be more soberly clad; the princesses in
crinoline ball gowns and fox-hunting attire. The general feeling is
that both design and costumes are terrific. We will play it first on
the thrust stage in the temporary Courtyard Theatre at Stratford
which, all who have seen it say, is a most exciting space. (I think
'space' and 'piece' are very arty-farty words. What is wrong with
'stage' and 'play'?) Trevor suspects there may be trouble with
sight lines.

We eventually go back upstairs and Trevor explains how he
wants to begin the play with a royal procession, showing Lear in
all his grandeur – a bit like how he started Kevin Spacey's *Richard*

II at the Old Vic, when we all came in wearing scarlet gowns as
in the House of Lords. We discuss whether we should adopt a
special way of bowing before royalty. Trevor tells a story of how
when he was directing *Sunset Boulevard* for Lloyd-Webber, Prince
Edward was working as an assistant for the Really Useful
Company. At the first production meeting Trevor casually asked
where his tea was. A red-faced Prince Edward got up, closely
followed by his bodyguard, and went down the corridor to make
Trevor a cup of tea. Sylvester McCoy attempts a joke by saying,
"That's why you'll never get a knighthood!" Sir Ian McKellen
whispers in Sylvester's ear, whilst *Sir* Trevor Nunn studies his
script.

Wayne Eagling has arranged two tickets for Dora to see first
night of *Giselle* at the Coliseum. I tell her that I would be pushed
to make it and she has gone with the handsome young actor,
Raymond Coulthard, currently playing the Maître d' in *Hotel
Babylon*. He's free for the evening as his partner Jenna Russell is
appearing in *Amy's View* at the Garrick round the corner. So I
have the evening at home by myself – is it a coincidence that
Chelsea are playing Wycombe on Sky?

Thursday January 11th

Bit miffed to find that the RSC, not Trevor, still expects us to be
in at 9.45 for a half-hour vocal warm-up, when most of us were
not called until 11.00. Can't see the point of it for us older ones; if
our voices aren't right now they never will be. Anyway, why
have a vocal warm-up if you're not going to speak?

At last we begin blocking the first scene in which Lear divides
his Kingdom between his daughters. This is usually done as a big
court scene, with Lear sitting on his throne in state, but Trevor
has decided to make it more informal: a family gathering in the
royal library. Lear is seated behind a large desk with a lectern to
his right, from which he will read a prepared speech that the
Gentleman hands him. The two elder daughters are seated

downstage of Lear with their husbands standing behind them. Cordelia: the favourite, stands close to her father. Downstage centre are a pair of kneeling cushions, where the proposed engagement of Cordelia – which Trevor thinks is what the scene starts off being about – will take place. So many directors waste time trying to work out in rehearsal how to move people round the stage, others let the actors feel their way around, but Trevor has planned it all already. Though I've been in four different productions of *Lear*, he makes it seem completely fresh and spontaneous. Am very relieved when Trevor suggests that I am Lear's secretary, and officially transcribe the details of his division of power in a writing case. It means I will be sitting down for most of that long scene. A veteran actor is always looking for excuses to sit down – it is usually very hard in Shakespeare. In Trevor's modern dress *Richard II* at the Old Vic, I hit upon the brilliant idea of having a shooting stick.

Ian is wearing a pair of extremely low-cut jeans, which suits Lear's eccentricity. They seem to cover only the bottom half of his buttocks and would be the envy of any 'hoodie'. I ask him if they were the pair the *Daily Mail* reported he wore at the party in Cape Town on New Year's Eve. He looks completely bemused and said he wasn't in Cape Town on New Year's Eve. You should never believe what you read in the papers.

Find Romola sitting alone, studying a text book in the shabby cubicle that passes for our green room. She tells me that she is about to take a degree in English Literature at the Open University. I am very impressed: she is obviously no brainless little starlet. Russell, who came into acting late and has very limited experience, comes up and tells me that Trevor has asked him to understudy the Fool. He is very concerned and doesn't think that he can do it. I tell him not to worry – I genuinely think he will be fine. I say I will go through the Lear/Fool scenes with him whenever he likes. Zoë Boyle – pretty, with a mass of Pre-Raphaelite red hair – is understudying Cordelia as well as Nina in

The Seagull. The old actor's adage is that the most important thing to take into consideration when casting Cordelia is her weight: Lear has to carry on her dead body when he is absolutely knackered at the end of the play. As we will have to do a full understudy run on stage sometime, I am glad to note that Zoë is a wisp of a young girl. It's her first job and I have no doubt she'll be fine as Cordelia, but Nina is the key role in *The Seagull* – would she be up for it if she had to go on in New York? The understudy casting is almost complete. Naomi will be understudying Regan and an actress called Melanie, who has a very white face and jet black hair, will be covering Goneril.

It is even more complicated as most of the understudies need understudies. Every permutation of circumstances has to be gone through in a long chain. For most people it is not the health of the person you are understudying you have to worry about, but someone else further up the line. John Heffernan, who plays the showy little part of Oswald, is understudying Edgar; Oswald's understudy is Ben Addis, who plays the King of France, who in turn is understudied by Richard Goulding. Thankfully I've only got to worry about Ian. Adam Booth, a big dour Yorkshireman, is understudying me.

Friday January 12th

Carry on blocking the early scenes. Trevor continues to be full of invention: as ever he strives to find the sense of every line. He's introduced a great deal of life and energy into the scene at Goneril's house by having Lear's knights dance like Cossacks to an accordion squeezed by Peter, who seems to have a talent for playing all sorts of musical instruments. I've been trying to find things to do which will help establish my character. I suggest today that I play the Gentleman as an old Cossack Sergeant Major – Trevor says no, as it would make the character too like Kent. Ian has a box which he sits on to take off his boots – when he storms out at the end of the scene it has to go with him.

Someone has to carry it off and bring it on again when Lear arrives at Regan's. I find myself saying, "I suppose I could take..." Trevor instantly agrees. I'm sure he was angling for it all along. The box is heavy, am I going to regret it? Naturally, I watch Ian very closely. He rehearses with a worried frown – his eyes dart around taking everything in. Richard Eyre, who directed him as Richard III, said that at first he fusses around and over-decorates, exploring all avenues before arriving at the truth. I think that sums it up very well. Sylvester, who plays the spoons with the London Concert Orchestra, appears to want to play them at every opportunity.

Have the afternoon free. I ask Ian if he would like me to go over Lear's lines with him as it would help me as well. He takes me to lunch in a fish restaurant on Clapham High Street and we go through the early scenes. In the text he says, "Come hither boy" and "Where's my fool?" several times. The confused little waiter keeps running up, like Manuel in *Fawlty Towers*, thinking Ian is addressing him. Ian is completely 'unstarry.' When we get to the end of the first three scenes he asks if I would like him to hear me. Naturally, I decline.

Very worried about Chelsea. Is Mourinho really going? What is wrong with John Terry, Joe Cole, Cudicini and Robben? Why won't Abramovich let Mourinho sign up some reserves? If we don't beat Wigan tomorrow we can forget about winning the Premiership this year.

Saturday January 13th

Very gratifying trip to Stamford Bridge with my eldest son, Rubin, to see Chelsea trounce Wigan 4-0. The title race is still on!

Tuesday January 16th

Had Monday off as Trevor was working on the Gloucester scenes which are almost a complete play in themselves. Bill, having spent time rehearsing with him, thinks our handsome American,

Philip Winchester, will be fine as he's got lots of energy when he acts. I'm not so sure. Edmund the Bastard may be a very showy part, but it is very difficult to pull off – very few actors have shone in it.

We continue working through the play following Trevor's direction and moves. He's toying with the idea of having the Fool hanged on stage. Ian is worried because next Monday we leave *Lear* for two weeks, to begin work on *The Seagull*. We will have blocked to the end by Friday but seem to be rushing through it – not having enough time to go back and cement things in. I have to confess I'm finding *Lear* very hard to learn.

Watch an old video of Olivier's television *Lear*. Very sad. Like watching Ali at the end of his career, taking too many punches. Realise that *Lear*'s curses mean nothing if they are just shouted: there is profound meaning in them all. But Robert Lindsay disproves my point and shines as Edmund and so does John Hurt as the Fool. The Gentleman isn't bad either.

Wednesday January 17th

Trevor's genius is that he makes something out of every scene. My little scene with Kent, for example, which would normally be just two blokes giving boring information explaining the plot, has become a dangerous rendezvous in no-man's-land. Trevor always says that he has telephoned "Bill Shakespeare" to get his approval, whenever he makes a slight amendment to a line. I suggest putting a small cut back in: "What? In the storm! i' the night?" and to my surprise and delight Trevor thinks it is a good idea.

The review of *Antony and Cleopatra* in *The Times* says Harriet Walter lacks the sensuality that Frances Barber brought to the role at the Globe last year. I point it out to Frances and she is elated. She has never worked with Trevor before and thinks he's wonderful. She's a really gutsy lady with a great sense of fun, but I wouldn't like to cross her. Romola and Monica by contrast seem far more reserved.

Slowly getting to know more of the company. Julian Harries, a big serious looking fellow who plays Albany and understudies Kent, is appearing in his own Christmas play at some small theatre in East Anglia. At the end of each rehearsal he tears across London on a push bike to catch his train from Liverpool Street. Guy is a heavy smoker and spends every available moment smoking in the cold street outside. Melanie does the same. How unlike the smoke-filled rehearsal rooms of my youth.

Spend the evening trying to learn more of Lear. It's difficult because so much of what he says is so similar. Or is old age catching up on me? I've never had any trouble learning lines before...

Thursday January 18th

Get up early and go to the dentist to have my bridge fitted at last. My diction seems to improve immediately. Ian is very concerned about *Celebrity Big Brother* as, it appears, is the rest of the country (he believes the inhabitants of the house are subject to brainwashing). As we still haven't got a Trigorin, who after all is the leading man in *The Seagull*, I suggest Trevor casts Jade Goody and lets her play it as a lesbian. Such is the cultural state of the country, she'd pack them in.

Trevor has nearly blocked to the end of the play. I am delighted that he has given the Gentleman a clear line to follow throughout. Although hardly anyone will notice, I have my own story to follow. Moreover I am by Ian's side all the time, apart from during the storm and the scene in the hovel. I will watch him like a hawk.

We leave *Lear* tomorrow then start *The Seagull* on Monday.

Friday January 19th

Head to Clapham on top of the bus mumbling Lear's lines. Young girl gives me such a piteous look – she must think I'm senile.

Thank God, the battle of the warm-ups has been won. They are now all voluntary. We are now into the final battle scenes and the stage management hand out some old dummy rifles from a wooden chest. Trevor is reminded of the very first professional production he ever did for the RSC. It was a play about soldiers and they were rehearsing it in a room overlooking Fleet Street. During the rehearsal period Winston Churchill died, and they realised that their rehearsal room would overlook the route of the funeral procession, which would consist of practically every head of state in the world. One day the stage management arrived in a taxi with dummy rifles in two cricket bags, carried them up and began to hand them out to the actors. Suddenly the door burst open and Special Branch detectives burst in screaming and lined them all up against the wall, thinking they'd discovered a sniper's nest – it was just a few months after Oswald had shot Kennedy. It took several minutes for a young Trevor to convince them of their innocence. Nowadays they would probably have burst in shooting.

Ben Delfont, the stage manager, who arrives at rehearsal each morning on a huge, glittering motor bike, calls a meeting to elect an Equity Deputy. Ian is concerned that so many actors don't bother to belong to Equity since Mrs Thatcher got rid of the closed shop. Before that you couldn't get a job without being a member and you couldn't become a member without having worked so many weeks. Every theatre or company was permitted to issue a limited number of provisional Equity cards each year. There was never enough and it forced many aspiring actresses to begin their careers in strip clubs and other places of low entertainment. I've heard that Judi Dench refuses to work with anyone who is not an Equity member and am therefore a bit surprised when young Romola shrugs and says she doesn't need it. Ian points out that she uses an Equity Contract, but she dismisses the thought with a shake of her head. I expect someone to say she is being selfish, but nobody does. On the other hand, it makes a refreshing change from the sanctimonious goodness that most actresses tend to affect. And Romola might well have a point: I'm not all that clear what Equity has ever done for me. Nobody seems keen to volunteer to be Equity Deputy. In all of my 46 years in the profession I've always avoided it and don't want to start now. Besides all the paperwork and time the role consumes, the Deputy usually manages to become unpopular with both the management and the company. Guy, who has done it before, eventually agrees. Ben Delfont then says we must also elect a Health and Safety Representative. I check there is no paperwork involved and volunteer for that.

Trevor is also completely engrossed by *Big Brother*: everyone will be watching Jade's expected eviction tonight. Trevor has to go to a family funeral on Monday so we will start on the understudy rehearsals with Gemma, the Assistant Director, and begin *The Seagull* on Tuesday. We still haven't got a Trigorin.

Saturday January 20th

Emil, my younger son and his family come for the weekend, which is partly ruined by Chelsea's loss to Liverpool and the inexplicable turmoil going on at the club. They seem to want to self-destruct.

Monday January 22nd

We finally make a start on the understudy rehearsals, which involve two thirds of the cast. Gemma Fairlie, our pretty young Assistant Director with a smile like Darcy Bussell's, is very helpful. It is strange speaking Lear aloud for the first time. We naturally begin with the first scene, which is mostly straightforward, especially for me as I spend much of it sitting behind my desk. All three daughters, even young Zoë, seem very good. Julian makes an impressive Kent, Seymour can do Gloucester on his head and big Adam, who understudies Guy as

well as me, makes a very menacing Cornwall. We do not as yet
have an understudy for Albany; it will be whoever they find to
play Trigorin in *The Seagull*. Young Richard Goulding, with the
leading role of Konstantin in *The Seagull*, covers both France and
Burgundy. Even for an old ham like me, it will be a rewarding
experience working with them. We will give a full understudy
performance, with costumes, lighting, etc, before an invited
audience at the Courtyard in May, so at least I will play Lear
once: something every actor should aspire to do.

Tuesday January 23rd

Today we begin work on *The Seagull*. Back to sitting round the
square of tables. Our Trigorin has finally arrived in the shape of
Gerald Kyd, and our acting company of 23 is complete at last!
Gerald, who is half Scottish and half Greek, looks like
D'Artagnan: darkly handsome, with long black hair, small
pointed beard, and an open shirt revealing a swarthy, hairy chest.
As the leading man in *The Seagull*, he has no lines in *Lear* but will
have to play a soldier and understudy Julian as Albany. That's
how an ensemble company should be. A rival production with
Kristin Scott Thomas has just opened at the Royal Court. Some
of the cast have been to see previews and, quite naturally, have
not been overly impressed. They say the casting was wrong:
Trigorin seemed younger than Konstantin and Arkadina should
be slightly past her sell-by date – Scott Thomas looked too
beautiful. They also did not like the set or the way Konstantin's
play within the play was staged in the First Act.

  Trevor spends an age expounding on Chekhov and Russian
drama. Nowadays, every production of Chekhov has to have a
new adaptation, usually done by a noted playwright such as
Michael Frayn or Christopher Hampton. Trevor thinks they often
put their own slant on things and are then reluctant to change
words and phrases that the actors find difficult to say or think
wrong for the character. To attempt to get back to what Chekhov

intended, Trevor has commissioned two brand new literal translations as a basis for our production, which means the company will be free to adapt as they feel necessary. Never knew that there were no definite or indefinite articles in Russian. The real title should be *Seagull*.

Spend the afternoon reading the play. Trevor appears to have cast it well. Young Richard Goulding, who has never acted professionally before, should make a good Konstantin, Arkadina's neglected son (apart from looking slightly too well-fed). Gerald Kyd is sexy as the philandering novelist, Trigorin. Romola is already moving as the betrayed Nina, and Frances Barber has all the qualities for a great Arkadina, the flamboyant actress. I predict she will outgun Scott Thomas as she did Harriet Walker as Cleopatra. Jonathan Hyde is suitably suave as Doctor Dorn, and Monica seems well cast as the embittered Masha. Ben Meyjes is her put-upon husband, Medvedenko, Guy is the oafish estate manager, Shamrayev, and Melanie his frustrated wife, Polina. To save Ian's energy for *Lear* he is sharing the undemanding part of Arkadina's brother, Sorin, with Bill Gaunt. They read alternate acts. Peter has a few lines as Yakov, the servant. It is a wonderful play and seems so straightforward after *Lear*.

I sense Ian is uneasy to be leaving *Lear* for two weeks. He is still fishing around, trying to find the character. *Lear* after all is the main feature and *Seagull* has really just been thrown in so that Ian will not have the near-impossible task of doing six or eight *Lears* a week. I hope I will not be involved in *Seagull* and have the evenings off, but sense Trevor has something planned for the dozen of us who are not down as any named character.

Wednesday January 24ᵗʰ

Still around the table. Some days Trevor speaks very softly and older ears find him difficult to follow. After lunch he loses me when he gets bogged down expounding the Russian 'decadent' and 'symbolist' literary movements, concerning the fate of Russia and the life of the people. I treated myself to a curry at lunchtime, as it is a very cold day, and struggle to keep my eyes open. I glance around the square and see that other people are in the same boat. Frances Barber is putting up a game fight but her head occasionally drops towards the tabletop. The odd eye is firmly shut. Guy Williams, who I think is going to be very funny as Shamrayev, for no apparent reason goes into a lengthy explanation of why the moon mentioned in the play would be waning not waxing. Later he tells me that he is a sailor. There are untold depths to him.

Ian is very concerned about the news today that the Catholic Church is refusing to allow gay couples to adopt. He has been a key campaigner for gay rights ever since he 'came out' 20 years ago, leading the opposition against Clause 28 and promoting civil contracts. Although he is left-wing, he has none of the political intensity of Corin Redgrave, who I think automatically assumed that I had the same radical views as himself. Ian is essentially a gentle person.

Thursday January 25th

The action of the play takes place on Sorin's country estate, and Trevor talks about houseguests in grand houses and the effect it has on the servants, hinting that he wants to have many servants on stage. My hopes of having *Seagull* nights off rapidly disappear. Trevor then recalls staying at Lloyd-Webber's grand house in the South of France, which occupies almost a peninsular and the servants there desperately running round to make a good impression. Guy announces he once ran a game reserve for Stephanie Powers in Kenya and says the frenzy of activity that ensued during the few weeks of the year she was in residence was very similar to Arkadina's arrival at Sorin's estate. Everyone is gob smacked: Guy has poked out eyes (albeit a dead sheep's) like Cornwall and has run an estate like Shamrayev. Trevor strokes his beard; "I never realised how perfectly I'd cast you."

Later try to learn more of Lear. Finding his diatribes against old age quite depressing and contemplate my own mortality. One of my oldest friends, Brian Eatwell, has died in Hollywood. I have written an appreciation of him that another old friend, Ian McShane, will read at Brian's memorial service in LA. Brian is the first to die of my close-knit group of friends who were founder members of the National Youth Theatre with me in 1957. A friend of Brian's in Hollywood has posted a very moving montage of his life on YouTube. I watch it and see my own life pass on parallel lines. I'd forgotten how beautiful Brian was in his youth.

Friday January 26th

The Seagull at the Royal Court opens to mixed reviews. *Evening Standard* critic Nicholas de Jongh, the *bête noire* of actors and always the first you read because his notice comes out a day early, has perversely given it five stars whilst decrying the performance of Kristin Scott Thomas as Arkadina. When I arrive at rehearsal most of the cast are crammed into the shabby little green room. Frances is in great form; she was up early checking the other reviews on the Internet. She quotes De Jongh on Scott Thomas' '*relentlessly one-noted performance*', with such good-natured humour that one cannot fail to warm to her. As other members of the *Seagull* cast come in, she greets them with "You've got a good one", or "They didn't like you," as if it were their own fledgling performances being reviewed.

Trevor blocks the first act and, as I feared, uses all the company. Again he shows his mastery in filling the stage. Julian, John, Adam and Philip are estate workers running the makeshift stage and effects of Konstantin's play within the play in the first act. Seymour, Ben, Russell, Zoë and Naomi are house servants, who come out to watch the play, supervised by me: the butler. It is a true ensemble; Philip Winchester, who plays Edmund, one of the leading roles in *Lear*, plays a non-speaking estate worker and understudies Trigorin. Already there seems to be a great feeling of camaraderie. I have worked out my business; I am a very old butler who will find himself a convenient cushion and fall asleep watching the play. Naomi, who has one line as the cook, suggests that she and the butler are married. I consent.

Whilst I'm standing at the bus stop at Clapham Common ready to come home, Timothy West appears out of the mist like a character in a spy movie. He is rehearsing an RSC production of *Coriolanus* nearby. To my surprise, he doesn't know where the main RSC rehearsal rooms are. He hasn't worked for the RSC for more than 30 years. We catch different buses and our conversation is cut short.

Am furious that my Sky receiver has broken down – they will not be able to come and fix it until Feb 6th – I'm going to miss a lot of football.

Sunday January 28th

Dora gives one of her kitchen dinner parties. The guests are: literary agent and author Andrew Lownie, his wife Angela, and Raymond Coulthard and Jenna Russell. Jenna is about to finish in *Amy's View,* and has been nominated for an Olivier for her performance in *Sunday in the Park with George*. She is a lovely, talented girl and we hope she wins. Her partner Raymond, who I first met when he played my son in a Rattigan play during a bleak winter in Dundee many years ago, was a stalwart of Trevor's ensemble at the National. Trevor had offered him the roles of Trigorin and Albany on the *Lear* tour, but he was under contract for *Hotel Babylon*, and anyway didn't fancy a year away from his lovely Jenna. I also suspect they are trying to have a baby. A pity – it would have been fun going round the world with him.

Wednesday January 31st

Back rehearsing after a few days off. Trevor is in terrific form as he orchestrates Madame Arkadina's departure. He finds a reason for the entire cast to be in the scene. I manage to invent what I think is amusing business as the butler, counting and ticking off the suitcases like a hotel porter. Trevor tells me to forget it: Russian peasants couldn't read or write.

Bill has a swollen lip. Yesterday evening, his mobile phone rang as he approached Clapham Common tube. As he put it to his ear a 'hoodie' came from nowhere, punched him in the mouth and tried to grab the phone. Bill, who is nearly 70, swung back. He missed, but it was enough to fend his attacker off and the young gentleman made his getaway sprinting across Clapham Common. Bill has spent several thousands on the bridgework to his front teeth and was very relieved to find that no damage had occurred. I've just spent £1,300 on mine. As I walk back from lunch my mobile rings; I see two youths running towards me and cowardly let it ring in my pocket as they jog innocently by.

Ian goes to lunch in a nearby Indian restaurant. He enters and finds it completely empty. He sits at a table and the waiter tells him he can't sit there, as it is a table for four. Ian asks him where he should sit and is pointed to a table for two in the window. Ian, quite naturally, doesn't want to sit in the window and asks if he can sit in the back of the restaurant. He makes for a table for four and the waiter again tells him he cannot sit there. Ian asks why and is told he'd better take his custom elsewhere. I don't suppose many restaurants in Manhattan or Hollywood would turn away Sir Ian McKellen.

My eldest son, Rubin, has got me a ticket for Chelsea's game with Blackburn tonight, but I can't go because Dora and I are going to dinner with Julian and Emma Fellowes. It is a crucial game. If we don't win we'll never catch United and maybe even lose second place to Liverpool. As I pass Woolworth's in Clapham High Street, I see that the DVD of *Gosford Park* is on sale at the giveaway price of £3. I buy a copy and want to take it with me to tease Julian that he's passed his sell by date, but Dora won't let me.

Delightful evening at the newly-refurbished Sloane Club with Julian and Emma. It is almost 20 years since I first met Julian, when we were both appearing in a production of *Rebecca* at the Churchill Theatre in Bromley. He was playing Jack Favell, the cad, and I was Giles, the bungling brother-in-law. It was the year of the hurricanes and Julian, as was (and still is) his wont, had gone to stay at a country house for the weekend. On the Monday morning he woke and saw to his horror that the drive was blocked with fallen trees. There were no understudies at Bromley and he phoned the theatre to say he was leaving immediately and would do all he could to get there on time. I and the rest of the cast arrived at the half that evening to be told of Julian's predicament by the stage manager. There were no such things then as mobile phones and Julian had last phoned from a garage off the M25 and was still not sure if he could make it. It was decided that if Julian had not arrived, we would start the play without him as he did not make his first entrance for 20 minutes. Then, if he had still not arrived, the stage manager would come on with the book and read Julian's part. We began the play, constantly looking anxiously towards the door where Julian, hopefully, would make his entrance. At last the moment came, the door burst open, and instead of the smooth cad in blazer and cravat, Julian burst into the room in shirtsleeves and a muck sweat. He was barely able to croak out his lines, having left his car parked on the double yellow lines and had dashed straight through the stage door onto the stage.

Success now positively oozes from Julian but he hasn't really changed. He is a vastly entertaining and knowledgeable conversationalist. Now he is working on a script of a film Scorsese will produce about the young Queen Victoria. The publicity machine is already pumping out the absurd story that Sarah Ferguson is going to write it. I ask him who will play Victoria and he says they are thinking of Emily Blunt, who was so good in *The Devil Wears Prada*. I hope she gets it and not some Hollywood starlet like Kirsten Dunst: who I found very hard to believe as Marie Antoinette. Julian has been taking the Director of the film, Jean-Marc Vallée, a French Canadian, on private tours of Buckingham Palace and Windsor Castle. He has really cornered the upper crust costume market; Spielberg also wants a script from him. On top of that his royalties from Disney's stage musical of *Mary Poppins*, for which he wrote the book, pour in from both sides of the Atlantic. Nevertheless, I insist we split the bill.

Get home and check on the Internet. To my great relief, Chelsea have won 3-0.

Friday February 2nd

Trevor has told us to wear old clothes, as we are going to have one of his 'fun' days. He usually has one in a rehearsal period – I suppose he feels that they break down our inhibitions and bond us together. Lots of directors seek ways to do this. Richard Eyre, Trevor's predecessor at the National, calls it 'mutual familiarisation', but we have been together now for more than a month, and are familiar already. Trevor pairs us off and we begin by telling fairy stories to each other, simultaneously listening to what the other person is saying, to increase concentration (listening is in fact a very important, and often neglected, part of acting). I am paired with Zoë and am very pleased with my fairy story:

Once upon a time, there was a little hobbit called Trevor. One day he was walking by the banks of the Avon, wearing jeans and a blue denim shirt, when a voice called down from heaven, saying, "My name is William. I have chosen to give you the secret of all my plays. You alone will be able to direct them as I conceived them, but you must always be humble and remain exactly as you are today." So young Trevor went to Shakespeare's Theatre and told the chief hobbit, Peter of the Hall, that he

knew the secret of Shakespeare and, lo and behold, Peter sensed his power
and gave the theatre to him. For the next 20 years, young Trevor directed
nearly every play Shakespeare wrote and formed the most famous
theatrical company in the world, but he always remained humble and
always wore the same jeans and blue denim shirt. He began to think that
he had done all that he could do.

Then one day he took a trip across the big ocean and as he walked
down a street called Broadway, a voice called down to him from heaven,
saying, "My name is Oscar Hammerstein…"

I don't think Zoë gets it, which is fair enough, as I can't
remember what she told me.

We then bond by forming groups, improvising situations and
displaying emotions such as being shipwrecked, missing the last
train home, or gate-crashing a party. It's a bit like a children's
party for grown-ups. I suspect most of us feel it is a waste of time
but we all enter into the spirit of the occasion. All directors have
their own methods, as do all actors, and there is no perfect way to
arrive at a performance. I heard that when the late, lamented
Michael Bryant was cast as Badger in *Wind in the Willows* at the
National, he was given some videos of badgers to take home so
that he could study their movement. Michael came back the next
morning and said: "You know, I've found out the most
extraordinary thing – badgers move just like Michael Bryant."

In the afternoon, we go through 24 hours on Sorin's estate.
We're not allowed to speak or make eye contact with one
another. We start at 5am and Trevor chimes the hours, about
every five minutes, on the piano. Trevor has given all the non-
speaking members of the company definite roles as servants, I
suppose he wants us to imagine what their various lives would be
like. As the butler, I manage to spend a lot of the time asleep in a
cupboard. I saw an illustration of a butler doing just this in a
book about life on a pre-Revolutionary Russian Estate. The
highlight of my improvisation is killing Shamrayev's barking dog

with a hammer at 2am, after Frances' Arkadina has screamed her complaints about the bloody noise for the third time. Trevor watches, stroking his beard. I wonder if he thinks we have got anything out of it. Will be glad to get back to *Lear* next week.

Jonathan Hyde lives in Bath and during the rehearsal period is staying with our mutual friend, Rupert Fraser, in Greenwich. I invite him to come home with me for a quiet supper but the evening does not turn out quite as planned. Perhaps my Martinis are too strong, but the evening ends with him having a heated discussion with Dora over Israel. Dora's father survived Auschwitz and she is very much pro-Israel: she has family and many friends there. I side with Dora, but nearly all actors are left-wing and therefore pro-Palestinian. It was different in the sixties when Israel was the underdog. I remember at the beginning of the Six Days War in 1967, during a rehearsal of *Macbeth*, Paul Scofield went round with a petition (in support of Israel) from the Hollywood director, Fred Zinnemann, for whom he'd just completed filming *Man for All Seasons*. As far as I can remember, everyone in the cast signed it. Times change. Decide to keep off the subject of the Middle East for the duration of the tour.

Saturday February 3rd

See *Seagull* at the Royal Court. Cannot understand why it has received such wonderful notices. To my mind the casting is wrong and the actors don't seem to act with each other. I also don't like the set: Sorin is supposed to be short of money, but he's not a pauper. Arkadina and Trigorin, a successful writer, would never stay in such a depressing, dilapidated hovel. Dora says it reminds her of a run-down property that one finds in France and has to spend thousands on to make habitable. Dora is a great fan of Scott Thomas, she thought she was wonderful in *Three Sisters* a couple of years ago, but as Arkadina she finds her cold and sexless; she poses and waves her arms around as if she were semaphoring. Naturally, at the egalitarian Royal Court, there is no plenitude of servants. Sorin has a much smaller estate and doesn't have a butler.

Monday February 5th

Meet Jonathan in Clapham High Street. He apologises profusely for the falling-out on Friday. I apologise equally profusely for the strength of my Martinis. All is well, but I somehow suspect that we will never become close friends. Spend the entire day on the opening scene. Ian is taking it easy but shows glimpses of his extraordinary vocal powers. His voice can excite like Olivier's.

Spend lot of time discussing royal protocol – in what order should Lear, his daughters and their husbands enter? We decide to follow the Queen: Lear and Cordelia come on last. I have a sudden inspiration and suggest to Trevor that the Gentleman/Secretary might be a priest. He pulls his beard and shakes his head: "If there's a priest in this play, we're fucked." I should have realised; Lear is not a Christian play: the Gods referred to are pagan.

In the evening, we do another understudy rehearsal of Lear. You only find out how difficult it is when you get up and try to do it yourself. The words are not so bad but I find I can't remember the moves, even though I've watched Ian all day. All the others have much work to do as well, but even in an understudy rehearsal all eyes are on me: I am covering Lear. I haven't played a big role since I did my one-man play, Falstaff, at the Cottesloe five years ago, but over the decades I've played most of the great Shakespearean roles – Romeo, Prince Hal and Hotspur (in the distant past) then Mark Antony, Brutus and Macbeth. I even went on with the book as Othello one night at the Young Vic when Kenneth Haigh went down with stomach problems. I reassure myself that nobody is better qualified to cover McKellen.

Tuesday February 6th

Go to a reception at the National for Nobby Clark's exhibition, *London Blues*. We tend to take Nobby for granted but he is a true artist – Hogarth with a camera. Meet fellow Chelsea fanatic Paul Blackman who now lives in New York. He tells me he knows a bar in Manhattan that shows all the Chelsea games live. Arrange to meet up with him when *Lear* hits Brooklyn.

Wednesday February 7th

Rehearse the big hunting scene at Goneril's house. Peter, Russell, Ben Addis, Adam, Gerald and Richard, who are playing Lear's knights as drunken Cossacks, throw themselves wholeheartedly into the scene and give it vibrant life. Sylvester having done little Shakespeare before is finding it difficult. He is playing the Fool as a sort of old music hall comedian and takes refuge in playing his beloved spoons at every opportunity, which to my mind holds up the action. Ian and Trevor are extremely patient.

Thursday February 8th

Ian wants to cut more of *Lear* – it always seems to be the bits I've learned. Trevor's main concern is that the RSC is issuing its own edition of the play, and the text of *Lear* the editor has sent him to ratify is based entirely on the Folio: completely different from our version. He recalls that when he directed *Timon of Athens* he helped Shakespeare out by secretly writing 220 new lines. Some critics said they understood the play for the first time.

Most lunchtimes, if Bill is not at rehearsals, I like to wander off by myself and read the sports pages over a sandwich or liver and bacon in the local greasy spoon. Several of the young ones, such as Monica, Romola, and the ever health-conscious Russell, bring in salads and health foods and eat them in the grotty green room; unlike my young days, when we would have liquid lunches in the nearest pub. Ian, Frances, Jonathan Hyde and

Sylvester usually have a proper meal in one of the many local ethnic restaurants.

I know how important confidence is in acting and have always made a point of encouraging young actors. I tell Ben Addis today how well I think he plays the small part of King of France, and also let Ben Meyjes know how impressed I am with the work he puts into his Edgar. I think I probably picked up the habit when I was directing at the National Youth Theatre. Mind you, I don't always practise what I preach. Apparently, when I was directing the NYT in a production of *Midsummer Night's Dream*, I gave up on a public-school type playing a fairy and told him to stand at the back and pretend to be a tree. I have since been informed that that fairy was Colin Firth.

I still don't know much about the young actors however, apart from the fact that Richard supports Tottenham Hotspur. So, surprisingly, does Melanie Jessop, whose black hair and attractive, but drawn, white face remind me of the old 'Keep Death off the Road' poster (but I suppose anyone would look like death if they supported Tottenham Hotspur long enough). She doesn't have a proper part in *Lear*, only understudying Goneril, but will play the substantial role of Polina in *Seagull*. Monica remains an enigma to me; I think she is going to be very effective in both her parts, but I find it very hard to talk to her. I suppose we have nothing much in common. I'm not surprised – I'm old enough to be grandfather to most of them and don't recall socialising with the old actors when I was young. Perhaps things will change when we move out of London and start the tour.

Walk along Clapham High Street and pass a cafe to see Naomi eating there by herself. She waves at me and I go in and join her. I like her and cannot understand why she always seems to be alone. I remember her being very upset when she broke off an entangled relationship when we were at the Old Vic. I ask how her love life is going. She tells me it's back on track. I hope it works out for her.

Friday February 9th

In rehearsal room watching Trevor directing Ian in the storm, when Jonathan Hyde comes in and announces that Ian Richardson has died in his sleep at the age of 72. There is a hush; Ian stands still and bows his head, looking like Don Quixote in silent prayer; Trevor sits down and holds his head in his hands for a full thirty seconds. He gets up and recalls that in 1967 Richardson played Vendice, the major role in *The Revenger's Tragedy*, a forgotten play by Cyril Tourneur that Trevor had rediscovered. It was Trevor's first big production at Stratford. Richardson, with his vocal precision and art of being able to turn on a sixpence, was one of the major reasons for its success. He went on to play nearly every major part in the canon during Trevor's early years as head of the RSC; Trevor is visibly moved. I remember hearing that Alan Howard, who played the other major role in that production, has recently been seriously ill with diabetes. Everyone in the room, apart from the stage management, is over 60; we sense that we are moving closer to death. It only seems like yesterday when I was the youngest member of the company in my first job at Leatherhead Rep and throughout the years there have always been generations of actors ahead. Now they have nearly all gone. The likes of me, Ian, Bill and Trevor are in the front line – it won't be long before we go over the top.

Decide to have a check-up on my heart before we go off on tour.

Saturday February 10th

Read Ian Richardson's obituary in *The Times*. Touched to see that *Coriolanus* was one of the roles he was most proud of – I understudied him and played Titus Lartius. We went on the RSC's tour of Russia with Peter Hall's production of *Macbeth*, known as 'the red carpet' because the stage was covered with it and most of the cast started the play beneath it. Paul Scofield was Macbeth, Vivien Merchant – then married to Harold Pinter – was his Lady, and Ian Richardson, Malcolm. In spite of that cast it wasn't the success we expected. I have a memory of going with Ian to Stanislavsky's apartment in Moscow on a freezing cold December day and being shown around by Stanislavsky's old valet, who was still surviving in Soviet Russia in 1967.

Wonderful afternoon at Stamford Bridge: Chelsea beat Middlesbrough 3-0.

Sunday February 11th

Watch BAFTA Awards on TV. No point in paying £90 to be there and sit up in the gods. Awards agree with my voting, apart from the girl in the James Bond film, Eva Green, who won the award for Most Promising Newcomer; I would have given it to Emily Blunt. Actors should not try to make jokes when they announce the awards; they always fall flat. Daniel Craig does it right – just announces the names. Ian is in good form. Glad Helen Mirren pays tribute to Ian Richardson.

Monday February 12th

Arrange to have a cardiac test as soon as possible. Trevor is letting me play my second scene with Kent with a touch of comedy. The Gentleman is becoming a bumbler.

A story is going around that the morning after Ian Richardson died, the telephone rang, and his widow Maroussia picked up the phone. A bright young lady from some office asked if she could speak to Ian Richardson. Maroussia replied she was very sorry, but Mr Richardson had just died. The bright young lady replied, "Oh, no problem!" Clearly, actors are dispensable.

Tuesday February 13th

Very depressing UNICEF report out today stating that British youth is the worst off among the prosperous nations. I think of what my grandchildren have compared to my own childhood or even that of my children. Rooms packed with toys and gadgets, ballet lessons, football coaching, private education. I then think of the hours their parents work to pay for it all and the lack of time they can spend with them. Sir Ian is also concerned and says he woke up this morning and thought of what he should do to help young people, then remembered he's Vice President of the National Youth Theatre; at least they're trying to do something. I know from my own experience in the early days of the Youth Theatre that a theatrical production is the best way of involving a huge number of kids with different backgrounds and abilities. More subsidies in the arts – about the only thing that this nation still does best – would save a great deal of money in the long run and add so much to so many young lives. Indeed it was my own schoolmaster, Michael Croft, who took me under his wing when my father died when I was 13 and opened my eyes to the theatre. He always wanted to give kids a chance to glimpse at the stars.

We spend most of the day on the long scene on Dover Cliff: perhaps the greatest scene in the play. It really plays itself, like a scene from Samuel Beckett; two old, broken-hearted men – one blind, one mad – contemplating mankind. Bill plays stoically behind his bandaged eyes as Ian runs the gambit with his voice and emotions, hardly ever saying a line the same. I come on to say my few lines and feel privileged to be part of it.

Wednesday February 14th

Finish rehearsing with Trevor at 6 and have a late understudy rehearsal with Gemma at 7. I mention to Klare, the assistant stage manager that I am going to go across the road to the pub and have a drink whilst I wait. She asks me if I am aware of the RSC's policy on drink and drugs; I'm not sure if she is joking. Even in the nineties, the green room at Stratford served beer and wine throughout the performance. Why can't they rely on actors

to behave responsibly? I'm sure it's part of some politically
correct theory that drink is just as dangerous as drugs and so both
must be banned. Sir Donald Wolfit would never do the second
act without his Guinness. On the other hand, I remember stories
of Richard Burton drinking so much beer whilst playing Prince
Hal at Stratford that he pissed in his armour; and Wilfred
Lawson sitting inebriated in the stalls at the Old Vic, where he
was supposed to be playing the Button Moulder in *Peer Gynt*,
nudging the lady sitting next to him and saying in his deep voice,
rich as port flavoured jam: "This next bit is going to be interesting
– it's where I come in." I am glad that I had a chance to work
with such characters; they were also great actors. In honour of
them, I decide to defy Klare and slip over to the pub for a quiet
half pint. Gerald Kyd, our handsome Trigorin, is already there.
He tells me he has split from his partner. First casualty of the tour
and we haven't even left London.

Good rehearsal with Gemma, she seems to know her stuff.
Confident I won't let anyone down if I have to go on. Naomi,
Melanie and Zoë are all good as my daughters, as are: Seymour
as Gloucester, Julian as Kent, Gerald as Albany and Adam as
Cornwall. Russell is very nervous but has a pathetic quality about
him that is right for the Fool – and at least he doesn't insist on
playing the bloody spoons.

Walk back along Clapham High Street. It's Valentine's night;
the restaurants are all full of lovers. Men and women, young and
old, black and white, are hurrying along the pavement carrying
bunches and pots of flowers. Love is in the air. It would be a
suitable subject for a poem by Betjeman. Go home for
champagne with Dora.

Thursday February 15th

Another young boy has been shot in Clapham near our rehearsal
room. I don't recognise the description of the run-down inner city
area that was described on the news on TV. At lunch go to my

greasy spoon and see a squad of tubby policemen and women in their yellow jackets ambling up the little lane opposite. As I walk back to the rehearsal room, I pass a pretty young girl carrying a bunch of flowers to lay in tribute to the shot boy. She is weeping. It is exactly the same spot where people were carrying flowers for a happier reason yesterday. One couldn't put it in a novel – it would be too sentimental, but it's true. Leave the turmoil in the streets and head back to our safe little world. We are so lucky to be working doing something we love.

I have now decided on wearing little, round glasses as the Gentleman, making him a fussy, nervous little man. I also acquire Lear's satchel to hang around my neck as well as my own. With the box I am now veritably burdened down, but it helps with the character. Trevor is slowly adding more and more detail. He gives his full attention to even the smallest part and the least important scene. Every line spoken must have a reason. He is like a painter, filling in every detail of a vast canvas. He introduces a sort of Cossack dance for the riotous knights. Gerald, perhaps because of his Greek ancestry, is particularly convincing. I try to get out of it, but Trevor insists I should take part, that is, until he watches my laboured efforts, "I work with New York and London's finest dancers. You're bloody terrible." We decide I will be a disapproving onlooker.

Tomorrow morning, at last, we will do our first run-through of *Lear*. Ian and the rest of us will discover much more about our parts and the play after we have done it.

Friday February 16th

Stephen Pimlott has died at 53. A lovely man; I was in his production of *Murder in the Cathedral*. I most admired him for bravely giving our dear friend Sheila Gish her last role, Arkadina strangely enough, at Chichester, when her face was ravaged with cancer. She played Arkadina with an eye patch, but conveyed more sex with one eye than most actresses can do with two (except Francis Barber of course).

We are all very nervous as we do our first run-through. It takes nearly four hours. Nearly everyone is uncertain of their lines; people forget moves and entrances; in my opinion Sylvester is still slow and Philip speaks too fast, but already, to me at least, it feels like a great production. Ian is exhausted at the end: he has played Lear for the first time. He is dissatisfied with himself – he wouldn't be a great actor if he wasn't – and is worried that we are going to have to leave it for another two weeks and go back to *Seagull*. After that, we'll only have two weeks before we go up to Stratford and begin the technical rehearsals. Trevor takes three hours giving us our notes. As ever he encourages, never rebukes, endeavouring to give everyone confidence. The rehearsal room is very hot and stuffy. I nearly drop off a couple of times.

Dora is giving one of her dinner parties around our kitchen table. Rozzie Metherell, who runs the education department at Covent Garden, rings earlier in the day to say that her husband, Charles, is ill so we have an empty place. I ask Ian if he would like to join us. He accepts. We walk down Clapham High Street arm in arm, like two old gents, and catch the 137 bus to Chelsea Bridge. He arrives at our flat in Pimlico exhausted. We put him to bed, to sleep for an hour before the other guests arrive. As he closes his eyes he quotes, "We'll go to supper in the morning."

He awakes refreshed and is in sparkling form. The other guests, Paul Roseby, the present Director of the National Youth Theatre and his partner James, Rozzie, and Davina and Larry Belling, who have previously met Ian at bagel brunches in Hollywood, are all delighted. We have another happy evening round our kitchen table, which goes on until well after midnight. Larry has written a play, *Nurse Betty*, based on his old father who married his nurse, 20 years his junior. He mentions it to Ian, saying that Sean Mathias, Ian's ex-partner, has read it and likes it. He asks Ian if he'd be interested in playing the leading role – Ian diplomatically declines. He is charming and extremely unpretentious, even though his name would guarantee the production of any play on both sides of the Atlantic.

Saturday February 17th

Wake up and listen in bed to Radio 5 Live. Sheridan Morley has died in his sleep. Three in a week! He had been sitting at our kitchen table in December. A huge, generous, gregarious character, I've known him all my professional life. Because we were more or less contemporaries, he was always of the mistaken belief that I had been at Oxford with him. He would introduce me to the other guests at the huge Christmas parties he and his wife, Ruth, would give, with, "You know David Weston? We were at Oxford together." It had gone on for so long I never had the heart to contradict him.

One year Ann Leslie said: "I don't remember him." Sheridan waved an expansive hand dismissively, "Oh, he was ahead of you."

I will miss him dreadfully. He had been ill with depression for a long time and he and Ruth had been planning to sell up and move to New York. I don't think he would have really been happy, moving away from London and his friends.

Dora and I go to BAFTA to see *The Good German*. Very slow and atmospheric in black and white; fell asleep. Dora likes it – it brings back memories of her childhood in post-war Vienna. On this occasion I find George Clooney bland, but then I'm only a man.

Go to Watford to see Christopher Luscombe's production of *Enjoy*, a more or less forgotten play by Alan Bennett. Never been to downtown Watford before. Arrive early and look for somewhere to eat. Pedestrian precinct: very depressing. No individuality, same chain stores as every other high street. Very relieved to find a Pizza Express, full of very nice families having a Saturday meal together. Haven't been to one for years but we are surprised how good the pizzas are. Meet Christopher at the

Palace Theatre. Again, we are pleasantly surprised; the newly-restored theatre is full, the seats comfortable, and the audience better dressed than in the West End. Christopher has directed the play very well and drawn excellent performances from his cast, none of whom I have ever heard of before. It just proves how many good actors we have. Not sure about the play though. Not your usual Alan Bennett; more like Joe Orton crossed with Pinter. It flopped when Joan Plowright did it in London in 1980 but, such is the way of the world, if this production and cast had done it at the Cottesloe or Donmar today I'm sure the critics would have hailed it as a lost masterpiece.

Sunday February 18th

Ruth Leon rings to thank us for our message of sympathy and says how much Sheridan always enjoyed coming to Dora's kitchen parties. Like Ian Richardson, he had gone to bed happy and never woke up: the best way to go. Ruth wants only a small, family funeral but there will a memorial service at the Actor's Church in Covent Garden followed by drinks at the Garrick on May 22nd. At Sheridan's request, Sondheim's 'I'm Still Here' will be sung.

Go to BAFTA feeling very distinguished now that my hair and beard for *Lear* have grown. Bump into Michael Walker, who tells me I look like a cleaned-up tramp. See *Fauteuils D'Orchestre,* a delightful French film that makes us want to jump on a Eurostar and spend a few days in Paris. It's a real 'feel-good' movie. I expect the critics will look down their noses.

Wonderful news: Jenna Russell has won an Olivier and the little Menier Chocolate Factory has won five Oliviers: more than the National, the RSC or the Royal Court. David Babani, who runs it, is a real 'wunderkind'. I first met him ten years ago, when I was doing my one man show, *Falstaff,* at Highgate School. The drama master asked me if this kid could help me with the lighting; the theatre seemed to the only subject he was interested in. David lit it brilliantly. He was producing his first shows before he was 20 and gave me a part in one of them. Babani is a showman in the traditional Broadway style: a British Ziegfeld.

Monday February 19th

Stanley Reynolds writes a rather grudging obituary for Sheridan in the *Guardian* but it is balanced by a very sympathetic one from Michael Billington in the same paper. I sometimes disagree with Billington, but this time I am completely on his side.

Needless to say *The Times* critic gives *Fauteuils D'Orchestre* only one star and says it was so boring that it had practically put him to sleep.

Trevor will be spending the whole of this week on *Seagull,* so I have most of it off.

Sunday February 25th

We spend the weekend in the country with Simon and Amanda Relph, who left Islington ten years ago to live in a picturesque old house in Wiltshire. Simon, a fellow Chelsea fan and an ex-president of BAFTA – and probably the reason I was elected to it – has produced almost as many films, (*Privates on Parade*, *Damage*, *Ploughman's Lunch*, and *Enchanted April*, etc.) as Didier Drogba has scored goals. On top of that, the bugger co-financed more than 57 films when he was head of British Screen and never found a single part for me in any of 'em. But filmmaking, like acting, is an addiction. Simon has had the rights of Sebastian Faulks' novel *Birdsong* for years and is still striving to get it made. He was at Cambridge with Ian and in fact played Hotspur in a famous production in which Ian first attracted attention for his performance as Justice Shallow. I remember Amanda as a sparkling young girl at RADA – she is now a dowager, deeply imbedded in country life. I love keeping in touch with old friends – that's the best thing about emails; they make it easy. There's an old poem Michael Croft used to quote:

'Experience all is of use – save one:
To have angered a friend.
Lose thy heart for a maid,
Another will love thee ere long,
But friendship's grave's the end.'

Come back via Waltham St Lawrence where our younger
son, Emil, is living. Dora wants to see the grandchildren, Mia
and Fabian, and I want to see the Carling Cup Final. Arrange to
meet Emil in a pub in Twyford that is showing the game on Sky,
but can't find it and can't get any reception from Emil's mobile.
End up reading *Just William* stories to Mia, impersonating my old
chum Martin Jarvis, another National Youth veteran, whilst
listening to the latest score on my faithful little radio which I take
everywhere with me. My disappointment is tempered by
Chelsea's victory over the 'Gooners'.

Tuesday February 27th

Another week on *Seagull*.

Celebrate Dora's birthday. Dinner party round the kitchen
table with Brenda Polan, Michael Hastings (who I was at prep
school with), Bertie Portal and his beautiful girlfriend, the actress
Janet McTeer. Have never met Janet before – why is it that the
best actresses tend to be so modest and charming? Bertie is one of
a dying breed; the archetypal English gent, related to Lord Portal,
one of Churchill's paladins of WW2. He is also a leading tri-
athlete and is about to take over Richard Hannay in *The Thirty-
Nine Steps* at the Criterion. They couldn't have found a better
man.

Wednesday February 28th

Take Dora to King Edward VII Hospital for Officers for her third
shoulder operation in six months. We forget her X-rays so I have
to dash back home to get them and miss the first act of the run-

through of *Seagull*. I only have to come in and watch Konstantin's play so am not really missed and I get to see the scenes I am not in for the first time. I'm sure that Frances Barber will give the performance of her career. The young ones, Romola and Richard, appear to have most to do, but that is only natural. They are both very difficult parts, but they have plenty of time. Tell Monica I think she is excellent as Masha – she shrugs enigmatically.

Dash back to hospital and wait two hours while Dora's operation takes place. Sit in her room learning Lear. Very relieved when a rather portly Irish nurse comes in and announces breathlessly that the surgeon says it has gone well. Wait with Dora whilst she comes round and eats a little supper. The hospital looks first rate. It sparkles like a luxury liner, with pictures of the Queen Mother everywhere.

Sunday March 4th

Dora comes home, very weak, with the arm in a huge sling. She must not move it for a month, yet today she insists on all the family coming over for lunch. Rubin, Emil, their wives and our four grandchildren. A happy day. A family puts everything into perspective; we are so lucky to have them.

Monday March 5th

We are back on *Lear*. It's surprising how many people keep forgetting things we have done before. Everyone is still uncertain of their lines and taking prompts. I'm not sure yet about Sylvester's Fool. He still seems to play the spoons at every opportunity, and being a natural comedian, puts in business and gags that seem to take forever but he is a really charming fellow. There is a childlike innocence and gullibility about him as he blinks hopefully behind his glasses. I'm sure he'll get it in time. I can see it's especially difficult for Ian, as he has to wait to deliver his next outburst, but he is so patient and never complains.

Do a run-through of the last scene, which is an act in itself. Goneril poisons Regan, Edgar kills Edmund in a very exciting duel, Goneril stabs herself and finally the heart-breaking climax when Lear staggers on with the dead Cordelia. Most of us, including me, have forgotten moves and business Trevor has given us. It is one of the rare occasions I have seen him angry. He doesn't shout – he sniffs in disdainful disappointment. I feel ashamed and unprofessional; maybe I have been concentrating on Lear too much and have been neglecting the Gentleman? Or is the problem that we keep switching between the two plays? Shouldn't be, done it enough times before at Stratford and the National – that's what playing in a repertory is all about.

Tuesday March 6th

Go to Stamford Bridge with Rubin for European Cup Game against Porto. At half-time we are a goal down and I am convinced we are out, but we come back in the second half and win 2-1. As we come out of the stadium everyone is ecstatic. A chap behind me says, "Get a move on, Father Christmas."

I turn, with all the dignity I can muster, and reply, "Do you mind? I am King Lear."

He looks bemused, then shrugs, "Silly old c**t!"

Thursday March 8th

Another run of *Lear*. Ian lets rip and the real performance begins to emerge. I can deliver Lear's lines with sense and feeling, but he can make them sound mint-fresh: that is why he is a great actor. As far as the rest of us are concerned, the first half is not good, but we pick it up as we go along. It is still 3 hours 40 minutes. We should go on working on it, but tomorrow we will go back again to *Seagull*. Time is now going very quickly.

Friday March 9th

It is like the first day of spring. Bill Gaunt and I slip away at lunchtime and have an illegal half pint of draught ale in the sun, outside a pub in Clapham Old Town. Once again, we reminisce as only old actors can. At one point I ask him, "Did you see the modern-dress *Henry V* at the National?"

He pauses, "I was in it... So were you!" Of course I was. We even played the first scene together. *'Old men forget and all shall be forgot!'*

Saturday March 10th

Last free Saturday for some time, as Trevor concentrates on the speaking parts in *Seagull*. Things will get really busy from now on: two weeks tonight, we will be performing our first public preview of *Lear*. Pity that Chelsea are playing away at Manchester City. Purposely avoid hearing the result and later watch them win 1-0 on Sky TV.

Monday March 12th

Still continuing with *Seagull,* although most people (apart from Richard, Romola, Frances and Gerald: the four leads) feel we should be spending all the time on *Lear.* I suppose Trevor knows what he is doing, but *Lear* is the reason why we are doing the tour and is by far the more difficult and complicated production.

Only come in during the afternoon for servants' entrance. Hot day; hotter in London than in Athens and the central heating in rehearsal room, despite global warming, is naturally at full-blast. Initially find it difficult to keep awake until Frances Barber lets rip. She is electrifying – you can't sleep when she's on song. Everyone is getting ready to depart for Stratford. The younger actors; Richard Goulding, Peter Hinton, Gerald Kyd, Philip Winchester and Ben Addis have now formed into their own little group and usually have drinks after rehearsal in the pub across the road. I'm sure they will leave a trail of debauchery behind them across the world. Even if I had the inclination, I would not have the energy. To quote Maurice Chevalier: "I'm glad I'm not young anymore!" I never see John Heffernan with them; he is fanatical about the theatre and dashes off nearly every evening to see a play somewhere. I think Ben Meyjes hurries back to his girlfriend, who works for some charity or other. As far as I can see, none of the boys seem to show any romantic interest in the female members of the company. I'm sure most of them would jump on Romola if they got half a chance, but she is beyond them, and already has a boyfriend who, I believe, writes for the *Guardian*.

Get the results of my cardiac test: everything is more or less fine. Excellent cholesterol level – blood pressure's slightly high.

Wednesday March 14th

We do an understudy line run of *Lear*. To my great relief, I more or less know it. I stop worrying about the words, which start to come naturally and I begin to feel the part for the first time. Am surprised and gratified when the mournful Melanie, who hardly ever speaks to me, congratulates me and says I was very moving. In fact nearly everybody was good, including Melanie herself, as were Naomi, Zoë, and Seymour, and I think John Heffernan and young Peter give as good performances as Edgar and Edmund as Philip and Ben, if not better. Not yet sure about Russell's Fool, but he certainly tries.

Thursday March 15th

Another full run of *Lear*. When scene follows scene in quick succession, even after all these weeks, it still seems unfamiliar. The venerable John Barton comes to watch. He looks very ancient now, and sits with a furrowed brow, like one of those trees in *Lord of the Rings*. Relieved to see he no longer chews razor blades, as he was reputed to have done in the sixties. Ian is brilliant in bursts but still has difficulty with some of the lines – is it because he has got so used to film acting? – but the production is gradually finding itself and Sylvester has quickened his pace.

Trevor, who seems slightly in awe of Barton (he was more or less running the RSC with Peter Hall when Trevor first appeared,) reports that the great man found it "one of the better *Lear*s of recent years".

Ian and most of us want to run *Lear* again tomorrow, but Trevor insists we go back to *Seagull*.

Saturday March 17ᵗʰ

Our last day in Clapham. We do a final run-through of *Lear*, the technical people who have come from Stratford sit and watch earnestly, taking copious notes. It has improved since Thursday. Ian starts tentatively, on one occasion I whisper a prompt in his ear, but when he gets to the scene where his daughters cast him out into the storm, he suddenly lets rip. In the great speech; "O, reason not the need…" his magnificent voice control makes it almost an aria, as exciting and moving as anything you'll ever hear in opera.

When Ian Holm stripped in the storm playing Lear at the National, I seem to remember some critics carping at the paucity of his member. As yet Mckellen has not revealed all, but he does so this morning with a vengeance: his magnificent manhood dangles in the dusty Clapham air. I watch the female heads of department avert their eyes like Victorian maidens. I'll never match up to him – in every aspect, Sir Ian's part is far bigger than mine. The run eventually ends with the technical people, who naturally see every show that comes to Stratford, applauding and nodding their heads in approval. We are all glad to be leaving Clapham. Trevor tells us what we all know: we have much work still to do.

Dinner at Patricia Hodge's, with Sheridan Morley's widow, Ruth. She has taken over most of Sheridan's writing assignments.

She is going to be based in New York but doesn't know what to do with Sheridan's library of 40,000 theatrical books. Sheridan was Noel Coward's literary executor. We are shocked when she tells us that as yet no British university wants Noel Coward's papers. They are wanted in America, but as Coward didn't want them to leave the country, they are now languishing in a cupboard.

Sunday March 18th

Terrible news: Dave Fournel, one of my truest and oldest friends and another founder-member of the National Youth Theatre, died in the night. Ring another old friend, Tony French, to tell him, and he tells me he has just been told his cancer is inoperable and that he has only a year to live. Very depressed and I am leaving home for Stratford tomorrow.

Stratford

Monday March 19th

Get up early and drive up to Stratford on the M40. It seems like such a long time since I first took the road to Stratford. I can remember that it was Richard Burton himself who advised me, during a break from filming on *Becket*, to make my career in the theatre and not to be seduced by films as he had been. He was dramatising things, as he always did – he positively revelled in being the biggest film star in the world, as he was at that time – but he also knew that most actors can only find a long and fulfilling career on stage. So, 40 years ago I rejected the only film offer I had on the table (the juvenile lead in a Hammer film about Rasputin) and began my first Stratford Season, playing Benvolio to Sir Ian Holm's Romeo. I can still see myself in 1967, brimming with the confidence of youth, and planning to work my way up the company; full of hopeful expectation. At least I can say I've gone the distance.

We all start off thinking we are going to be stars – the realisation that we won't comes at different times. Some poor souls leave drama school and never get a job, others quickly find they can't stand the constant rejection and disappointment. I still held on to the belief that I had that special quality until I was well into my thirties – always thinking that the big break was just around the corner. When I finally realised that it was not to be, I made a conscious decision to soldier on in the business, no matter what. I loved acting and being an actor too much, I would take whatever came. I am so glad that I did – especially with this new adventure about to unfold.

Flat's not too bad. Lovely views over the Avon, but the

carpet and oven are dirty. It is in a modern block, part of a development built on land sold by the RSC about 20 years ago. I can remember the big old house and lovely garden that was once here. Part of the deal was that the RSC was given a block of flats, which the RSC rents out to its visiting actors. They pay you £125 subsistence for living away from home, and promptly take it back, and more, in rent and commodity charges. I'm on the ground floor next to Ben Meyjes. Monica, Melanie, Guy and Trevor's assistant director, Gemma, are all above. I'm sure we will get to know each better now we're living in such close quarters. Lady Sainsbury, who is on the RSC Board, has lent Ian her beautiful cottage on Waterside. Bill is bringing his two beloved cocker spaniels with him so has rented one of the RSC's little houses with a small garden, almost opposite the stage door. Others are renting various properties the RSC owns around the town, whilst some are staying in cheaper, privately-rented accommodation. Guy, our intrepid Kenyan, is living in a caravan. John Heffernan has the cheapest accommodation of all as he is staying with his mother who lives in Stratford.

In the afternoon we all assemble at the Courtyard, the temporary venue for all the main plays here at Stratford until the entirely rebuilt RST re-opens. Though it looks just a functional brick building from the outside, the auditorium has a real Elizabethan feel about it.

There is nothing glamorous backstage at the Courtyard: it was never intended to be the main house, so there is not much room. I go upstairs to the plain, brick-walled dressing room. I'm sharing with Lear's two sons-in-law, Guy and Julian, as well as Seymour, big Adam and John Heffernan, who is going to be very good in the sneaky little part of Oswald. I've never really managed to break the ice with Seymour in all the years I've known him. I ask him what happened to a girlfriend I had here in Stratford in 1967 – I'd always suspected he was rather keen on her. "She was my first wife," he growls. I make further attempts at conversation and discover that he supports his home town Colchester United and Liverpool – and hates Chelsea.

The younger actors share two more rooms along the corridor. The girls are all crammed into one on the ground floor, where Jonathan and Sylvester share a small room, as do Ian and Bill.

We begin technical rehearsal which, knowing Trevor, will go on for days. We stagger slowly through the first scenes. Everyone tries to adjust their own performance to the theatre: we will have the audience on three sides of us. Trevor constantly fine-tunes positions, whilst Ian's eyes dart everywhere as he seeks out the most effective spot to deliver a line.

My evening is made by Chelsea winning the FA Cup replay 2-1, which I watch intermittently on the stagehands' TV.

Because of Union regulations, Trevor has to stop at 10. Some things have changed for the better: when I started in 1961 at Manchester Library Theatre, technical rehearsals went on all night. Most of the cast opt for a drink, but I'm too tired. I go back to my lonely little flat and wish I was back in Pimlico with Dora.

Tuesday March 20th

Cold night. The noise of the rushing Avon waters on the weir outside keeps making me want to pee. Wake up lonely and freezing.

Technical rehearsal continues. It becomes apparent that the design of the Courtyard, which will be repeated in the RST when it is rebuilt, is faulty. The thrust stage has terrible sight lines so unless the actor is moving, he blocks the view of large numbers of the audience. Trevor is forced to put most of the action towards the back of the stage as if there's a proscenium arch. One begins to wonder what was wrong with the original RST: it was good enough for Olivier, Gielgud and Scofield. So many great productions were created in it. Only my opinion of course, but isn't it a case of ill thought-out change for the sake of change? And what a waste of millions! Talking of waste, four musicians will be touring the world with us. As their music is played a long way from the stage and is only heard by the audience through speakers it could so easily have been recorded, but, unfortunately the original charter of Stratford theatre stipulates that every production must have live music. Fortunate for the musicians, however.

Discover, in the close proximity of the crowded dressing room, some of my fellow players have BO. Hope it won't get worse in the tropics.

Go to The Black Swan (or 'Dirty Duck', as it has always been known since thirsty actors as far back as Sir Frank Benson – and probably much further – started stumbling the 100 yards there from the stage door). Memories of the Summer of Love of 1967 flood back, but now the young, nubile, dolly barmaids have been replaced by hairy, butch Australian blokes. Pam, the formidable Brummie manageress, with whom you had to find favour to get an after-hours drink and be part of the scene, has long departed. Can't help but feel it's lost some of its charm.

Wednesday March 21st

Our first preview performance is only three days away and there is a slight feeling of unease as we stagger through lighting cues, sound cues and scene changes. So much is expected of this production. In the back of my mind I recall the *Macbeth,* always an unlucky play, which Peter Hall did here with Paul Scofield in 1967. That was going to be a definitive production and it too was scheduled to go around the world. We rehearsed for a few weeks, things were going well, then Hall got shingles. The production was postponed and never recovered. It got a lukewarm reception and we got no further than Moscow. Will history repeat itself? I am having trouble with the Gentleman's 60-odd lines. I've never had trouble before or really worried about the magical way lines go into an actor's brain. Every veteran actor fears that one day this magic will leave him. I've heard a certain dame resorts to

Eye Q tablets from Boots.

We eventually get to the end of the play and start again from the beginning as Trevor polishes and cleans up. Everyone seems very quiet and tired, but that is normal after three long days of technical.

Thursday March 22nd

A better day. In our dressing rooms we find our costumes waiting for us on rails, together with a pretty dresser. We put them on for the first time. What we originally saw as sketches now look superb. Ian is dressed in a scarlet and gold coat in the first scene; Jonathan and Bill, as Kent and Gloucester, are accoutred as Russian grand dukes in black and silver; the three daughters are glamorous in décolleté ball gowns. Romola, naturally, is particularly ravishing. Frances' dress has a high collar, made of dark lace that makes her resemble the Wicked Queen in *Snow White*.

All round the auditorium, laptops gleam in the dark, as lighting, sound and music all fit into place. Trevor is constantly reworking positions. He discovers that an arrowhead formation works best on the thrust – you cannot be upstaged as in a normal theatre. I have never known him to be so nervous. He was always calm at the National, even in *Troilus and Cressida,* when we got so far behind with the technical that we had to do the first preview without dress rehearsing the second half.

We have real rain in the storm, which floods the front row.

Friday March 23rd

Ian is having his hair dyed pure white and I am suddenly asked to stand in for him, in the scene where Lear wakes from his madness and recognises Cordelia. Am relieved to find I know the lines and am touched at the end when Romola whispers: "Well done, David." In the evening we do a full dress rehearsal. It is very frantic working out how one gets to either side of the stage to make one's entrances. In this case it's even more frantic as the Courtyard is not built like a normal theatre. One is always terrified of being off: a worse nightmare even than drying on stage. As well as the usual entrances from the sides, we also use the two vomitaries that thrust out right through the auditorium. I even have to make a couple of entrances through the lobby, as does Ian, past gaping tourists. I see a couple of Americans casually take photos of him as if it has been laid on as a photo opportunity. The show is long (all Trevor's productions are), but goes better than I'd expected, though I still don't find poor old Sylvester funny, even with his music hall costume and various props, including a fool's head which he uses as a sort of ventriloquist's dummy. Like all comedians he desperately needs an audience.

Tomorrow the previews begin, before the critics come in and the show opens for real. An audience will judge for the first time the fruits of our 12 weeks of labour – I have no doubt we'll be ready. As I drop off to sleep I realise that, from now on I will be expected to play Lear at the drop of a hat if anything happens to Ian, no matter that I have had barely a couple of rehearsals. I'm relieved to find that it doesn't worry me. I am more or less secure with the lines: imagine the nightmares if I weren't.

Saturday March 24th

First preview. Trevor spends the day giving us notes and making final adjustments. A sense of keen anticipation is all around the building, which grows gradually throughout the day. All too soon we find ourselves standing nervously in the wings, and then the moment finally comes. The musicians begin to play Stephen Edis' stirring Russian music from the depths of the building. Seymour and I, at the head of the waiting procession, watch the red cue light gleaming through the darkness. It turns to green; we each take a deep breath and then walk firmly out to centre stage, before turning down towards the waiting audience. The rest are coming behind us, with Ian far at the rear: we are under way at last.

Everything fits into place. Ian rises to the occasion, as I knew he would, and is wonderful. But others come up as well: Bill is rock-firm as Gloucester; Frances and Monica are suitably evil as the wicked daughters; Ben Meyjes works his arse off as Mad Tom; Philip looks dashing in his costume and fights a good duel; Sylvester manages to get a few laughs, as does John Heffernan as Oswald. Everybody else, including the Gentleman, puts all they can into it. There is a great feeling of excitement and the audience is completely enthralled. I feel very proud to be a member of this company. Even though the show is three hours and 40 minutes, there are cheers at the end. Trevor is delighted and relieved; we each get 'Treved' as we come off stage. Everyone seems happy, but we must remember that this is only a preview. The first night and the all powerful critics: Billington, De Jongh, Nightingale *et al* – the big hurdle – is waiting round the bend.

Drive back to London, get home in the early hours.

Monday March 26th

After a restful Sunday, drive back up to Stratford on the old road, via Henley, Woodstock and the Cotswolds. A lovely spring morning. Apart from the speed cameras, nothing much has changed: England is still beautiful. One of the bonuses of touring is that you see a lot of the country. I once drove through Sussex on a sunny day with the sultry Kate O'Mara, who told me that her idea of heaven would be to drive through the English countryside for eternity.

Arrive in Stratford to learn that Frances Barber has fallen off her bike: a female American tourist stepped in front of her in the High Street. She has dislocated her knee and her voice is tired, but insists she will not be off. There is a scurrilous article in the *Daily Mirror*, headlined, *'Gandalf Waves his Wand'*, claiming that some members of the audience were shocked at Ian's nudity and complained that they hadn't been warned. I can't believe it. Probably phoned in by some would be journalist on the make. Trevor is very happy and relaxed, however, and gives us four hours of notes. The only real problem is that the show, like most Nunn productions, is too long: he says it must come out at under three and a half hours. He will give us the cuts tomorrow. I wonder how much of the Gentleman will go?

Tonight's performance is naturally a bit flat. As well as being the second night, it is a theatrical tradition that Monday performances are always bad, as are Friday nights in the West End, when wives drag their reluctant husbands along from the City. Am slowly finding my personal rhythm backstage – how much time I can spend in the dressing room etc, which will not be a great deal. Apart from the storm and hovel scenes, I am on all the time that Ian is on, plus my two scenes with Jonathan Hyde. Meet Russell in the corridor behind the stage and realise that we both have about 15 minutes free before he comes on as the Doctor. Decide to run our Lear/Fool scenes every night at this time. He is terribly keen and nervous. He tells me about his Italian boyfriend with whom he is about to enter a civil partnership (apparently his ex-wife, who taught him to act, is coming to the ceremony). I realise I can go over my scenes with Gloucester, Edgar and Kent with Seymour, John and Julian in the dressing room.

Tuesday March 27th

The RSC has bowed to the power of the *Daily Mirror*: there are now signs attached to the doors, alerting patrons that this production of *Lear* contains gunshots, strobe lighting and a glimpse of male nudity. I watch two elderly ladies reading it – they nod approvingly.

We wait apprehensively as Trevor gives out the cuts. I lose six of my most poetic lines:

'This night, wherein the cub-drawn bear would couch,
The lion and the belly-pinched wolf
Keep their fur dry, unbonneted he runs,
And bids what will take all.'

And:

'Sorrow would be a rarity most belov'd,
If all could so become it.'

Can't complain – everybody has lost something. Although I can't help but feel more time would be saved if Sylvester would cut down a little on his beloved spoons. The cuts won't be implemented until they are rehearsed in tomorrow – needless to say that tonight I feel I speak the lines perfectly for the first time. Frances bravely limps about with a stick and the performance is the best yet.

Wednesday March 28th

In the afternoon we put in the cuts. It seems simple, but one gets used to the established rhythm. In the performance I stumble on one line and then Jonathan Hyde, as Kent, dries because of the different cue I have given him. Later on I refer to Edgar as Edmund, which makes the plot ridiculous. Even though hardly any member of the audience would have noticed (apart from Trevor), I feel very unsatisfied. Am I getting past it? With all the cuts we have only saved three minutes. Naturally, Ian varies his speed with the emotion of the part and I think he is actually getting slower.

I arrange tickets for Henry Goodman, who won an Olivier for his Shylock under Trevor's direction. Afterwards we have drinks in the Duck with his friend, a fellow student at RADA, who is now a director of the Habima Theatre in Israel. As far as I know they are the first theatricals that have seen it. I am a little disappointed as I sense they are not overly impressed. Henry says the cast seem to be straining to push the words out – which is true because we are battling with the acoustics and sight lines. His Israeli friend says the same architects are building a new theatre for the Habima in Tel Aviv and it has the same problems. Again I wonder if all this money is being wasted. Will the new RST be Shakespeare's Millennium Dome? Ian joins us. They have much to talk about as Ian has done his one-man show in Israel, though nothing much is said about *Lear*. An amusing moment when Ian notices the actress Janet Suzman, Trevor's first wife, chatting at another table with a dark-haired young man. Ian assumes he is Janet and Trevor's son: his godson, whom he has not seen for years. He goes over to say hello to the young man, and after a very deep and friendly conversation, finds out it is not his godson after all.

Thursday March 29th

Morning free – spring is really in the air. Go for a gentle jog along the Avon and meet Bill walking his two beloved cocker spaniels. Suddenly, Stratford seems once again the beautiful place I remember from my salad days. In the afternoon Trevor, still worried about the length, makes us do a speed run: rushing through the play at double speed, without props or costumes, as if we're in a silent film. He says that whenever he has done this before, the play has always lost a minimum of six minutes. There seem to be great worries about audibility: perhaps Henry and his friend were right. We all have an hour of vocal exercises with Cis Berry, the doyenne of RSC speech. She makes us project our voices from various parts of the auditorium. I decide that, as I haven't had any vocal problems for half a century, I will speak as normal.

Performance goes smoothly with another great reception at the end. Trevor tells us over the Tannoy that, despite his speed run, we have put on a minute.

Friday March 30th

Today is the funeral of David Fournel. I can't get down to Kent so at 11.15, when the funeral is due to take place, I go into the gardens of the RST and throw a white rose, as David was a Yorkshireman, into the Avon, expecting it to go downstream towards the Holy Trinity Church. The current takes it no further than the 'Dirty Duck', where it comes stubbornly to rest among the reeds. David always did find it difficult to pass a good pub.

At the Courtyard Trevor continues to make minor adjustments. Poor Frances is still battling on with the stick, in considerable pain. She has never been off in her life and, like most seasoned pros, is determined not to break her record.

Best performance yet. Afterwards we all go to dinner with sponsors' guests. Tables laid out around the gallery in the Courtyard lobby. Good food and wine. I sit at a table full of hard-headed lawyers who are overwhelmed by the play. I'm quite at home with hard-headed lawyers – my eldest son is one.

Saturday March 31st

Brave Frances did further damage to her knee in the performance last night and is now weeping in agony. It's clearly far more serious than I thought – it had all seemed like a joke at first. I admire her guts, but she would have been better advised to have missed a few previews and rested it. Not sure how long she can go on like this.

Drive back to London after show.

Sunday April 1st

Dora and I go to Bill Gaunt's surprise 70th birthday party in the beautiful garden of his home in Chiswick. Full of actors and actresses who I remember as beautiful juveniles, all envious that Bill and I have got such a fantastic job. Suddenly everyone has become stout and aged. It would be too unkind to mention names.

Monday April 2nd

Return to Stratford to learn that Frances' knee ligaments have gone completely. She must have keyhole surgery and will be off for anything up to six weeks! Melanie Jessop, her understudy is on and will also play Madame Arkadina in *Seagull* until Frances is fit. Even bigger news is that the powers that be (Trevor or the RSC) have decided to cancel the critics invitation for the official first night of *Lear* tomorrow. I cannot believe that we have been rehearsing solidly for three months and aren't now going to officially open! I think it is a mistake, and all the others in the dressing room seem to think so too (although actors are a funny breed and you never can know what they really think at a time like this). Goneril is an important part, but it is not Lear. In any case, an understudy taking over at short notice is part of the excitement and romance of live theatre. Ian is in favour of the postponement and thinks that the critics should review both *Lear* and *Seagull* on the same day, after the latter previews. I wonder if this will be what happens.

Melanie takes over seamlessly from Frances and gives a thoroughly professional performance. Naomi takes over Melanie's small part, of the woman who leads the blinded Gloucester and will also play Melanie's very good role of Polina in *Seagull*. I am pleased for her; she is a frustrated actress, longing to act. Now, she will have weeks under Trevor's direction.

Tuesday April 3rd

Our scheduled First Night. After a morning off, we meet for Trevor's notes at 2.30 which last throughout the afternoon.

Dora arrives up from London with my friend Hugh Futcher; it is good to see the old rogue again.

Needless to say it is a strange first night. Most people aren't sending the usual Good Luck cards or presents, but even though the critics are absent, we are still nervous because the house is full of friends, agents and casting directors. Nerves provide all the stimulus we need and it feels like a vibrant performance.

The first night party in the Duck is still on. The old, timber-framed inner sanctum which the formidable Pam only allowed her favoured few to enter has been replaced by a large, characterless brick room. It is very crowded, as the cast appearing in *Coriolanus*, the final production in the old RST, are also present. Dora is recovering from her operation and looks very glamorous. Both she and Hugh have a great time chatting to handsome young actors. Dora finds Philip Winchester charming. She and Hugh both think it is a magnificent production and, for the first time, I am totally convinced it will be a huge success.

Wednesday April 4th

Strange to have no reviews to read after a first night, although Benedict Nightingale writes a long article in *The Times*, echoing my feelings that we should have let the critics in. I'm not called today as Trevor is rehearsing the speaking parts in *Seagull*, so am free to enjoy another beautiful spring day in Stratford. Dora and I walk along the banks of the Avon and are happy to be alive.

At the theatre gradually getting to know more about the other occupants of my dressing room. I talk most with Guy, when he's not outside in the yard smoking. He has a very inquisitive and open mind. John Heffernan spends most of the time reading the arts pages in the newspapers; he has a great pile on his dressing table – he seems to see everything that is on. Julian is always on his laptop, writing the next Christmas play for his East Anglian company. Adam is a big quiet Yorkshireman in his late thirties, who weighs every word he utters. He worked as an architect before becoming an actor and has a nice girlfriend with a well paid regular job in the City: just what an actor needs. Discover to my amazement that Seymour and I shared another girlfriend in the dim and distant past. I can't see what any girl who liked me would see in Seymour, or vice-versa. We have very different characters and tastes. He tells me that when Trevor took his first RSC production of *The Taming of the Shrew* to LA in 1968, he, Seymour, was driving a hired car on the freeway with his girlfriend (not one of mine) beside him on the long front seat, and Trevor sleeping in the back. The young lady was smoking a cigarette and suddenly some burning tobacco fell onto Seymour's leg. His foot automatically slammed down on the accelerator and they shot across the highway, only missing the oncoming traffic by a hair's breadth. What would have happened if they'd hit an oncoming car? The world would have been deprived of Trevor Nunn – no *Cats* or *Les Mis*. It would undoubtedly have affected our trade balance.

Thursday April 5th

Tomorrow we will have a complete day off, as the RSC do not play on Good Friday – I suspect it's because they would have to pay us double time. Dora likes our little flat overlooking the Avon so much, she decides that we will spend tomorrow going to IKEA in Birmingham, to get some things to make it more habitable. I groan at the thought.

After an uneventful *Lear* we watch TV together in our cosy little room. Through the window the moon sparkles on the waters of the Avon. Life feels good.

Friday April 6th

I have found every visit I've ever made to IKEA painful. Dora and I usually end up having a row. On one occasion I forgot to offload everything from the trolley into the boot of our car and left half of it behind. Today is no exception; we get lost for over an hour trying to find it on the Birmingham ring road, then spend a fortune on pots, pans, glasses and rugs that we'll never use once we get back to London.

Sunday April 8th

Have lunch with my step-niece Sarah and her husband, Lloyd
Dorfman at their beautiful house in Hampstead, which was once
the home of Gerald du Maurier (famous actor and father to
Rebecca author, Daphne du Maurier). Sarah and Lloyd are both
great patrons of the arts: Sarah has just endowed a new green
room at the Festival Hall in memory of my step-sister, Audrey,
and Lloyd's company, Travelex, sponsors the £10 ticket scheme
at the National. Indeed, I can remember rehearsing the modern-
dress *Henry V* with Nick Hytner the day the deal was resolved. It
was just before the invasion of Iraq. Nick was putting together a
scene he'd devised, which entailed the shooting of the French
prisoners. Nearly everyone who was not speaking at the time was
kneeling very uncomfortably at the back of the stage with a
sandbag over their head, pretending their hands were tied
together. Suddenly, Nick's secretary burst into the rehearsal room
and said that the sponsor was on the phone. Nick apologised and
told us to wait, saying the entire season depended on this phone
call. He came back 20 minutes later with a huge smile on his face,
"This wonderful man, Lloyd Dorfman, head of Travelex has
agreed to sponsor the entire season. I was afraid he would pull
out because of the war."

I pulled the sandbag from my head and said, "Do you realise
I am a member of his family? If it was an Italian family I
wouldn't be here with a sandbag on my head. I'd be playing the
bloody Duke of Exeter at least." Nick Hytner had stopped
smiling. I don't think we have the same sense of humour.

Fellow guest is a charming man by the name of Land. His
father was a Jewish immigrant who came here in the thirties and
was so grateful to his adopted country that he called his company
'Hope and Glory', so that when he answered the phone he could
say, "Land, of Hope and Glory."

Monday April 9th

Drive back to Stratford early to escape the bank holiday rush. *Lear* is now fully grounded-in and I think it is a truly magnificent show, although until the critics give their judgement we won't know whether we have an official hit or not. It seems that Ian was right – it has been officially decided that they will review both plays on May 31st – the original planned press night for *Seagull*. It seems as far away as when we started rehearsing on January 2nd.

Flat in Stratford now seems very empty without Dora, who is heading off to Israel for ten days. Go for a drink in the Duck after the show. Ian sits there quietly, in regal splendour, with most of the cast clustering eagerly around him. It is very noisy. In recent years I have become slightly deaf in one ear and can hardly hear what anyone says, but everyone seems happy and relaxed. Meet Jonathan Hyde's wife, Isabel, a Scottish opera singer who will be accompanying him on most of the tour. She is charming and warm.

Tuesday April 10th

We, the non-speaking members of the *Seagull* cast, are called to rehearse with the main characters at the spanking new RSC rehearsal facilities, which are situated in a very dreary part of Stratford, surrounded by a retail park. I'm not sure how long the RSC will occupy this place – hopefully only until the new theatre is built. The charm of working in Stratford was always the pleasant ambiance; you could walk out of rehearsal straight into the gardens by the Avon. The new complex is clean and soulless; long corridors of blue carpet, like in a private hospital. Also very stuffy, and with this warm spring weather it's hard to keep awake.

At the rehearsal Trevor spends a lot of time on Melanie, who is getting very good in both of Frances' parts. She has not yet got

Frances' confidence and sense of fun as Arkadina, but there is not much to choose between their Gonerils. I'm sure she is going to feel it when she has to relinquish the roles. The only time I've ever taken over, for any length of time, was in *Love for Love* at Chichester, when Derek Jacobi went down with appendicitis on the opening night. He never came back and I played it for the entire run. I know how I would have felt if it had been taken away from me. You can't help it: you begin to feel the part belongs to you. Seeing *Seagull* again after several weeks only makes it seem better and of course it will improve further before the first previews in just over two weeks' time. I wonder which show the critics will prefer.

Tonight is the last performance of *Lear* until April 27th. Trevor is in to see it, for the first time since last Tuesday (the first night that never was). He has fingers in many pies as usual: he is setting up the transfer of *Rock and Roll* to Broadway, as well as preparing a student production of *Cymbeline* at Oxford. Again Ian leads us all in what feels like a magnificent performance. Almost the entire audience gives a standing ovation at the end – and they aren't all Americans, who seem addicted to them. I heard Dustin Hoffman couldn't ever understand why he never received a standing ovation for his Shylock in London – long and loud applause, yes, but never a standing ovation. On the night Laurence Olivier died, the story goes, Leigh Lawson, who was playing Antonio, suggested that Hoffman should say a few words in tribute at the curtain call. Hoffman agreed and after receiving his normal loud and long applause, he dutifully stepped forward and said, "It is with great sorrow that I announce the death of the greatest actor in the English-speaking world, Laurence Olivier." At this, the entire audience rose and stood in silent homage. As Hoffman left the stage, he whispered to Lawson, "You've gotta fuckin' die in this fuckin' country to get a standing ovation!"

As Winston Churchill is reputed to have said: "If that story isn't true, it ought to be!"

Trevor is delighted with the performance and, after taking care to give special praise to Melanie and Naomi, invites us all to dinner at the Duck tomorrow night.

Evening is crowned by Chelsea's magnificent performance against Valencia – which nearly matches Ian's as Lear.

Wednesday April 11th

The entire company, with the exception of the fortunate Sylvester (who is the only one not in *Seagull* and will have a week or so off) spends a very long and hot day in the rehearsal rooms. Trevor keeps giving the non-speaking members more and more to do. We now have to change the scenery as part of the action in character. Trevor also devises a little sub-plot, whereby my Butler is now under threat from Peter's cocky young Peasant, who eventually takes over my position in the last act. Peter himself is a very self-assured young man, straight out of drama school, with shoulder-length black hair, cut in a style reminiscent of Lord Farquaad in *Shrek.*

We all have supper with Trevor at the Duck, apart from Sylvester and Philip, who has flown to Madrid to attend the premiere of *Fly Boys*, a film he has recently made. We're at two long tables in the back room. Trevor presides over one; Ian the other. Food is not too good – standards definitely seem to have dropped since Pam's day. Then, at least, you could always get a decent steak and chips. Begin by sitting next to Ian, who is extraordinarily humble. He thanks me for a little note I gave him today – Sorin mentions the personal telephone he has in his office, I pointed out it must have been an extraordinary thing in provincial Russia at that time. Ian asks me to go through Lear with him and point out any other things I have noted: I am very flattered. Later I move on to Trevor's table, where Peter and some of the younger ones are hanging on his every word as he gives them the fascinating story of how he came to write the lyrics for '*Memory*' which has subsequently been sung by every major diva in the world.

Thursday April 12th

Begin technical rehearsals for *Seagull*. I think Stephen Edis' music creates the ideal atmosphere and mood. He did the same thing with *Summerfolk* at the National. I'm sure one day he will write the music for an Oscar-winning movie.

Frances arrives from London on crutches; she couldn't keep away. She has given up her own accommodation in Stratford and is moving in with Ian, who, most unselfishly considering all he has on his plate, has offered to look after her. Frances immediately regales us with a number of hilarious anecdotes, including one involving her balancing on a bedpan with her leg in traction. (By an extraordinary coincidence, her surgeon was a Dr Shakespeare). There is no chance of her going back on stage for several weeks yet: Melanie will play the first previews of *Seagull*. Melanie hugs and kisses Frances profusely, but it will be difficult for her to play Frances' parts whilst Frances herself looks on. I feel sorry for Naomi. Nobody seems to notice that she has taken over the difficult part of Polina, and is doing it very well. I resolve to be nicer to her, but we hardly meet during the evening except onstage. Once a play begins to run, you barely see some people because you are always on at different times. Every night I notice Ben Meyjes and Monica, who play husband and wife in *Seagull*, whispering together as they wait to go on, like the married couple they play on stage. There is no hint of romance though. Ben, a young man of impeccable morals, would make a worthy vicar or missionary and, typically, has a girlfriend who works for Amnesty International.

I was looking forward to spending long periods of time reading in the dressing room. Realise now, however, that with all the servant business that Trevor is putting in, I will have just as many entrances as I have in *Lear*.

Saturday April 14th

At lunchtime I catch sight of Trevor in busy Marks & Spencer, dressed as ever in his shabby blue denim shirt and jeans, holding a sandwich and a bottle of fruit juice. He looks bewildered as he surveys the long line waiting for the quick checkout tills. An old lady behind me whispers to her neighbour: "That's that there Trevor Nunn." When he gets to the top of the queue he fails to see the light flashing.

"Number six!" is yelled over the Tannoy.

Trevor looks mortified. "Oh, I'm so sorry," he murmurs as he creeps shamefacedly to the till.

Sunday April 15th

My younger son Emil is spending the weekend with me, as his wife Lindsay and their children, Mia and Fabian, are in Portugal with her parents. Lovely Sunday with Emil – we've not spent a day alone together for years. Beautiful weather again too. We sit outside the flat by the river and read the papers. Snide article by Richard Brooks in *Sunday Times*, '*Farcical scenes at the RSC over its star-studded King Lear and Seagull. Nunn's decision not to have press night until end of May, three weeks before it closes. Is this Nunn's revenge on whining critics?*' 'Star-studded'? Not sure about that. Who is a 'name' apart from Ian and Frances, and perhaps Romola? No mention of the fact that this is only the beginning, that we are going off on a world tour and then will do a full season in London as well. Besides, perhaps reviewing both plays on the same day might not be such a bad idea. It will make it an event, an opportunity to show that we are a real ensemble.

There still appears to be this ingrained prejudice against Trevor. It was apparent when he ran the National, just as successfully, in my opinion, as Nick Hytner (upon whom the press never fails to lavish praise). Trevor even left the National with a surplus. The great problem with running the National is filling the Olivier. Trevor did it by putting on big musicals. He believed a 'national' theatre should cater for all tastes and many of the elitists, perhaps jealous of the fortune Trevor made with musicals, resented it. They seem to forget that Richard Eyre, Trevor's predecessor (who enjoys near beatific status) started the trend with *Guys and Dolls* and *Carousel*. Hytner has been fortunate because the sponsorship of Travelex and its £10 a seat scheme have enabled him to put on affordable, highbrow fare for younger audiences.

On our way to lunch in an excellent pub, away from the tourist hordes, Emil and I meet Gerald with an attractive young lady, who he introduces as his new girlfriend. She is an actress and will be coming over to join him on the tour when we get to Australia – he's not wasting any time. Emil and I later visit another pub to watch Chelsea beat Blackburn in the FA Cup semi-final. Day only slightly spoiled in the evening, when Gemma kindly comes to hear my Lear. Perhaps I've drunk too much celebrating Chelsea's victory, but I don't know it half as well as I thought I did.

Monday April 16th

Wake up worried about Lear. It is one thing listening to Ian every night, but what I really need is to speak it myself, get my tongue around the words, rehearse a scene again and again with Gemma and the other understudies, which, due to us doing both plays at once, I haven't yet had a chance to do. True, we will have five days of rehearsal before I perform in the understudy run on May 4th – but what if Ian is off before that?

Have morning free so decide to go out to the Rollright Stones; a miniature Stonehenge in the Cotswold Hills. In 1959 when Charles Laughton was attempting Lear he would often drive out there at night with Ian Holm, who was playing his Fool, to rehearse the storm scene. Holm told me about it when I was playing Benvolio to his Romeo in 1967. He said that

Laughton, who by then lacked the energy and strength to play Lear on stage, was awe-inspiring when he declaimed his speeches under the stars. One night, after a few drinks (drink-driving rules were far slacker in those days) Holm drove me out to the stones and gave me his impersonation of Laughton doing Lear. It was an experience I shall never forget: Holm seemed to defy the very elements. He spoke the words as if he were inventing them for the first time, as the stones stood round us in the moonlight. The local legend is that they were originally a king and his knights, turned to stone by a witch – that night I swear some of them moved. I never saw Holm's acclaimed *Lear* at the National, but I'm sure it had its origins at the Rollright Stones.

I hope that perhaps some of the magic will rub off on me, if I say the same lines in the same place – besides, here at least I will have the opportunity of really letting rip. I contemplate taking Russell with me but decide it will be better if I am alone. It is a fine spring morning as I find the stones, park the car by the side of the road, climb over the stile, and stand in the middle. They look far smaller than they did that night. A few sheep gaze at me from an adjoining field. I gaze up at the heavens, take a deep breath and bellow: "Blow, winds and crack your cheeks...!" At that exact moment, a tour bus comes up the hill and disgorges a load of American students, who proceed to clamber over the stones around me. Every single one seems to find them 'awesome'. They pose, take photos and drape themselves around them. An attractive girl asks me to take a photo of her and her boyfriend. My inspiration dwindles and I decide to drive back to Stratford with the speeches undeclaimed.

Rehearse *Seagull* in afternoon. Trevor comes back from visiting the old RST for the first time in nearly 20 years. Extraordinary that he hasn't seen a production there in all that time. He says the auditorium (which will be gutted), has better sight lines than most theatres in London and New York. Every seat in the house has a clear view of the stage.

Tuesday April 17th

First preview of *Seagull* but there's not much sense of occasion. After full houses for *Lear*, bit of a shock to play before only 50%. Bill is playing Sorin for the first two nights and apparently the bookings are much better for the performances when Ian is on. Bill is excellent but the show doesn't go as well as I had expected. Melanie, is very nervous, and stiffens up as Arkadina. I sense she slightly loses the audience halfway through. We all thought Guy was so funny in rehearsals – Trevor's face would crease up whenever he watched him, but he doesn't get many laughs tonight. Romola looks beautiful as Nina and acts from her heart. She is certainly moving, but does her voice occasionally grate? Have she and Richard enough experience for such difficult parts? But then Trevor has never been afraid of putting his faith in young talent – he found Ben Wilshaw playing small parts at the National and made him a star by casting him as Hamlet at the Old Vic. Trevor has tried to increase the drama, putting Konstantin's attempted suicide onstage along with dramatic music, but will the critics attack him for meddling with Chekhov? Frances and Ian both sit and watch – a bit like United, playing without Rooney and Ronaldo. This is still very much a work in progress.

Wednesday April 18th

Both Ian and Frances think the lighting during yesterday performance was too dark. You must be able to see faces clearly for comedy, which makes up most of the play. A laugh often depends on the slightest nuance of expression. A long afternoon as Trevor gives three hours of notes and us non-speaking servants just sit there. We would be better employed doing understudy rehearsals for *Lear*. House is still only half full for tonight's performance – what will it be like when Ian takes over tomorrow?

Melanie is still showing signs of nerves.

Follow Chelsea v West Ham in dressing room on my little radio. They do it again: 4-1! How long can they keep this up?

Thursday April 19th

Ian takes over Sorin and the house is nearly full. I'm not onstage so I can hardly tell, but there is a general feeling in my dressing room that Bill gives the truer performance. But the audience is there to be entertained and Ian has them eating out of his hand, getting laughs at every opportunity. Very warm reception at the end. Being a servant without lines is beginning to get tedious already, but soon we will be playing both plays alternately.

Friday April 20th

In the dressing room Guy, John Heffernan and Julian note that Ian is making a lot of noise on stage, tapping, and coughing: inventing extra business. Is he finding Sorin too small a part? I was taught at RADA that there were no small parts, just small actors – but then some actors can't help being bigger than others.

Trevor tells us he is leaving us to get on with it for a few days – his head is too full of *Seagull* to see it clearly any more. We've had him watching over us nearly every day for the last four months; usually you open a play in four to six weeks and then rarely see the director at all after that – it will be good to have a little break. I wonder if he's slipping over to New York to do some casting on *Porgy and Bess*?

Beginning to get bored with Stratford. No desire to go to the Duck every night, as most of the cast seem to do. I find it noisy and uncomfortable. Ian goes after practically every *Lear*, because he has to unwind after such a performance, and Bill goes because he is a draught beer drinker, but I, having rather less to unwind, would rather go back to my flat, have a Martini, watch TV or read. Am I boring old fart? I wasn't always. I fondly remember walking into that same bar 40 years ago with my Dalmatian dog and my fire engine red Mini parked outside. In my youthful folly and vanity, I considered myself to be the very epitome of an up-and-coming actor. The Beatles had just released *Sergeant Pepper*, and throughout that summer girls came to England from all over the world looking for romance. If they couldn't find an actual pop star, a Shakespearean actor from Stratford was high on their wish list. It was, perhaps, a unique moment in sexual freedom – the pill was freely available for the first time and things like AIDS had never been heard of. In these days of political correctness, am not too ashamed to admit that I drove many young ladies back to the thatched cottage I was renting at Ettington, including one of Peter Hall's nannies (maybe that was one of the reasons I didn't make as much progress in the company as I'd hoped).

I remember, years later, I met one of the young ladies in question in Regent's Park. I was playing Theseus in *A Midsummer Night's Dream* at the Open Air Theatre and was exercising my son's Yorkshire terrier between shows. She looked at me, shook her head sadly and said; "David, your dog has shrunk."

Glad Dora is coming back from Israel tomorrow.

Sunday April 22nd

Drive to London early in the morning in time for breakfast with Emil, Lindsay, Mia and Fabian who all stayed with Dora last night. A quiet, happy day – spoilt only by Chelsea's failure to beat Newcastle.

Monday April 23rd

Dora drives back to Stratford with me where we discover the surgeon has left stitching in her shoulder. She will have to go back to London tomorrow to have it removed.

Stratford is full of gentle Indians who are performing a magical version of *A Midsummer Night's Dream* at the Swan. Dora sees *Seagull* and likes much of it but thinks Romola waves her hands a little too much and has difficulty hearing her in the last act. She also thinks Richard needs more variation as Konstantin, but says Melanie is very good. I have to say I agree, Melanie has now shed her nerves and looks very beautiful with a white turban around her black ringlets. Dora also thinks Gerald is sexy as Trigorin and Monica excellent as Masha. Ian plays Sorin so house is nearly full.

Tuesday April 24th

Dora, back in London, phones to say the surgeon saw her and said the stitching was nothing to worry about. Mounting boredom with Stratford. I suppose it's only natural – it must be my sixth summer in this town, though it must still be an exciting place for most of the younger ones. I'm sure some will look back on this as I remember the summer of '67. Remind myself of the exciting tour to come.

Feel sorry for Bill – every time he plays Sorin the house is only a quarter full.

Wednesday April 25th

I rehearse Lear on the stage at last. It goes well. Gemma is a good director and very encouraging. I know the lines and realise I can play him. All the others, including Russell, are coming on fine. We will do a full understudy run, with full lighting and effects, on May 4th – I must say I'm looking forward to it. As it will probably be the only time I play Lear, I decide to go for broke and send off a general email, inviting all my old cronies to come up and see me. Most of them, the non-acting ones, are retired and have plenty of free time. Also suggest to Dora that she brings the granddaughters, Mia and Charlotte. They are only seven but I'm sure it will be something they'll remember.

After the grandeur of Lear I return in the evening to the banality of my silent Butler, but still it's been a good day, especially as Chelsea beat Liverpool 1-0 in the first leg of the European Cup semi-final. Seymour is not best pleased.

Thursday April 26th

This weekend is the big annual celebration for Shakespeare's birthday. Ambassadors will come up from London and parade through the streets of Stratford, to lay wreaths on the Bard's grave. It is also being combined with the RSC's open day on Sunday; which will include workshops, sonnet readings, forums, culminating in a final recital in the old RST before the interior is gutted. Nearly all the leading actors and actresses from the past 40 years will be taking part. Lynn Darnley, who is organising some of the festivities, asks if I will read Prospero's 'Ye elves of hills...etc' in Holy Trinity Church on Sunday morning. I don't think she could get anyone else.

Friday April 27th

This evening we go back to *Lear*. Sylvester returns and it's good to see his warm, friendly face again. Trevor persists in giving us notes from the last time we did it, a couple of weeks ago. In the evening a refreshed Ian gives a magnificent performance. It is good to play to packed houses again and have some acting to do – even the Gentleman has his moments.

Sunday April 29th

A grand birthday celebration indeed. It is rather like an old Ealing Comedy or a period play on Sunday night television. The dignitaries of Stratford, clad in Tudor gowns and caps and led by the town band, parade to Holy Trinity on a beautiful spring morning. Decide to address my Prospero to members of the congregation directly, as 'elves of hill', 'demi-puppets', etc. I find I am saying: "You, whose pastime is to make midnight mushrooms" into the eyes of the wife of an African ambassador. She doesn't look amused – does she think I'm accusing her of taking hallucinatory drugs?

Final performance in the old RST; Donald Sinden, Judi

Dench, Harriet Walker, Anthony Sher, Juliet Stephenson, Michael Pennington, David Warner, Simon Russell Beale, Roger Allam, Toby Stephens and of course Ian, plus many others speak on the old stage for the last time. Again one wonders why this magnificent auditorium is being gutted. The acoustics are good, the sight lines are perfect and the seats are spacious and comfortable. As Patrick Stewart closes the evening with Oberon's final speech from *A Midsummer Night's Dream*, our company, and the Indian troupe currently playing in the very same play in the Swan, appear at the back of the stage, holding candles which we blow out on: 'So goodnight unto you all'. It is a very emotional moment.

Afterwards there is a fantastic party in a giant marquee by the Avon as fireworks burst overhead. Delicious food and wine is provided by expensive caterers; even the disco music – to which some are dancing on the specially-laid wooden floor – is not too loud. Everyone is there; Judi Dench, gracious and warm as ever (like us, she cannot understand why the old theatre is being destroyed) and Sir Donald as usual telling fantastic stories in that wonderful, fruity voice – including one that I've not heard before. When he first came to Stratford in 1946, the actors rehearsed in suits and ties and he was mortified to have the part of the Dauphin in *Henry V* taken away from him because he woke up late on the first day of rehearsal and didn't have time to shave! But, despite both of these national treasures and Michael Pennington reminiscing with me about our distant days in the National Youth Theatre, the highlight of my entire day is meeting the footballer, Dion Dublin and his charming wife. Contrary to my expectations (he has a reputation for being one of the hardest footballers around, he even played for a time with a broken neck), he is soft-voiced and very cultured (and, to Dora's delight, loves the ballet.) He, in turn, is very impressed with my knowledge of football. He once played in the Premiership for Manchester United, now he plays for Norwich City in the

Championship: I was once a promising young actor and played leading parts – now I play the Gentleman and understudy Sir Ian McKellen. I think we sense we have something in common: we are both veterans hanging on to the job that we love. We arrange to meet again.

Monday April 30th

Today I reveal all. I have done it once before, at the National in Trevor's production of *Speer*. It was a very dramatic moment at the beginning of the play, based on an historical fact. When the convicted Nazi war criminals first arrived at Spandau prison, the Russian guards made them strip naked and put on concentration camp uniforms. There were seven of us all told. I was playing von Shirach, head of the Hitler Youth, but all the attention was on Alex Jennings as Speer. Even so, there was a lot of discreet rope-pulling amongst the rest of us before we stepped on that stage. The size of one's member is a matter of concern for most men, and today my old friend will be hanging out on his own from a cold start. The dropping of my trousers has to be rehearsed, to get the timing right. Russell, as the Fool, has to make sure he can pull them back up. Feel very embarrassed with Gemma directing: a bit like having a blanket bath with an attractive nurse (not that I've ever had one). The moment finally arrives. I note that Klare, the deputy stage manager who is on the book, has lowered her eyes. I take a deep breath, then begin to howl; "Off, off, you lendings. Come unbutton here!" and reach for my flies. Suddenly, a door opens in the gallery and a party of schoolgirls enter on a tour of the theatre. Like a Hollywood diva, I scream for the set to be closed.

Thursday May 3rd

Have concentrated on Lear every waking moment throughout the week. Every night I listen to Ian's constant changes of inflection and watch him like a hawk. Why am I doing it? I know Ian will never be off, and no matter how brilliant I am in the understudy run, I know it won't make a scrap of difference at this late stage of my career. I guess I just I want to prove I can still do it. 20 years ago when there were still reps, I might have gone off to Westcliffe or somewhere and given my Lear. Unless I do it over a pub or play it on the fringe somewhere to two men and a dog, tomorrow will be my only opportunity.

Go over my scenes with Russell backstage – he has developed a simple innocence to his Fool that is quite touching. Find the scenes with Mad Tom the most difficult to remember; Tom talks such nonsense that I'm never sure when my cues come. Run them through with John Heffernan in the dressing room at every opportunity. Melanie, naturally, is too busy performing Frances' parts, but Naomi is always keen to do Regan with me.

The RSC casting department customarily attend the understudy runs. Most of the others are anxious to impress, in the hope of being awarded bigger parts in the future. I'm not at all bothered – the casting department seems to change every year or so and then another bunch of people you've never heard of take over. Anyway, I've realised I don't want to come here anymore; I've done it all and like my home too much – though foreign tours are a different matter. But Trevor and Ian have promised to attend and I want to show them and my faithful friends what I can do.

Disaster: Chelsea crash out of the Champions League to Liverpool yet again – Seymour has the final laugh. Fear this season Chelsea, like Lear, will lose all.

Friday May 4ᵗʰ

Today I perform Lear, probably for the only time. I sit at Ian's place in his dressing room and apply some white to my eyebrows. It is a sobering thought that this is the only make-up I need to play the old boy. Have Ian's dresser, who has done the past three Lears at Stratford; Robert Stephens, Nigel Hawthorne, and Corin

Redgrave. Both Stephens and Hawthorne are dead and Corin has suffered a stroke – I hope that's not some sort of omen. The dresser is kind and motherly as she slowly helps me into Ian's regal costume: black trousers, polished boots, gold-trimmed waistcoat and the scarlet Cossack coat, then finally the huge golden gown with train. She places Ian's heavy crown upon my head and I look at myself in the mirror and see a king.

The beginners call comes over the Tannoy and I make my way to the stage. Somebody whispers that Trevor, Ian, Frances and rest of the cast are all in the sparse audience. Though many of my old cronies have come up from London, there cannot be more than a hundred in total. When an understudy run takes place in London, the cast expect their agents to attend and bring other casting directors with them, but Stratford is too far away. Regardless of the size of the audience, though, I am about to play Shakespeare's greatest role before Ian and Trevor, two of the most discerning judges of Shakespearean acting in the world. To paraphrase the Bard: their approval will *'o'erweigh a whole theatre of others'*.

Steven Edis' now familiar music wafts up from the musicians' room at the back of the building, and the play begins. Today, instead of leading the procession, I am bringing up the rear. The spotlight is beaming down on me as I raise my hands to the heavens and silently bless my court and daughters, who bow and prostrate themselves before me. Before I know it I have led the procession off stage and am being assisted out of the gown and crown, whilst Seymour and Julian do the short opening scene. The music plays again and I sweep back on stage with Zoë on my hand. The court bows as I regally sit behind my desk. I look around their anxious faces before uttering my first line: *'Attend the Lords of France and Burgundy, Gloucester.'*

I've always believed that big parts are easier than small ones. If you make a mistake, you have plenty of opportunity to get back on track – in a small part you only have the one chance. As

I begin the big speeches the words flow out of me – the passion of
Lear takes over: I am no longer lurking supportively in the
background. Scene follows scene; I am in the middle again,
dominating the stage. I feel pain, grief and rage. My trousers drop
and I stand in the rain, as 'a poor, bare, forked animal.'

Around me, I am aware that every understudy has come up
trumps. Seymour, like Bill, is a rock as Gloucester; Melanie
repeats the excellent performance she now nightly gives with Ian;
Naomi, without Monica's idiosyncratic mannerisms, is excellent
as Regan; Zoë is simple and moving as Cordelia; Russell doesn't
get many laughs but makes a good stab at the pathos of the Fool;
John Heffernan and Peter, in my mind, are equal to Ben Meyjes
and Philip as Edgar and Edmund, and Ben Addis is also very
good as Oswald.

At the interval, as I am recovering from my drenching in the
storm, Nobby Clark bursts in with his camera to take photos of
me in costume. I have the well-earned rest that Shakespeare
thoughtfully wrote into the play, before the dresser adorns me
with flowers and herbs for the great mad scene on Dover Cliff
with the blind Gloucester. Before I know it I've got through to
the end and I'm staggering on with the dead Cordelia in my
arms. I whisper the final words; "*See there... See there...*" and it is
over.

Immediately, Ian comes round to congratulate me and says
that I have now truly played Lear. Trevor gives me a hug and
tells me he is proud of me. I am temporarily brought down to
earth when my old school friend, P.R.R. Jackson, comes in and
says he doesn't know why I bothered to drop my trousers. Walk
back from theatre across the greensward with my two
granddaughters in each hand, Dora and Rubin on either side, and
20 loyal friends following – things don't get much better. Dora
has provided cava and snacks and we have a great party for an
hour before I go back to being the Gentleman for the evening
performance. I am no longer the King, but still feel contented and

satisfied.

Saturday May 5th

We have begun doing matinees (one mid-week and one at the weekend): two performances of *Seagull* – one with Ian one with Bill. In our dressing room we sing; *'Whose 'Sorin' Now?'*

Sunday May 6th

Snide article in *The Observer* complaining about the RSC's 'Phantom *Lear*' – presumably because the critics have not been allowed to see it. They interview members of the audience and the only thing they seem to complain about is the 'piped music'. To think we are spending a fortune taking a live orchestra round the world!

Chelsea can only draw with Arsenal and so finally lose the Championship – but they go down magnificently, fighting hard with only ten men.

Monday May 7th

Germaine Greer was sighted in the audience one night last week and has written, what I consider, a vindictive and scurrilous article in *the Guardian*, headlined:

'So Ian Mckellen drops his trousers to play King Lear. That sums up the RSC's whole approach'.

The old girl begins: *'The most memorable moment, for many of us the only memorable moment, in Trevor Nunn's latest production of* King Lear *is when Ian McKellen drops his trousers and displays his impressive genitalia to the audience.'* She is woefully inaccurate, when she describes the packed and enthusiastic audiences that we have had as: *'most don't have English as their first language – a minority of geriatrics who haven't got out of the theatre-going habit, and a majority of teenaged school-trippers bussed in from various grim hostelries in the environs of Stratford.'* She seems to have a long-standing dislike for the Trevor, Ian and the RSC. '*The production is as perverse as anything Trevor Nunn has ever done...when it comes to inexplicable dumb shows, Nunn is your man.*'

She cruelly mocks Ian's acting and doesn't seem to have been at the same play we've been working on for the past four months.

What will *The Guardian*'s revered critic, Michael Billington, think about having his thunder stolen?

Tuesday May 8th

As we pass the RSC Press Office, a lady comes out. I ask her what they are going to do about Germaine Greer – she looks sheepish and says they are looking into it. I wonder.

Meet Roger Howells, who has been a stage manager up here since the days of Anthony Quayle in the fifties. He tells me it is the first time he has noticed that the Gentleman has a clear line through the play. Very gratified. Email from Davina Belling – who sat through both Ian and my performances of *Lear* last Friday – saying that Germaine Greer should be shot.

The Gentleman sits at the back of the stage for most of the long first scene, supposedly writing down Lear's edicts. Gerald and young Richard, as attendants, stand a few feet away. Tonight I hear Richard sniffing and become aware of a noxious smell. I look up and think I see a faint suspicion of guilt creep across Gerald's handsome face, or is it drifting in from the wings? At that very moment Romola breaks away from Lear and walks straight into the miasma – I'm certain she thinks it is me. Farting on stage is not altogether uncommon. I remember the line of soldiers that used to stand on guard under the night sky in the interminable French camp scene in *Henry V* at the National. They became so bored that each night they managed to fart in sequence. When I was young I heard old actors tell tales of a renowned Dame – perchance the aptly named Marie Tempest – who would never quit the closed confines of a box set without leaving a pungent remembrance behind.

Thursday May 10th

Now everyone is getting in on the act. 'Trevor Nunn's Folly –
The Real Tragedy of King Lear' is splashed across the front page
of today's *Independent*. Inside is a two page spread headlined:
'This Great Stage of Fools – It's a Bloody Tragedy.' Adrian
Hamilton, who as far as I can make out is a political
correspondent, only really has one point; that if it isn't considered
good enough for the critics to review, the public should not be
asked to pay full prices for the seats. He also says it is very unfair
that Melanie won't get any notices for her Goneril or Arkadina,
and then proceeds to give a review of both plays. He thinks that
Ian is a good, but not great, Lear and overacts as Sorin, whilst
Trevor's production is inferior to the one Richard Eyre did at the
National in 1997. There is no mention that May 31st was always
going to be the opening night for *Seagull*. Now that the original
opening night of *Lear* has been postponed (misguidedly I admit),
surely it will be more exciting to see an ensemble tackle both
great plays on the same day? Besides, the critics all have their
diaries filled with other opening nights. As for Melanie, well,
when I took over from Derek Jacobi at Chichester ten years ago,
I played Tattle for the entire run and the critics were never invited
to that. I suspect some critics are miffed that a nice little swan to
Stratford, with expenses, was cancelled and now they will have to
do two for the price of one.

The Guardian is now inviting those readers who have seen
Lear to blog their own reviews in. Of the ten they publish, only
one is favourable. So many 'bloggers' (what an awful word) seem
to be envious of Trevor and Ian, but who is selecting the blogs?
Are they genuine theatre-goers? It is all very hard to believe from
the thunderous reception we receive every night. Things are
spinning out of control and it is all down to the simple accident of
Frances falling off her bike. But then we wouldn't have had all
this antagonism if Trevor (or the RSC, or whoever) hadn't
insisted on postponing the opening night. I know most of the cast

also feel it was a mistake.

Friday May 11th

Some support from the press at last! Nice piece in *The Times* about Trevor by Jane Wheatley: *'Director of precious talent – the man many consider the finest theatre director in the world'*. She quite rightly points out *'the half-sublimated envy'* many critics feel for his wealth and his ability to mix classics with popular theatre, letting audiences enjoy both. She quotes Benedict Nightingale, an excellent critic (and fellow Chelsea supporter): *'What distinguishes Nunn is an intelligence that never lacks human sympathy and never forgets that both captains and cabinet makers may be in the same audience'*. Very true.

Saturday May 12th

It is a seven-minute walk from Avonside to the stage door. Following the matinee, I go home to eat with Dora and then walk back with Ben Meyjes, who is living in the flat next door. He appears to be a thoroughly decent young man – I am genuinely impressed with the hard work he continually puts into his Edgar, and tell him so. Perhaps we walk slightly slower as we are talking – it is probably the first conversation we have had – and we arrive, at the stage door two minutes late at 6.27 instead of the official half at 6.25. To my amazement Ben Delfont, the stage manager, puts us in the show report for missing the half. It is the only time this has happened to me in my entire 47-year career. My only consolation is that there are seven other names in the report and my name is next to Sir Ian McKellen's.

Sunday May 13th

Back in London to look after grandchildren. Nobby Clark brings round the photos he took of me as Lear. He is a great photographer – manages to make me look like Lee Marvin.

Monday May 14th

Ian shows me a copy of a response to Greer from a master at a famous public school, which *The Guardian* (perhaps unsurprisingly) didn't publish. It is in fact our very first favourable notice. The gentleman in question stoutly defends Ian's '*heartbreaking performance*' and Trevor's '*poised interpretation of the play in which every word is clearly spoken, almost every speech inflected with intelligence and feeling.*'

He goes on to liken Dr Greer's concern with Ian's penis with that of the teenagers he'd seen gawking at Daniel Radcliffe's in Equus the previous week.

We do a full dress rehearsal of *Seagull* for Frances as she will take over Arkadina on Wednesday. She is extremely brave, obviously in great pain, but still manages to sparkle glamorously. I feel great sympathy for Melanie. She has made the part her own, got used to being Trevor's leading lady and suddenly is discarded, pushed back to being Polina and all Trevor's attention is naturally on Frances. Melanie looks very unhappy, but she could be getting into character: Polina is supposed to be frustrated. Naomi seems to have accepted the loss of Polina better. She is now down to only one line as the Cook.

Wednesday May 16th

An eventful day. Rubin, my eldest son, rings to tell me he has managed to get me a ticket for the Cup Final. I regretfully inform him I will be doing a matinee of *Seagull* that afternoon. "Can't you pull a sickie? You don't say a bloody word!" He is a hard-headed lawyer who considers I haven't done a proper day's work in my life. I know they would get on perfectly well without me and I wouldn't be missed at all, but I would never knowingly miss a performance. It was worse in 1966: I had a ticket for the World Cup Final but was just about to go up to the Edinburgh Festival to act in *The Winter's Tale* with Laurence Harvey. Things weren't going too well and an extra Saturday rehearsal was called. So I wasn't at Wembley on that magical afternoon, but in a seedy ballroom on Strutton Ground. At least I was playing Florizel, the juvenile lead, meaning I spent much of the play with my arms around a lovely young actress called Jane Asher. (Actors always remember their worst reviews – they are burnt like acid into their brain. Although I had some favourable ones, the one from this I can still quote is: '*Jane Asher is not helped by her chubby Florizel*' To think – I missed Bobby Moore's triumph for that!)

The brochures of the luxury hotels we will be staying in around the world are pinned on the notice board – everyone seems impressed. Meet Trevor in the corridor and ask him if he has any notes from the understudy run, in case I ever have to go on as Lear. He again tells me I was excellent and that he made full notes on my performance which he will give me when he gets some time – I wonder if he ever will.

At the company meeting following the matinee, Denise Wood, the RSC producer for the British part of the tour, tells us that we will be playing in the New London Theatre when we get back to London in October. It is the only West End theatre with enough wing-space to accommodate two productions and moreover, as it was partly designed by Sean Kelly (who, contrary to most theatre architects, actually was also a great theatrical designer), it can be adapted to fit our staging. Trevor breaks in to say that it was considered a white elephant when it first opened. Nobody knew where it was, at the unfashionable end of Drury Lane. When he and Lloyd-Webber were struggling with a musical about cats, having just lost Judi Dench as their leading lady, it was the only theatre they could find. Everyone predicted disaster, but *Cats* ran at the New London for 23 years. It was the only theatre in London with the sign: 'No entrance whilst the stage is in motion.'

Young Peter, who is becoming increasingly self-assured, even though he has missed a couple of entrances, asks if we can do another understudy run of *Lear* in London. Denise agrees immediately and Trevor says that it's an excellent idea and that we should do an understudy performance of *Seagull* as well. Denise agrees again. Nearly everyone seems pleased – it will be far easier to persuade agents and casting directors to attend a performance at a West End theatre, especially towards the end of the run when people will be anxious for their next job. I don't say anything, but am secretly thrilled at having a second chance of playing the old bugger.

Denise then mentions the unfavourable publicity about the postponement of the first night of *Lear*. She says that the RSC have decided to keep a dignified silence. They decided to postpone as Melanie had had only one day of rehearsal. It had been very difficult to find an alternative date, as the run at Stratford was completely sold out and because the critics have their own diaries planned well in advance. Trevor says he'd written to Charles Spencer, Chairman of the Critics' Circle to explain the predicament, inviting them to see *Lear* on the same day as the arranged first night of *Seagull*, May 31st. As Spencer had been ill and would have missed the original first night, he said he was delighted with the arrangement. It was only later that Spencer became aware that other critics were not so happy. Nevertheless, the furore in the press is being stirred up by the arts editors, not the critics. They never published the RSC's explanations – that this is only the beginning of a world tour and that Trevor had originally decided to hang back the press night of *Seagull* because there had been two recent productions at the National and at the Royal Court.

Michael Boyd arrives from London to see Frances' first performance as Arkadina. He wears a tight-fitting seventies-style leather jacket and addresses us in a school masterly tone. He says our hard work deserves success – nothing about both being wonderful productions – and proceeds to cover the ground that had already been covered.

Frances gives a very brave performance, especially when she
has to tumble to the floor in her passionate scene with Trigorin.
She is obviously limited in her movement and has lost some of
the vitality and fun she found in the rehearsals back in Clapham.
I'm sure she will get it back before the opening night. Melanie
was very good but Frances has an extra quality that makes her a
leading actress. I suppose it is the same difference between Ian
and me – but an actor's vanity always convinces him that he
possesses that quality. It really comes with confidence, but in
order to get that confidence you have to play the roles and be
acclaimed.

Thursday May 17th

We have now been rehearsing for nearly five months without
officially opening. Trevor spends the entire afternoon working on
bits of *Lear* and giving fresh, perceptive notes. I continue to be
amazed at his energy and enthusiasm. The other night he was
sitting watching *Lear* in the back row, making notes with a small
torch pen. Next to him was an American lady, who glanced at
him from time to time. When he returned to his seat after the
interval, he took out his notebook and smiled apologetically at
her. She leaned forward and asked encouragingly; "Are you
thinking of directing this play?"

Ian gives one of his finest performances to date, full of
invention and spontaneity. After the show, I spot Jeremy
Paxman waiting sheepishly among a group at the stage door to
see Ian, like a small boy who's about to meet Santa.

Friday May 18th

Ask Ian what Paxman thought about the production. Ian replies,
acidly: "He said it was great fun." Indeed, a strange comment to
make on Shakespeare's greatest tragedy. Ian had only agreed to
meet Paxman and his friends because Paxman had gone to the

same Cambridge College, St Catharine's, and had said that *Lear* was his favourite play. I suggest that Paxman may have been a bit overawed. "Nonsense – this is a man not cowed by prime ministers or presidents."

Another great performance by everyone with dutiful standing ovation from self-satisfied Americans, but we still won't know if we are officially a hit until the critics review it. It feels strange still being in limbo after all this time.

Saturday May 19th

Cup Final day. Years ago, I read Norman Mailer's book about the Ali/Foreman fight in Africa. A witch doctor told Mailer that, in order for your warrior to conquer, you had to do something brave yourself so that it would rub off on him. Mailer describes crawling along a ledge from one window to another on the 20th floor of his Kinshasa hotel. I was staying at my friend P.R.R. Jackson's house in Portugal, some nine years ago, when Chelsea were playing in the Final of the European Cup Winners' Cup. I decided to copy Mailer and go from one first storey window to another. It was only about 12 feet from the ground and within easy reach. As I was straddled from one window to another, I caught sight of a horrified lady staring from her bedroom in the house opposite. I could think of nothing else except to give her a feeble wave. Since then, I have confined my 'bravery' to a run and I dutifully jog along the Avon to give energy and power to José's boys – although without Carvalho and with Essien playing out of position, plus the injuries to Ballack and Shevchenko, I am fearing the worst.

Chelsea 1 – Manchester Utd 0. To paraphrase Lear: 'It is a Cup which doth redeem all sorrows that ever I have felt.'

Sunday May 20th

Drive back to London. Receive an invitation to attend a reception hosted by Prince Charles at Clarence House – no idea why I have been chosen. Regretfully decline the invitation because on June 13th, the day in question, we have another bloody matinee of *Seagull*. A pity, but I'd rather have gone to the Cup Final.

Monday May 21st

Drive back to Stratford with Bill Gaunt. Bill says several people who have been up to see *Lear* have their reservations. We will see in ten days from now, when the critics will finally deliver their verdicts.

Receive a joke text message from David Warner, saying Michael Boyd has decided to postpone the opening of his *Falstaff* until he puts on more weight.

Tuesday May 22nd

Trevor flies from New York to rehearse Frances back into *Lear*; Ian says you can only win an argument with him when he's jet-lagged. The energy and industry of Trevor, for a man in his mid-sixties, is astounding. As well as the pressure of opening these two productions, he is casting the transfers of *Porgy and Bess* and *Rock 'n' Roll* to Broadway. He is battling with American Equity, which insists he holds open auditions before he casts the people he wants.

Frances bravely insists on kneeling, which Goneril does several times in the play. Trevor turns a blind eye and assumes she's alright because she doesn't complain.

Back in London, Dora attends the celebration of Sheridan Morley's life at the Gielgud. Says it was very moving, very theatrical. Another event I've missed – still I'm glad to be working.

Wednesday May 23rd

Frances is finally back as Goneril, poor Melanie is reduced to playing the Country Woman and Naomi no longer has a single line. Ian, though, is really doing his bit as a leading man – he truly leads the company (one forgets he led his own very successful Actors' Company for several years). Today at the half he goes round all the dressing rooms, making sure everyone is in good spirits. Something I don't remember Kevin Spacey doing at the Old Vic – at least not among the older members of the company.

Extra drama backstage. One of the young actors is off. Instead of hanging the Fool, the climax of the first half, he was playing chess in the Green Room. To make matters worse, his friend, realising he wasn't there, went to fetch him and was off as well. All actors have a 'being off' story – they dread it even more than forgetting their lines. My favourite is of Sir Robert Atkins, the old-style actor/manager, who ran the Open Air Theatre in Regent's Park throughout the forties and fifties and had to rely on the donations of wealthy patrons. If they had a daughter who wished to go on the stage he would often cast one in the unimportant role of First Fairy in *Midsummer Night's Dream*. One night he was onstage as Bottom, complete with ass's head, when the current girl did not appear. He stormed off into the bushes and found the young lady, tying up her shoelace. "It's no good looking for yer entrance, duckie," he is reported to have bellowed, "you've missed it."

Thursday May 24th

The missing actor, rather touchingly, puts a handwritten letter on the notice board, apologising and promising to mend his ways.

Seymour has been complaining about being very tired – not surprising as he understudies Sorin in *Seagull* as well as Gloucester in *Lear*, and has been continuously rehearsing since January. He sees the company doctor who tells him he has caught a virus and must rest. So Russell plays Seymour's role of Curan and Adam takes over the Doctor from Russell. Russell is rapidly becoming my favourite member of the company. He's very gay, with the face of a clown, the body of a champion middleweight boxer (which he hones every day in the local gym), and a heart of gold.

It is Ian's birthday. Richard Clayton provides the usual cake at the interval and we all sing '*Happy Birthday*'. When Ian was a pupil at Bolton Grammar School in 1957, he camped (in tents!) with friends just outside Stratford, to see Olivier as Macbeth and Gielgud as Prospero; 13 of his old friends have come again tonight to see Ian's Lear and to celebrate his 68th birthday with him at the old Falcon Inn. I wonder if any of them ever thought they would see him play Lear at Stratford, half a century ago?

I realise I am the second oldest in the company after Bill.

Friday May 25th

Understudy run of *Seagull*. I go in to fulfil my silent role as Butler: I am about the only servant left as all the others are understudying the main parts. Seymour is still ill, Bill Gaunt has gone to Yorkshire to see his actress daughter, Tilly, in a play and Ian is about to be interviewed by the distinguished American critic, John Lahr – there isn't a Sorin in the house. Gemma asks me if I will read it as the others are raring to go, and their parents, friends and lovers have come to watch. I agree without hesitation. I would never want the show not to go on (I once went on with the book as Othello, when Kenneth Haig had stomach trouble at the Young Vic). Gemma takes me through the moves in the first act and I realise the part is more complicated than I thought. I go to my dressing room to look over the script when, to my relief, it is announced over the Tannoy that Ian has put off his interview and will play Sorin with the understudies: a generous gesture. Ian still loves acting; he still has his enthusiasm, which is a precious thing.

So John Lahr, looking just like his father, the Cowardly Lion in *The Wizard of Oz*, watches the run and becomes the first official critic to catch a glimpse of either of the productions. As with

Lear, the understudies are very good; Zoë is very fragile and vulnerable as Nina, John Heffernan, in my mind, is a more natural Konstantin than Richard (it is rumoured Trevor very nearly gave him the part in the first place). Melanie and Naomi have, of course, now played Arkadina and Polina many times and are excellent.

Saturday May 26th

Ian is very nervous tonight. His ex-partner, Sean Mathias, who has directed him several times – most recently in *Dance of Death* opposite Helen Mirren, and, in sharp contrast, as Widow Twankey in *Aladdin* at the Old Vic – is seeing his *Lear* for the first time. Ian had invited Dora and me for drinks in his house by the Duck after the show, but spends so long in his dressing room talking with Mathias that we decide not to wait.

Monday May 28th

Ian apologises profusely for keeping Dora and me waiting on Saturday, I tell him it not to worry in the slightest. He is very flat as Lear tonight, I can't quite put my finger on why. Did Sean Mathias not like his performance and give him notes? It's only natural for a director to disagree with another's interpretation – but my money would always be on Trevor. Nevertheless, I think we have rehearsed too much and too long; we should have opened as planned. I once read a book by a very verbose American actor who said that actors are like baseball pitchers: they have to deliver perfectly every night. He is wrong: in baseball the coach can always make a substitution if his man is having an 'off' night – that isn't really an option in the theatre.

Tuesday May 29th

Trevor spends over five hours giving us notes on the last performances he saw of both plays, but still hasn't time to go through all of his comments on *Seagull*. I think some of us are numb with notes.

Tonight is our last performance of *Lear* before the critics finally see it on Thursday afternoon. Better than last night but it still lacks some of the excitement and buzz it had a few weeks ago. I'm sure that on the day Ian will pull out all the stops and be magnificent. Bill is excellent as Gloucester, his years of experience playing countless parts in rep theatre shine through, but Sylvester, Philip and several others are still not completely there yet and poor Frances is still having difficulties with her knee. Although we are playing *Lear*, Trevor is floating about backstage giving notes to Romola and Richard on their *Seagull* performances. He slightly gambled casting them and I think he is worried. It's Richard's first job after drama school; he seems a lovely young man and I hope he pulls it off. Romola, who didn't even go to drama school, is vastly experienced as far as filming goes, but professionally has only appeared once on stage before, and the play in question only lasted a few performances.

Wednesday May 30th

Another cold, damp day and we are stuck indoors for the duration, preparing for the big day tomorrow. Robert Hardy – who has been a true and loyal friend since I first worked with him when he played Coriolanus on television in the early sixties – will be driving over from Oxfordshire, and Sarah and Lloyd Dorfman are coming up from London to see *Lear* in the afternoon; whilst Nobby and Lynn Clark and P.R.R. Jackson will join Dora in the evening for *Seagull*. In between, Dora will give another small party in our flat.

After an uneventful *Seagull*, I have just remarked to the others in the dressing room that at least we will be spared a vocal warm-up before the first of our press performances tomorrow, when Ian's voice comes over the Tannoy asking as many of us as possible to join him on stage in the morning at 11.30. Nobody says a word.

What will the critics finally make of our first night after having been kept out for so long like a pack of hungry wolves? They may well not be able to resist tearing us apart.

Thursday May 31st

Press day at last. Dash around Stratford buying cards and organising my Good Luck presents for the rest of the cast. Julian Harries, who spends every spare moment he has in the dressing room on his computer has kindly made copies of a recording on the history of the RSC that I put together more than 20 years ago and is no longer on sale. It contains anecdotes and reminiscences by Donald Sinden, Peggy Ashcroft, Anthony Quayle and Ian Holm, among others, and I think that the young actors may find it interesting. I get to the auditorium just before 11.30. Usually less than half a dozen of the keener ones turn up for the warm-ups. To my amazement, the entire company is there, standing around in a circle, stretching and umm-ing and aah-ing under Lynn Darnley's instruction. Poor old Bill is standing apart, doing as well as he can with his arthritic foot. Frances is also there with her still painful knee. I shamefacedly slide in and take my place. At the end Ian calls us into a tight huddle. We stand together in silence – almost as if we are in church.

I know at that moment why I have persisted with my career, in spite of all the disappointments and pitfalls over so many years. I am an actor; I love nothing more than being in an ensemble of actors. At this moment we are a brotherhood, united against all the critics who wait eagerly to humiliate us. We don't do it for money, and very few of us will find fame, but we share something that few other professions can enjoy. I strive to think of something appropriate to say and come out with: "Perish the man whose mind is backward now!" It gets the desired laugh from all.

We no sooner get back to our dressing rooms when Trevor's

voice comes over the Tannoy, asking us to join him on stage. We all troop down again and go into yet another huddle, where Trevor thanks us all for our hard work and says that, lest we should subconsciously slack off and give a matinee performance, we should all think it is seven in the evening. By that reckoning, we won't start *Seagull* until one in the morning! Trevor has been with us practically every day since the beginning of the year, he has been the most important influence in our lives, we have drunk in his every word, but now, as far as these productions go, we will probably only see him two or three more times. He has *Rock 'n' Roll* and *Porgy and Bess* to do in New York and his next project has been announced in the papers today: a mammoth new musical of *Gone with the Wind*. His appetite is insatiable.

Presents are waiting for us all at the stage door. Ian and Trevor each give everyone a bottle of champagne and card. Ian's card to me reads:

'My dear David,
You are my rock in Lear – not just onstage but knowing you are ready in emergency and always there with support and helpful notes. Keep it all up!
Much love and enjoy what is to come.'

Trevor's is slightly more mundane: *'Great work mate. Deep thanks.'* I am slightly hurt there is no mention of my *Lear*, but I suppose he has so many other things on his mind. John Heffernan's card more than makes amends: *'I will never forget the devastating impact your performance had on me and everybody else watching in that final scene. It was completely heartbreaking. I really hope we get the chance to do the play again before long. Your performance deserves to be seen.'* Ben Meyjes thanks me for perking him up at difficult times; Ben Addis says he has learnt so much from working with me; Richard Goulding thanks me for my encouraging words about both his performance and the future prospects of Tottenham Hotspur.

Nice messages from all the ladies – even Romola says how honoured she is to work with someone of my experience. Bill and others give bottles of wine; Sylvester has bought everyone a little Russian Doll. I go round each dressing room and hand out my recordings and wonder how many will be listened to.

Then it is time for the curtain. We are completely united as only a good company can be and give an electric performance. Everyone tunes their concentration to the highest pitch and the whole play goes without a hitch. Ian is on top form, full of fresh invention and deep emotion. We finish to a great ovation, but for half of the company; especially Frances, Richard, Romola, and Gerald, the biggest test is still to come.

In between the shows Robert Hardy, the Dorfmans, P.R.R. Jackson, Nobby and Lynn have champagne in our little apartment, as the sunlit Avon flashes by. Lloyd Dorfman has never seen *Lear* before and is quite overcome by it, which, as he's a hard-nosed businessman, is an achievement indeed. Robert, now a sprightly 80-year old, played my part to Sir John Gielgud's *Lear* in 1950, and Edmund to Charles Laughton's in 1959. He thinks Ian's is the finest *Lear* he has ever seen. There must have been someone in the Gielgud production that had seen or acted with Irving, and thus with a few more leaps we are back with Burbage and Shakespeare himself. Robert, or Tim as he likes to be known by his friends, spent the summer of 1951 up here, playing Fluellen to Richard Burton's *Henry V*. He was also with Burton both at Oxford and in the RAF during the war and was one of his closest friends.

The Dorfmans tell him that they live just around the corner from where Burton used to live in Hampstead. This prompts Tim to tell them a story that Dora and I have heard many times before, from when Burton had just left his first wife Sybil and was living with Elizabeth Taylor in the Oliver Messel suite at the Dorchester. One night, Sybil came down to pour out to heart to Tim and his wife Sally in their little house in Chelsea. Sybil, unlike her husband, was not a drinker, but on that night she insisted on consuming large quantities of Crème de Menthe Frappé. Tim at the time was very hard up, paying for his own divorce, and only drove a tiny minivan. In the early hours, Tim helped Mrs Burton into his van together with his Dalmatian, Troilus, to take her home to Hampstead. As they drove up Park Lane, Sybil looked up and, seeing the lights blazing in the Oliver Messel suite, cried out in her heavy Welsh accent, "There he is, Tim. Up there with his fancy woman."

Tim, always the epitome of the English gentleman, replied, "Do you want me to bring him back, Sybil?" Her eyes filled with tears, "Oh, Tim, if only you could." At that Hardy swung the diminutive van into the forecourt of the Dorchester and got out, with Troilus at his heels. In the lobby the carpets were rolled-up, ready for the cleaners to wash and polish the floor, but even at that hour there was an assistant manager at the desk, immaculately dressed in tie and tailcoat. Tim went up to the desk and said, "My name is Robert Hardy, I'm an old friend of Richard Burton. Please tell him I must see him."

The assistant manager regarded him suspiciously, "I'm afraid I have strict instructions that Mr Burton is not to be disturbed."

Tim drew on his aristocratic heritage, "Tell him who it is, he'll see me immediately." The man still refused, so Tim insisted on seeing the Duty Manager.

Eventually after much persuasion and imperious acting on Hardy's part, the Duty Manager agreed to see him. He came out of his office and demanded, "What can I do for you, sir?"

At that moment Hardy saw, out of the corner of his eye, Troilus lifting his leg and peeing copiously over the expensive rolled-up carpet. Tim's confidence ebbed away as swiftly as Troilus' pee. "Oh, it doesn't matter, I'll come back in the morning." Tim still maintains that, if Troilus hadn't peed, Richard Burton would never have married Elizabeth Taylor.

Before we know where we are, the curtain is going up on

Seagull. I admire Frances' guts and endurance – the critics and everyone else will definitely be keeping a special eye on her, on top of that she is battling with pain and lack of movement with her knee. The pressure is really on her but she gives a star performance as Arkadina (although Ian steals the show with his comic, but touching, Sorin).

We began rehearsing on January 2nd – tomorrow is the first of June – we have officially opened at last.

At the party afterwards in the Courtyard lobby, everybody seems to be thrilled with both plays. Are we a hit? You can never tell until the reviews are in front of you in black and white. Meet Richard Clifford, Derek Jacobi's long-time partner, who jokingly tells me that Derek is busy doing all the films that Ian cannot do because of his commitment to *Lear*.

Friday June 1st

The first reviews appear, thanks to the Internet. Michael Billington's headline in the *Guardian* reads: 'McKellen's moving, majestic Lear uncovers a naked humanity.' He sticks a well-aimed barb in Greer's rump, perhaps guarding his own sinecure, by affirming: *'only those with dirty minds will be dismayed by McKellen's nudity.'* Benedict Nightingale awards it five stars in *The Times* and Quentin Letts, although unable to resist weak jokes on Ian's *'public exposure'* is very favourable in the *Mail*. Only Ian Taylor in the *Independent*, who questioned the production when it was first announced in January, and the dreaded de Jongh in the *Standard* are negative. De Jongh though, does like *Seagull*, especially Romola – *'it owes much of its devastating impact to her'*. But it seems it is not in his waters to be thoroughly pleasant; he goes on to say: *'a direct hit was spoiled by Frances Barber's vulgar, brawling, burlesquing of Arkadina whom she turns from famous actress into something more like a music hall turn.'*

Saturday June 2nd

Charles Spencer's review of *Lear* in *The Telegraph* is a two-edged sword. It gives us five stars, saying: '*it is one of the most lucid, powerful and moving productions of this great tragedy I have ever* seen,' but though it goes on to heap praise upon Ian, for some unaccountable reason it develops into a personal attack on Trevor, even declaring like a hooligan that: 'he needs a good kicking.'

Sunday June 3rd

All out war seems now to have broken loose, as Imogen Stubbs has jumped to her husband's defence and spoken out against the critics for giving Trevor a rough time.

The headline in Sunday Telegraph read 'Wife of Lear director wants to give critics a kicking.' The article began *'The actress wife of the director Sir Trevor Nunn has launched a remarkable defence of her husband and his much-heralded, but blighted, RSC production of* King Lear. ...[She] *said she felt her husband had been subjected to a "vituperative Niagara of words" since the decision to abandon the planned press night on April 3 when Frances Barber, who plays Goneril, needed surgery after a road accident.'*

In response to the journalist who called Trevor "a fool", "a prat" and someone to whom he would like to give a "good kicking", Imogen said: *"My husband hasn't uttered a syllable in print and has done nothing to be worthy of such bile,"* she said. *"These things hurt. To quote Shakespeare; 'Am I not a woman? What I think I must speak'."*

I have to say I agree with her 100%. For years there has been an animosity towards Trevor, as if the critics resent his success and the money he has made. It was the same when he ran the National and filled the Olivier by putting on popular musicals. He said then that a National theatre should be for everyone, something the intellectuals could never accept. As far as money goes his productions, especially mega-hits like *Cats, Les Mis,* and *Starlight Express* have earned millions for this country. He has often kept the West End going, and has given large amounts of his royalties back to the RSC and the National, indeed I heard he largely funded the ensemble season we did at the National from his own pocket. Even in the excellent reviews we are getting, underlying resentment against him can be detected. Ian is coming out much better.

But you can never please the critics. Tim Walker in *The Sunday Telegraph*, giving his verdict on what he calls: '*the most talked about play of the year*', attacks Ian for being *too* good. Even though he describes Ian's performance as '*a breathtaking tour de force, an act of unmistakable genius, the crowning moment in a great classical actor's career*', he continues, '*but, oh dear, doesn't the old boy know it? All his words have the right resonances, he stands in the right places and technically one cannot fault his performance. But not for one second did I believe I was watching Lear. I was watching McKellen as Lear.*'

Utter nonsense, but I shan't be too critical; he does give me the only notice I am ever likely to get in this production: '*One's principal impression of the supporting players was of the range of enormous iron-grey quiffs on display. William Gaunt, as Gloucester, has an even bigger quiff than McKellen, which seems to me tantamount to lese-majesty. Jonathan Hyde's Kent has a pretty big one too, though the most lustrous belongs to David Weston as the Gentleman.*'

Susannah Clapp's headline in *The Observer* reads: 'A crowning glory for McKellen.' She is largely positive, but cannot resist the old potato:

'*The double bill looked impregnable. And then it went wrong. Frances Barber…damaged her knee in a cycling accident: in a press release that made travellers on foot sound like Godzilla, the RSC explained that she had been 'knocked off her bicycle by a jay-walking pedestrian'. She went on with rehearsals – until, the damage having been aggravated, it turned out she needed an operation. At which point, the press night for* Lear *was postponed. In a big way. Though the public had been paying full price for tickets, the production was deemed not to be ready for critics, Barber's understudy, Melanie Jessop, having apparently never rehearsed with McKellen (why not?)'*

Oh, come, Miss Clapp. Do you know nothing of how theatre functions? There is never enough time to rehearse the principals, let alone the countless possibilities that could arise from anyone being sick. Why did not all the other understudies rehearse with Ian? Or Frances? Or Bill? Or Sylvester? You are complaining of a nine week postponement – do you want to wait a year?

So often if you get a good notice in a daily, the weekly version of the same paper will be diametrically opposed, or vice versa. *The Independent on Sunday* is a case in point. Kate Bassett declares the production was well worth the wait: '*It marks the high-calibre return for this director to the company that he ran for almost two decades, and McKellen is giving what is, surely, the performance of a lifetime.*' But towards the end of her paean she notes: '*This production does have its weaknesses. Nunn's use of swelling orchestral music – like a cinematic soundtrack – is obtrusive and sometimes cheesy. A few of those playing bit parts are sorely below par too...*' My Sunday is ruined.... Does she mean me???

Monday June 4th

With the war in Iraq getting worse by the day, global warming killing the planet and Blair in his final hours, *the Guardian* devotes its third editorial to – understudies!

Referring to the delayed critics' night and the fact that we had already been performing for a number of weeks, the article said:

Spare a thought...,amid the delayed critical plaudits, for the understudies who have nobly borne the brunt of the two plays since Easter without press notice. Melanie Jessop, standing in for Ms Barber in both roles, did most of the shows but has received none of the critical accolades. Similarly, Naomi Capron, who filled in as Polina while Ms Jessop took on the larger role of Arkadina. It was an unfortunate accident for Ms Barber, but Sir Trevor's response was mean both to the public and to the understudies. As it happens, they did a superb job, as many packed houses will confirm. Understudies work hard with no expectation of reward. If accidents happen they should be allowed their moment in the critical sun.'

Sir Ian's understudy heartily concurs!

On *the Guardian* count we have scored 8/10 with the critics. I sometimes think critics read their own intellectual interpretations into actor's performances. I think all most actors set out to do is understand what they are saying and portray their feelings as honestly as possible.

Run into Frances outside the supermarket, who's looking like a bag lady with her crutch, ragged jeans and workman's cap. She's on her way to yet more physiotherapy. She's as tough as old boots and needs to be. She is certain the press were out to get her and Trevor because of the delayed first night. Even critics like de Jongh, who have always praised her, seem to have gone out of their way to be as unkind as they can.

Tuesday June 5th

The Guardian, it seems, cannot leave us alone. In an interview with Paul Arendt in today's edition, Brice Pitt, emeritus professor of old age psychiatry at Imperial College, is quoted as saying:

"[McKellen's] *descent into madness felt very accurate. It's dangerous to make psychiatric diagnoses in plays, but I thought McKellen's performance was consistent with a vascular condition rather than Alzheimer's...In vascular dementia you tend to see a stormy personality.*

The storm on the heath can also be brought into the pathology. It's possible that Lear became hypothermic, or even suffered pneumonia. In any case the next time we see him he's delirious.

How would I treat Lear? Well, I don't think spending alternative months with Regan and Goneril is a viable plan. The main thing would be to find him a good home."

Ian, needless to say, has not consulted any psychiatrists in his work on the role.

I have read that Shakespeare's knowledge of all types of sickness increased once his eldest daughter, Susanna, had married Dr Hall, a local physician.

Thursday June 7th

Trevor has broken his silence and written a letter to the *Telegraph,* explaining the decision to postpone the opening night was made by the RSC, not him. Because the production was sold out an extra 'critic's performance had to be arranged, and it was the RSC again who decided to have a double press showing of the Lear and Seagull on the same day.

I don't really understand why Trevor felt he had to explain himself; after all his successes why does he worry? But I suppose he is an artist and all great artists are insecure. Olivier was terribly insecure, even developing stage fright towards the end of his career. Why has Boyd remained silent? He is, after all, the head of the RSC. Trevor is only a visiting director. Surely Boyd should come to the defence of his company and the director he employed?

I'm surprised how little the other actors seem to care about the brouhaha – but we are all selfish beasts at heart. I'm convinced that none of the animosity would have happened if we had simply opened as planned.

Sunday June 10th

Drive down to London in Bill's car with Ian. Dora meets us at

Bill's and after coffee in Bill's beautiful garden we drive Ian to Sloane Square to catch the District Line to his home on the Thames in Docklands. Unsurprisingly, the District Line is closed for repairs, so Ian, the multimillionaire, reluctantly decides to go by taxi. You can take the boy out of Burnley...

John Peter, whose review for some reason has come out a week late, gives us five stars in *The Sunday Times*:

'King Lear *ranks with Nunn's best work, and Ian McKellen now enters the pantheon of the greatest Lears of the past 50 years: Scofield, Sinden, Stephens, Holm. Nunn's genius as a director is in his handling of characters. He can find their deepest urges, secrets and confused ambitions, the things they know about themselves and the things they don't...The company acting is impeccable.*'

That really is our final notice, as far as the English national press are concerned. They have all been positive apart from De Jongh and John Temple in *The Independent*. After Ian, Monica has come out best in both plays. She certainly draws attention to herself – her Regan has a very noisy orgasm each night as Gloucester's eyes are pulled out, and her alcoholic Masha constantly sniffs her snuff box and stumbles about as she crosses the stage. She fidgets as she acts and makes strange patterns with her speech – which is very effective. When I congratulated her the other day she gave an enigmatic half smile and told me she never reads her notices. Many actors claim this and I don't always believe it. I know that Ian, Frances, Bill and Trevor read them all, and so do I.

Monday June 11th

This morning we have to assemble outside the American Embassy at 8am for interviews to obtain our employment visas. As well as the acting company, there are technicians and wardrobe staff that we have not met before. Despite the fact that we were told we would not be allowed to bring bags into the Embassy, Naomi arrives with two, both large and stuffed to capacity. There is no sign of Ian – I wonder if special arrangements have been made for him. At last we get through the initial search and walk round the fenced perimeter. Policemen patrol with guns, it feels like the Berlin Wall. We have been specially booked in at 8.30, but nobody seems to be expecting us. A gigantic American asks if we are the Royal Dance Company. I ask him if he thinks I look like a dancer, but he doesn't seem to have a sense of humour. Ian comes in late, looking very bedraggled and confused: he's being treated no different from the rest of us. Some of the Embassy staff are giving him queer looks – Sir Ian smiles at them benignly – the Americans whisper anxiously among themselves – I begin to think that we may be about to have an international incident – are they about to eject this strange old man as being an undesirable? Then one gives a sheepish smile, another gives a tentative wave. I realise, with relief, that they have just recognised Gandalf. The rest of us sit and fret and wonder if they have found any anti-American activity in our past – Sylvester recalls he once protested in Grosvenor Square during the Vietnam War – but at last, after having our fingerprints scanned again, our documents are duly stamped and we are deemed worthy of entry into the 'Land of the Free'. It was so much simpler when I went to Moscow with the RSC in 1967. Even though the Cold War was at its height, an official from the Embassy came up to Stratford with our visas and handed them out in the green room. I suppose there were no terrorists then, only nuclear warheads and the Red Army.

Now *Private Eye* is getting in on the act. There is a colour photo of Blair superimposed over one of Ian in his red Lear costume, headlined: 'King Blair: Tragic tale of a ruler who announces that he is going to give up power and goes completely mad at the ingratitude of his successors and everyone else.'

They have a half-hearted cast list of:

King Lear: Tony Blair
Fool: John Prescott
Macbeth: Gordon Brown
Yorrick: Ming Campbell

I would have added Tessa Jowell and Cherie Blair as Goneril and Regan, Alistair Campbell as the Bastard, and Jack Straw as Poor Tom. But who could be Cordelia? Claire Short? Tony would never be able to carry her on.

Wednesday June 13th

Getting fed up with Stratford now and looking forward to the tour. Frances, who has toured New Zealand before, puts a bit of a dampener on things by telling us that Wellington is a bit like Birmingham on a wet Sunday and Auckland is even worse, with the highest suicide rate in the world.

Lear appears to be getting better and better. Sylvester is growing in confidence after a couple of good notices – *The Independent on Sunday* says he was *'remarkably droll with the mania of Ken Dodd'* – and he is beginning to get more laughs. Ian gives an electrifying performance tonight; even the English rise to the standing ovation. Perhaps Hoffman was wrong: you don't have to 'fuckin' die' after all!

Friday June 15th

We attend a special meeting giving us details of the tour. We will be given a per diem rate of $75 dollars on top of our salaries, to cover meals and expenses – more than enough. Especially as there is on the schedule a plethora of receptions, cocktail parties and dinners, including a special reception at the New Zealand Parliament, presided over by the Prime Minister, Helen Clark, with whom Ian has become extremely friendly during the protracted filming of *Lord of the Rings*. We are told that no representation of smoking is allowed on stage in New Zealand – I will not even be allowed to have an unlit pipe in my mouth in *Seagull*. Ian protests that his performance as Sorin is based on his smoking; Frances tells him to have a few words with his pal, the Prime Minister.

Everyone seems ready to leave Stratford. It is no longer the idyllic place of my youth in the summer of '67. Everything is a mess; the RST now looks like a building site, surrounded by red boarding and an iron fence. One of the old dressers described the unnecessary tower they are building as 'the incinerator chimney'. To my mind, all the charm of Stratford has gone – it is has become no different from any other town. The old inns are now shops that hardly ever seem to do any business, or else have become cheap and garish. Pam, who ran the 'Dirty Duck' for decades, could be a bit of a tyrant, but I found it a far more pleasant place under her. The once idyllic greensward on the bank of the Avon behind the RST is now full of groups of ear-ringed oafs and overweight ladettes – some with children in prams – drinking Export Lager out of cans, which they leave strewn over the grass together with their cigarette butts. The willow in remembrance of Vivien Leigh weeps. In the sixties, there was a sense of evangelism about the RSC, they really believed they were creating something worthwhile and unique. Actors such as Ian Holm, Ian Richardson, Eric Porter, Roy Dotrice, Alan Howard, Norman Rodway and Brewster Mason spent years with the company, honing their craft. Now young actors seem to use it as a jumping-off point for what often proves to be an all-too-short career in television soap. Where did things go wrong? They can't blame it all on Mrs Thatcher.

Sunday June 17th

Dora has driven up to spend the weekend with me. We read the Sunday papers on the greensward outside my flat. The press, it seems, can never resist a chance to knock Trevor. Today there is a report in the *Sunday Times,* stating that Trevor paid £27,000 for a painting he thought was a genuine Damien Hirst. Keith Allen claims it was painted by Hirst's son and Allen's own 10-year old boy. Trevor will hate being depicted as a fool; but having seen Keith Allen on *Parkinson* last week, I take everything he says with a pinch of salt.

There is a flicker of sunshine so Dora and I drive to Broadway for lunch, in her open-topped Beetle. The Cotswolds are as beautiful as ever. In the afternoon we go to the first showing of Tony Sher's documentary: *Murder Most Foul*. It is about the horrific murder of a young actor in Cape Town, who was about to come to Stratford with Janet Suzman's production of *Hamlet*. It is very moving and finally convinces me not to go on holiday to South Africa. Sher suggests that the all pervading crime and violence is the legacy of apartheid. I think of Lear's line: 'Is there any cause in nature that breeds these hard hearts?' I had never really met Sher before. He is a brilliant and charming man, with a vulnerability I had not expected.

Monday June 18th

The last week in Stratford: it cannot end too soon. The wet weather continues.

The *Mail* follows up on the fake Damien Hirst story. Trevor is quoted as saying:

> "*I sold the painting privately a few years before for £20,000 more than it cost. But how Keith or Damien Hirst could work out which one my untitled painting was is beyond me. I put it on the wall in the kids' playroom, but when they got older, there was no need to keep it.*"

My seven-year old granddaughter Mia has left some of her paintings behind in the flat. I jokingly suggest to Dora that I take one into rehearsal tomorrow and ask Trevor to value it. Dora strongly advises me not to.

Tuesday June 19th

We spend the day back at the dreary rehearsal complex, re-blocking both plays for the proscenium stage of the Theatre Royal in Newcastle. Trevor who (naturally) we haven't seen since the first night, is back and in a buoyant mood, very pleased with the reviews and relieved all the fuss over the delayed opening is finally over. At the end of the day, he announces that there is a strong possibility of *Lear* being made into a television film after we finish at the New London in January. It depends on everyone being available and whether the producer, Richard Price – who has filmed several of Trevor's previous productions – can raise the money.

Lear grows and grows. That is the unique pleasure of acting Shakespeare on stage; each night, there are infinite discoveries to be made. I am still finding things in my small part of the Gentleman. Ian continually gives different readings and stresses, in all of which he finds tragic meaning. Another thunderous reception.

The lugubrious Richard Wilson is in the audience. He is a fellow Stonewall activist and afterwards Ian takes him out to dinner. Wilson, apparently, says hardly anything about the play (not even, "I don't believe it"). Alan Bennett has pointed out that 'Going Round' is a ritual peculiar to the theatre: vicars don't go round to congratulate each other after a service or judges after a sentence. It's always difficult finding something to say to a friend after a show. "Well, you've done it again!" is always a safe bet.

Wednesday June 20th

Watch the video of *Macbeth* that Ian and Trevor did more than 20 years ago. It remains the best interpretation of the play I've seen, and I've seen all too many, as well as having played practically every part in the play. I even did a one-man version in Texas. Ian and Judi Dench give faultless performances. Ian is an entirely different being to the Lear I stand beside each night – with his sleeked back hair he is like a ravenous wolf – evil seeps out of every pore.

Thursday June 21ˢᵗ

Last *Lear* in Stratford. After the performance Corin Redgrave, Stratford's most recent Lear, waits in the corridor, rather touchingly surrounded by Malcolm Tierney and a posse of aging members of the Workers' Revolutionary Party. Corin seems to have recovered remarkably from his stroke. I hear him generously tell Ian: "It was the finest Lear I've ever seen."

Sir Michael (his dad, and another great Lear) would not have been entirely pleased.

Friday June 22ⁿᵈ

In Marks & Spencer an attractive woman in her fifties approaches me:

"Mr Gaunt, I thought you were wonderful in *The Seagull*."

"I'm afraid I'm not Mr Gaunt, I'm Mr Weston."

"Oh, I'm so sorry."

"It doesn't matter; people have been saying we're alike for the past 40 years."

"You must be flattered."

I call upon a line from *Lear*: "Not altogether so." She leaves me looking confused.

Tonight there seems to be some sort of tension in the ladies' dressing room. As far as I know, there have been no affairs within the company as yet. Most of the older ones are married and the rest all have regular boy/girlfriends. The exceptions are Monica, Melanie, Ben Addis, Philip and of course, Ian. With no romance intended, Philip, who declares he is a Christian and is not interested in premarital sex (which must be a relief to Jonathan Hyde as Philip is reputed to have gone out with Jonathan's very attractive daughter at drama school) and Monica plan to go to

Fiji in the spare week between New Zealand and New York.
Young Peter was going to go to New York a week early, to meet
up with his actress girlfriend. However, she has just been offered
a job touring Ireland in a play about the Bog People, and to
Peter's chagrin has accepted it rather than spend a month in
America with him. Monica seems a touch disappointed that
Philip has now invited Peter to go to Fiji with them.

Russell is having his wedding before he goes up to Newcastle.
He tells us not buy him a present: he'd rather have cash. He'll
need it – he is taking his husband-to-be, an Italian postgraduate
student, around the world with him and I suspect he is footing
the bill. He's upset that his mother, who is very religious, will not
be attending the ceremony, although his ex-wife will.

Go into Duck after show for farewell drink. Surprised to see
quiet Ben Addis sitting at a table surrounded by attractive girls.
Apparently he is the 'Don Juan' of the company – has them
eating out of his hand. He plays the small part of the King of
France well and I think he should go far.

Saturday June 23ʳᵈ

Last day in Stratford. Everyone is busy packing, eager to get
away. Ian says he will give me a lift down in his taxi so Dora will
not have to come up and fetch me.

Lady Sainsbury of Turville, wife of the ex-Labour minister
and Deputy Chairman of the RSC brings Tessa Jowell, who lives
nearby at Shipston, to see last performance of *Seagull* at Stratford.
Ian takes me to have drinks with them after the show in the house
next to the 'Dirty Duck' that Lady Sainsbury had lent him during
his stay. Tessa is nicer and sexier than I expected. I am surprised
that she has driven herself to Stratford in her own car. Ian asks
her, with the rumoured cabinet reshuffle, if she expects to be in
the job by the end of next week. She says she loves being Minister
for Arts (who wouldn't?) and has taken all her phones off the
hook. She and Frances Barber commiserate with each other over

their treatment by the press. Jowell she says she does not read most of the papers because they are so cruel; Francis complains as bitterly about the theatre critics, which she reads avidly. *The Daily Mail* is considered the worst of all. As a long-term *Mail* reader and the only person present ever to have voted Tory, I decide to keep schtum.

Afterwards Ian and I drive back to London together. He asks me how I am going to spend Sunday; I tell him both my boys and their families are coming for lunch. I sense Ian is going to spend his Sunday alone. His protégé, Nick Cuthell is studying art in Florence and he has no regular partner at present. He plans to see the new musical version of *Lord of the Rings* at Drury Lane on Monday.

We don't have to go to Newcastle until Thursday morning. Four free days in London!!!

Monday June 25th

Wake up determined to make the most of these last few days of normality before the tour begins. I walk along the King's Road with Dora and realise, once more, how lucky I am to live in London. We go to BAFTA to meet Roly Curram and I can't help but notice how many of the female members are overweight. For the most part they are not actresses, but production assistants, make-up supervisors, wardrobe mistresses and continuity girls. I put their general obesity down to location catering, which I have enjoyed on many an occasion – some actors say it is the only time they get a decent meal. The first thing they do when they arrive on set at some godforsaken hour is to have a bacon roll. They later have a full English breakfast, plus cereals and toast. After biscuits at coffee break, they then have a three-course lunch which normally consists of something like steak and kidney pie, or roast meat, veg and plenty of roast potatoes, huge servings of apple crumble with lashings of cream or custard, rounded off with great wedges of cheese and biscuits. At tea time they are given cakes and buns, and if, God forbid, they go on after five o'clock, they can keep up their strength with plates of thick-cut sandwiches. The ladies I see before me, who have spent many more days on location than most actors can ever dream of, have paid the price with the size of their behinds.

We see touching French movie: *The Singer*, starring Gérard Depardieu and the beautiful, talented Cécile de France. It makes me hungry for French food, so Dora and I go to our favourite restaurant, La Poule au Pot for escargots and skate in black butter. It's one of the last restaurants in London where you can smoke – next week it will be against the law.

Tuesday June 26th

Dora and I go down to The Abbey School in Reading to watch our granddaughter Mia in an improvised entertainment. Mia is beautiful, though I can't hear or understand a word the kids are saying – but mustn't be overcritical, the kids and their parents obviously enjoy it.

Wednesday June 27th

We see *La Vie en Rose* at the Chelsea Cinema. Moving and evocative, with an Oscar-worthy performance from Marion Cotillard, whom I have never heard of before. We go home full of nostalgia, drink champagne and listen to an old LP of Piaf's concert at the Olympia in 1960. CDs and iPods will never match the pleasure of handling a big, glossy record, complete with beautiful painting of Piaf by her young American lover, Doug Davis, on the cover. Tomorrow I will go north. Dora will not accompany me on this section – she rarely ventures further north than Marble Arch...

Newcastle

Thursday June 28th

Get up at 5am to catch the Stansted Express for an 8.15 flight to Newcastle. Meet Peter at the check-in. He has just flown back from the South of France, where he has been staying with his girlfriend.

Julian Harries and I have both booked into the Rosebery Hotel in Jesmond, one of the better parts of Newcastle. On its website it professes to be an elegant Edwardian jewel which is often patronised by Prunella Scales. I presume that, after Fawlty Towers, she would know a good hotel from a bad one. Julian is arriving on a later flight and I arrive at the hotel at 11am to find it completely shut. I ring the phone number on the door and someone tells me a code to punch in, and then instructs me to open the drawer in the table in the hall. This I duly do and find an envelope with my name on it; inside is a key to Room 10. I have specifically asked for a large room and agreed to pay extra for it. I open the door to 10 and find that I have indeed got a large room, but it is filled with beds: a large double and two singles. Not a table or chair in sight.

I unpack and catch a bus to the town centre. The Theatre Royal is a beautiful building, designed by the great Victorian architect, Frank Matcham. As in all Matcham's theatres, the acoustics are superb. You stand on the stage and you can hear your voice fly clearly to the furthest reaches of the auditorium. The old-fashioned proscenium stage, with its modest apron suits the play far better than the thrust of the Courtyard – again I cannot understand the folly of destroying the old RST.

Trevor is already at the theatre, busy working on the lighting and sight lines. The scenery, props and costumes have all come up by road from Stratford. The theatre has a sensible amount of dressing rooms and Seymour, Guy and I are sharing one on the top floor. I don't expect Guy will be up there very much – he will be smoking in the street outside the stage door at every opportunity.

We spend a long day re-blocking – adapting the play to the type of staging most of us are more familiar with: that is, acting with all the audience to your front, instead of a third of them looking up your arse. Am very tired by the time we finish at 10 and decide not to adjourn to the pub with Julian and others in the cast. Come out of the theatre to find pouring rain. No sign of the 'five minute' bus service that was promised on the Rosebery's website. Walk down the Jesmond Road in the downpour, being drenched by passing cars splashing in the overflowing drains. Get back to the hotel, still no signs of life, climb up to my lonely dormitory and wonder what on earth I am doing here.

Friday June 29th

Get up and at last find some staff, cooking breakfast. Complain about my room. Am shown a better one which I can have next week. Over my breakfast, which I am sure Prunella Scales would not have considered healthy, I read a snide little piece in *The Times* by Hugo Rifkind:

> '*Theatres have a reputation for ruthlessly taking theatre critics' quotes out of context. Actors usually are above such things. Not always. Sir Ian McKellen quotes on his website a review of* King Lear *by Tim Walker in* The Sunday Telegraph: '*McKellen's performance is a breathtaking tour de force, an act of unmistakable genius, the crowning moment in a great classical actor's career…' Strangely, Sir Ian omits the following: 'but, oh dear, doesn't the old boy know it?… Not for one second did I believe I was watching Lear…I was stuck in a theatre with an immensely self-satisfied actor.'*

It makes me angry. I am sure Ian's website is run by two devoted female fans of a certain age and the inclusion of the quote in question has nothing to do with him.

I go back to my bed-filled room, turn on the BBC World Service, and hear the Singapore correspondent reporting that Sir Ian will not be allowed to reveal his 'big boy' in the Far East. Apparently, onstage nudity is not allowed in Singapore unless all the audience are over the age of 21.

At the theatre we finish re-blocking and in the evening embark on the first show of the tour. We give a full-blooded performance. In front of us the northern audience sits in rapt silence. Thanks to good old Frank Matcham's acoustics and the fact that we are facing them all for most of the time we are speaking, they can hear almost every word. During the performance I notice a middle-aged man sitting on a chair in the wings, watching Ian with spellbound devotion. Bill tells me that he is an American fan, a professional photographer, who runs Ian's website. Well, I was almost right.

At the curtain we receive thunderous applause, but not a single standing ovation – that Americanisation has not reached Newcastle yet.

Afterwards, a reception is held in the Circle Bar to mark the 30th anniversary of the RSC's yearly visits to Newcastle. As with nearly everything positive concerning the RSC it was Trevor's innovation. He delivers a sparkling speech from notes; he seems genuinely pleased that the RSC's close relationship with the city of Newcastle has endured and continues to prosper.

Lady Sainsbury has come up for the occasion. With the cabinet reshuffle in mind I find myself saying to her: "Tessa has been given the poisoned chalice. I'm sure the Olympics will be as big a disaster as the Dome." I'm getting more like Victor Meldrew by the day.

Saturday June 30th

A free day in Newcastle. Very upset by the latest attempted terror attack in London, I decide to visit the much vaunted Baltic centre – the Tate Modern of the North. Millions of pounds of government and Lottery money has been lavished on the old waterfront along the Tyne. Dignified commercial buildings have been converted into a plethora of bars and restaurants. As well as the ubiquitous Chinese restaurants and Tandooris there are many quasi-Italian Trattorias, serving what can only be described as a peculiar, northern version of pizza, over-topped with cheap, processed cheese. They already look tatty. I think renovation of an inner city needs more than cheap bars and eating places.

I cross the Millennium Bridge, which admittedly puts London's to shame, and climb up to the Baltic. Again no expense has been spared on the building, but in truth there seems to be nothing worth seeing on all its floors. It is a Saturday in late June and, I would think, one of the busiest days of the year, but there is hardly anyone here. The huge car park is less than a tenth full. I look for signs for active art classes for children or lectures to involve the community, but can find nothing, apart from an expensive gift shop. It is pretty much lunchtime when I reach the magnificent restaurant on the top floor – five waiters turn to me in hopeful anticipation – it is completely empty. Since the inception of the National Lottery so much money has been spent in a profligate flood on the building of new museums and centres for the arts around the provinces. The problem is there is then usually very little money left for the running costs, especially such seemingly unimportant matters as artists' and actors' wages (although funding for new marketing and publicity departments always seems to be available.) They are often built because of the vanity of local dignitaries, anxious to leave their mark, but so many have floundered through lack of attendance. It is fashionable to knock the resources that are spent on London – but only London has enough tourists, gays and Jews to keep such places open.

I walk across to the Sage Concert Hall. It is equally impressive from the outside, resembling a colossal silver slug or beetle. There are many people in the building, enjoying the views and drinking coffee. I read in the brochure that the Sage has delivered more than 72,000 music education sessions both in the building and the surrounding area. On top of that, they have music lessons for gifted young musicians, a flourishing youth orchestra, and a further five youth ensembles, delivering high-level training and performance experience. A much better use of funds. I scan the list of future attractions that will grace these magnificent halls. There are the Northern Sinfonia and Opera North, but as far as I can see no exciting names, only relics from the past such as Nana Mouskouri and Glen Campbell.

In the evening we play to another packed house. Because there are no vomitaries – the unpleasantly-named entrances coming through the auditorium – as there were in the Courtyard, I have to lug the heavy box through a side door in the stalls and clamber up steps to the stage. I glimpse the audience through the curtain as I wait for my cue. Solid-looking citizens all, and a good mix of all ages. They are once again completely rapt in the play; they appear to be far more intelligent and dedicated than most London audiences.

At the curtain call an amazing thing happens: solid, northern people cheer and slowly begin to stand. And not in the self-congratulatory, exhibitionist American way, but as a genuine tribute to what they perceive to be a great performance of a great play that is part of their heritage. I am quite moved.

Afterwards I am picked up by friends Paul and Leslie Fallon. In the past, when I have played Newcastle I have stayed with them in their beautiful house in Gosforth, but they have recently moved to Horsley, a dozen miles outside the city, where they have converted an eighteenth-century farmhouse and where I will spend the weekend. An old pro gradually builds up a network of friends across the country with whom he can stay in comfort when on the road.

Half the year is gone, and we have only got as far as Newcastle.

Sunday July 1st

Leslie and Paul have created something worthy of a spread in *House & Garden*. I wake and look out over newly laid lawns to rolling, distant hills. There is so much space in Northumbria, and this is only a few miles from the city centre. Paul is a cousin of the actress, Fiona Shaw, and a Liverpuddlian – I hold neither fact against him. He has spent his career in hospital and prison administration. I only got to know him because he was on the RSC digs list and I hit lucky. I find him a fascinating companion because he has such an inquiring mind and always has the ability to see around every problem. He is an expert on so many things; from clocks to bees. Leslie used to run a successful children's wear shop in Newcastle and has exquisite taste.

We spend a day in the rain, driving through unspoilt countryside, walking the Wall and visiting the gardens of Newbrough Hall and Newbrough Lodge. At Newbrough Lodge a sturdy, grizzled gardener stands alone in the rain. The water drips from the brim of his hat as he steadfastly stands by his stall, selling plants for the Red Cross. Paul asks him how many men it takes to look after such a magnificent garden. His face breaks into a proud smile: "Just me and the Lady, four days a week. She herself gets down on her knees and weeds the lawn." He contrives to suggest a beautiful friendship – or perhaps a more mature version of Lady Chatterley and her lover.

Monday July 2nd

Trevor has returned to the North and we spend the day re-blocking *Seagull*, which because of sight lines, is more complicated than *Lear*.

To explain, mainly to myself, why young Peter replaces me as Butler in the last act of *Seagull*, I have decided the Butler is developing palsy and make my hand shake during rehearsal as I pour Arkadina's wine. Hawk-Eye Nunn notices at once and asks why I am doing it. I proudly explain, thinking he will appreciate my trouble and invention. He shakes his head firmly: "If I let you get away with that, by the time I see it again in Melbourne you'll be completely paralysed."

I ask: "He's a good Butler, so why does the Butler lose his job?" Sir Trevor pulls on his beard; "He got too big for his boots and was demoted."

We are given our contracts for America. American Equity, unlike its British counterpart, is a strong union and we have to be temporary members whilst we are in the States. That means we have to be paid at their minimum level, which is more than double what most of us, even those way up the pay scale, are getting here. Jonathan Hyde is infuriated to see that the RSC, with British Equity's approval, has insured our lives for the paltry sum of £37,500. Again it shows how little actors are valued – Frank Lampard earns that in a day.

I had complained again about my dormitory and go back to a better room at the Rosebery Hotel.

Tuesday July 3rd

We finish re-blocking in the late afternoon and Trevor calls us all together for a final talk as after today we won't see him until we reach Melbourne. After that we will see him in New York, LA and, of course, when we get back to London. This is the first time I've been in one of Trevor's touring productions and we are certainly seeing a lot of him – he usually disappears onto his next project as soon as the critics have delivered their verdict. He gives a short, but inspiring, talk on why theatre is the most exciting of all the performing arts, that you never know whether tonight is the night it will be perfect. He explains that familiarity makes everything clearer and you become more confident, more relaxed – but you must never do it differently just for the sake of change. I ask him if there is any news about the film. He sniffs and says that the money is there if we film it in Russia, but he doesn't want to film in Russia because he thinks the technicians are bad. I think most of us are disappointed – making a film in Russia would be an exciting finale to the year.

Seagull plays to a packed house and has a wonderful reception. Frances says it is so much easier acting in a proper theatre: acting in the Courtyard is like acting in a Samuel Beckett play, up to your head in sand. I have to agree. You have no control – and no idea how two thirds of the audience are reacting.

Paul and Leslie come to the play and drive me back to my hotel. On the way we drive down Osborne Road and I think I am in Italy or Spain. The whole road is lined with open restaurants, bars and hotels and there is an air of gaiety. Newcastle continues to surprise me.

Wednesday July 4th

Another free day. I wander around Jesmond and it could be Hampstead. Beautiful parks and fine streets of well-kept Victorian and Edwardian houses. Have lunch in Santana's, an Italian restaurant in the Jesmond Road. Delicious sea bass – as good as anything I had in Puglia last year and only £5.95.

The Theatre Royal education department has arranged a session on *Lear* tomorrow for students, before the matinee. Ian, quite naturally, doesn't want to do it before a performance of *Lear*, so Gemma asks me if I will. I am only too delighted to accept as I haven't uttered a word of Lear out loud since the understudy performance in May. Gemma says we will discuss Lear's first big speech in the opening scene and then go into his relationship with Cordelia. Zoë will stand in as Cordelia, as Romola has to do Nina in the evening.

Thursday July 5ᵗʰ

Get in early at 10.45 and Zoë and I go through things with Gemma – a well brought up gal whose mother is a judge. She is always bright and enthusiastic and seems to know what she is doing. Before long the young lady in charge of the education programme comes into the green room and tells us that our audience is waiting. I am expecting to find at least a couple of hundred kids sitting in the stalls. We go on stage and find just 18 people – half of whom are in their fifties. I cannot believe the schools did not want to come. For all they knew they would be getting Sir Ian: bad organisation by the education department. As in nearly all subsidised theatres, there are huge numbers of administrative staff and they appear to outnumber the artistic team tenfold – but to my mind rarely display the same level of professionalism. Being true professionals, however, Gemma, Zoë and I do our stuff as planned, which is gratefully received by the meagre audience – but what a wasted opportunity.

After the matinee of *Lear* I join Frances in The Godfather, a nearby Italian restaurant. She tells me that it had been arranged for Trevor to be interviewed at the local BBC radio studio for a link-up to the USA. He got there, waited 35 minutes and nobody knew who he was. When at last someone appeared who had a vague idea, they could not establish the connection to America. The BBC man then said to Trevor: "Well, just guess the questions you think they will ask you and we can record your answers."

What a way to treat a man who ran the RSC for 17 years. Apparently Trevor was furious when he got back to the theatre, and I don't blame him.

Armistead Maupin, the American author who together with Harvey Milk's lover, Scott Smith, is said to have persuaded Ian to come out of the closet, is in Newcastle for a book signing at the local Waterstone's. Ian invites the cast to a party in Maupin's honour at the Northern Counties Club, where Ian and Frances are staying. I am an avid reader and am surprised (and a little ashamed) that everyone but me seems to have heard of Maupin and his *Tales of the City* novels. Even Russell Byrne, whom I have never seen reading anything has heard of Armistead Maupin. I am even more surprised to find that Waterstone's has shelves full of his books.

After the show we go to Hood Street, which is only a block away from the Theatre Royal. There, among the usual city centre betting shops, estate agents and employment agencies, I find a truly unexpected gem. The Northern Counties Club is like a time warp back to Edwardian England. Once inside, among comfortable leather armchairs, polished tables and sparkling silver, one could easily imagine oneself in Pall Mall. The businessmen who once made up the bulk of its members have long since gone from the wharves and offices along the Tyne and now it is forced to open its doors and offer accommodation at £70 per night to all and sundry – even to women, as Frances proudly points out. There is an open bar on Ian's account and delicious old-fashioned northern sandwiches, with thick slices of beef and ham. Actors are known for never refusing free food and drink, and nearly all the cast are present. There is a happy atmosphere, although there doesn't seem to be a lot to say – are we running out of conversation so soon? Things liven up when Ian arrives with Armistead Maupin, his young husband, Christopher Turner, and the American writer and critic, John Lahr. I had written to Lahr several years ago, pointing out an error he had made in his book *Prick up Your Ears*, but neither of us can remember what it was. Armistead is charming and sounds like Tennessee Williams. Resolve to buy one of his books tomorrow.

Friday July 6th

Today the papers are full of Al Gore and the 'Live Earth' rock concerts tomorrow. I cannot believe how much electricity is wasted at the Theatre Royal, which is run by Newcastle Council. The lights seem to be on all the time. In our dressing room, which is only occupied by Guy, Seymour and me, there are no less than 43 light bulbs, plus the emergency light over the door. If I want to light my own make-up place, another 18 bulbs switch on automatically. I walk along corridors with overhead lights every few yards and pass empty rooms with electricity blazing whilst daylight streams through the windows. This must be the case in every large public and commercial building in the civilised world. What is the use of an old lady switching off her little lamp at home when there is such waste all around? Gloucester's line from *Lear* comes to mind: 'We have seen the best of our times.'

There is no doubt about it: I am a boring old fart.

Saturday July 7th

Last day in Newcastle. Although the theatre has been packed for every performance and the audiences have been so appreciative, I am happy to leave the North and, like Doctor Johnson, believe the happiest road is that which leads to London.

At the theatre we are each given a copy of a letter from a lady from the St James Theatre in Wellington, New Zealand, saying that they are finding it very hard to sell tickets for *Seagull*. She says that the Wellington public have no interest in Chekov and the 3000 Russians who live there have no desire to see *Seagull* performed in English. The RSC have already told her that they could not change their performance schedule, but she points out that the Monday performance of *Seagull* has only sold 174 tickets in a theatre that seats 1560, and urges, that as the theatre is a non-funded charitable trust and will face financial difficulties as things stand, we change the Monday performance of *Seagull* to *Lear*, ending: '*who plays the lead is of no concern to us…*'.

Does this mean they want me to play *Lear*? I hardly think so. The Monday in question is when Bill was booked to play Sorin, and I rather think she means *Seagull* still wouldn't sell even if Ian was playing it. Indeed only 583 tickets have been sold for the only performance he is billed to do.

Frances, quite naturally as she is leading lady in *Seagull*, is furious, but I have some sympathy for the lady in NZ. I think it illustrates the arrogance of the RSC, living in their feather-bedded world. It was the same attitude that made them pull out of the excellent deal they had made with the Barbican and the City of London. The only reason why we are doing this tour is that the world and his wife want to see Sir Ian McKellen as King Lear. Productions of Chekhov's plays, however excellent, are ten a penny – but at the same time Ian cannot be expected to perform Lear every night; he has to recharge his strength. There is no way we can give extra performances of *Lear*, unless I do it – which unfortunately is highly unlikely.

Richard Clayton comes round beaming nervously to give us our final travel instructions for our flights to Singapore on Monday week. Ian and Frances are leaving early, to spend a week in a luxury health resort on an island in the South China Sea. It's a complete freebie and all Frances has to do is write a favourable article afterwards.

London

Sunday July 8ᵗʰ

Get up at 5am to catch the first Easy Jet flight to London. Share a
taxi with Guy Williams, who missed the corresponding flight last
Sunday, when he went home for the weekend – we are both
determined not to lose this one. Such is my haste to check in that
I leave my mobile in the taxi. Only realise this when I have gone
through check-in. Can't find Guy, can't find public phone box
either, as everyone now uses mobiles. Manage to borrow mobile
from nice northern lad. Phone taxi company and am relieved to
learn that the driver has already reported he's found a phone. Tell
taxi company to hold it for me. Flight is called; get to gate and
can't find my boarding pass. In my consternation over phone
can't remember where I've put it. Am refused entry to plane and
told to wait. I watch desperately as everyone else pours aboard.
At the last moment I find boarding pass in my shirt pocket.
Melanie is also on the plane looking glum; she doesn't seem to
want to talk. Am quite relieved as I am getting to the end of a
very good book. On arrival find Stansted Express is closed for rail
repairs so get on a bus driven by a Polish driver. Reach London
to find all roads are shut because of Ken Livingstone's brainwave
of inviting the drug-drenched Tour de France to start in London,
so have to guide Polish driver round back streets. Soon have a
convoy of coaches following us. On arrival at Victoria, the driver
and some of my fellow passengers thank me profusely.

Get home ring Paul Fallon in Horsley and tell him about my
phone. He rings back within an hour: he has already collected my
phone and tells me that a friend of his, Lady Beecham, will bring
it down to London tomorrow. It will be left in my name at Local

Government House in Smith Square, just over a mile from my
home: Paul is a remarkable man.

So glad to be home. From now on Dora will be with me all
the time.

Spend afternoon in Dulwich with Dora and Georgie and
grandchildren. Rubin is away in Kiev on business. In evening
Dora and I watch Darcy Bussell in Kenneth MacMillan's ballet
of *Three Sisters* on Sky, music by Tchaikovsky, augmented with
Russian folk songs. Excellent. We both think *Seagull* could be a
wonderful ballet. A future project for Sir Trevor Nunn?

For the past three weeks I have been struggling through *The
Religion*, a 750-page saga about the Siege of Malta, and have less
than 50 pages to go. I was reading it on the way from Stansted
and now realise, to my acute frustration, that I left it on the coach
whilst I was distracted, guiding the driver. I will now have to go
to Waterstone's and read the last page to see how it ends. After
that I will try Armistead Maupin: his books are shorter.

Monday July 9th

At 5pm I go to the desk at the Local Government Office and as
Paul promised, my phone is waiting for me.

In the evening Dora and I go to BAFTA and see *Moliere*, the
French version of *Shakespeare in Love*. Only partially successful,
but it has in it a wonderful Italian actress, Laura Morante.
European actresses are so much more interesting than their
Hollywood counterparts – their faces seem more real. Dora
thinks it is because they have a more down-to-earth upbringing.
Meet Roly Curram and his pregnant daughter Kay, who's
looking as beautiful as her late mother, Sheila Gish.

Tuesday July 10th

Drive up to Worksop with Richard Hampton to see our old
school friend Tony French. Tony has been told his stomach
cancer is inoperable and may not be here when I get back from

the tour. Richard is probably my oldest friend: we were at prep school together in 1949 and he was the leading actor in the early days of the National Youth Theatre. He played Hamlet, Henry V and Richard II. He went on to be the president of the Oxford University Dramatic Society and was a member of Olivier's first National Theatre company. He is now a balding 70-year old. We drive up the M1, laughing at old times and remembering old acquaintances.

As we pass Nottingham, I proudly bring out my satnav which my son Emil bought me for Christmas, and punch in Tony's address. The soft voice of a lady called 'Jill' promptly tells us to leave the motorway at the next exit. We blindly follow her instructions, although I notice that the sign says Chesterfield. I look at the map and can plainly see that we should have come off at the following exit 30, which leads directly into Worksop. Suddenly, Chesterfield's famous twisted spire comes into view. Richard has never seen it before. I give Jill the benefit of the doubt and decide she must be taking us on the scenic route. She then takes us onto the A619, the Worksop Road, but after a mile or so she suddenly tells us to take the next left. We do and finish in a cul-de-sac on a housing estate. By now I have lost my temper and am yelling abuse at the bitch. The satnav offers different voice options and I decide to switch to 'Tim', believing that men always read maps better than women do. 'Tim' comes on stream but promptly tells us to turn left down a little country lane. We decide not to follow his advice and shortly drive over the motorway at exit 30, despite 'Tim' telling us to turn around at the first opportunity. When we get to Tony's house, the bugger proudly announces; 'you have reached your destination'. No bloody thanks to 'Tim' or 'Jill'.

Tony has hardly any hair and has to wear dark glasses, but is still as tough as teak. He was a fine middleweight boxer at school, and is as cheerful as ever. Only the eyes of his lovely wife Beryl reveal the suffering they have gone through. Richard and I take them to lunch in a country pub. The countryside around Worksop is beautiful, being part of the 'Dukeries'- an area where the estates of several Dukes once converged. Worksop itself doesn't look as run-down as when I was last here, ten years ago. Then, it was still suffering from the closing of the mines, now, Tony tells us, it is the sandwich-making capital of England. All the M&S and Sainsbury's sandwiches are made here. From digging coal miles underground to buttering bread; I wonder which job the miners prefer?

Afterwards we go back to Beryl's comfortable home and talk about old times as we overlook Tony's carefully-tended garden. He has spent nearly all his adult life in Worksop, having been a lecturer at the local college. Compared to Richard and mine, his life could be considered humdrum and banal, but his home is hung with photos of his three children and six grandchildren – they are all well and happy. Tony has been happily married to Beryl for almost 50 years. He has many friends up here. One cannot hope for more in life than that.

I kiss him when we leave, feeling I will never see him again. I tell him a story Guy Williams told me about a friend of his who, having been told he had only six months to live, went to Brazil determined to fuck a black woman before he died and is still fucking her five years later. Tony is still laughing as he stands in the road waving us goodbye.

Richard and I decide to forgo the services of both 'Jill' and 'Tim' but still manage to miss exit 30 and end up in a traffic jam outside Chesterfield, with another perfect view of the famous spire.

Wednesday July 11th

Ring Davina Belling to say goodbye. For a girl who was slung out of RADA at the end of her first term in 1957, Davina has come a long way. It wasn't really her fault – in those days, there were far more girls than boys at the academy and Davina was given the role of Oberon, King of the Fairies: a very hard part for a 17-year old doctor's daughter from Bournemouth to make much of. She is now a highly successful producer of films and television on both sides of the Atlantic and pretty much knows everyone worth knowing. She recently employed me in her BAFTA award-winning children's series *The Giblet Boys*. I tell her our first stop is Singapore and she promptly tells me she will be in touch with her friend from there, Ling Lee Long. Within an hour or so I receive a long email from the lady, giving intricate details on shops, sights and restaurants – Davina never fails to surprise me.

Read Armistead Maupin's first novel: *Tales of the City*. Not overly impressed. Gay Steinbeck. Understand now why Russell has heard of him – but why is he so popular in Newcastle?

Friday July 13th

Spend most of the day making final preparations for departure. Now it comes to it, I'm not sure I really want to go. I'm always like this just before I go abroad. Unlike Dora, who thrives on travel, I think I've seen enough of the world. London and the Home Counties suit me fine. Dora arranges tickets for Emil and Lindsay to take Mia to *Fiddler on the Roof* and we look after Fabian. Mia is so excited – it is her first grown-up night at the theatre. Her evening is made when she meets Tevye himself, Henry Goodman, after the show in his dressing room and he signs her programme. The grandchildren will grow so much whilst we are away, and we will miss those precious months of their childhood. Julian Glover has told me that he turned down this tour for that very reason.

Saturday July 14th

Take Fabian to Stamford Bridge for the first time and buy him a Chelsea kit. Can't wait for new season to start, though I will miss the opening games. Thank goodness for the Internet! Not sure how Chelsea will do this season. So glad Mourinho has stayed, but looks as if Robben will go. Don't really mind as I never really warmed to him – like a selfish actor, I feel he always played for himself and not the team.

Singapore

Sunday July 15th

Hang about all day, waiting for our evening flight. I always like to travel early otherwise you waste the day waiting. As instructed, we get to Terminal 4 three hours before the scheduled flight. Dora is claustrophobic and needs to sit near the front of the plane. She booked two seats together at the bulkhead months ago, so we are rather perturbed to find that Quantas have placed us apart and towards the rear. Dora does not give up on such things easily. A supervisor is found who informs us that our booking was cancelled because of a wheelchair passenger (although we never see a trace of a wheelchair during the entire flight). After much hot debate we are finally assigned two seats together in the middle of the plane. It is only when we get through security that I realise the company are on two separate flights. Half are on a British Airways flight that is due to leave an hour before ours. There is an air of confusion. We learn there was no room for Bill Gaunt, Sylvester and Romola and now they have missed the flight entirely. Considering they have the most important roles after Lear, it is a complete cock-up.

Once aboard, we are informed that two passengers have lost their passports and we wait for an hour whilst their bags are removed from the hold. Dora tells the stewardess she is sure that there is more legroom on British Airways. The stewardess must have been informed of the cock-up with our booking because she apologises and sweetly offers us a glass of champagne. I have just settled down to watch *300* on the little screen before me when the stewardess returns and offers us a curtained-off row of seats at the front of the plane, normally reserved for the crew. The only drawback is that these seats have no in-flight entertainment. Dora accepts at once and I reluctantly leave my Spartans, still uncertain if their magnificent stomach muscles are the result of digital enhancement. We enter a little dark tent, freezing with air conditioning, in which Dora sleeps peacefully in her padded overcoat whilst I, dressed in my polo shirt with Singapore temperatures in mind, endure a cold and sleepless night.

Monday July 16th

Because of the time difference we lose Monday. I feel a bit like those who rioted in the eighteenth century when the calendar was brought up to date, crying: "Give us back our ten days!" We wake up and arrive in the evening at an immaculate and friendly airport. I see the name Changi and realise this is the site of the notorious Japanese POW camp in WWII. Now the immigration officer welcomes us and offers us a sweet from the bowl on his desk – how unlike the surly brutes we'll no doubt encounter in New York. We are met by both Richard Clayton and Jeremy Adams, the RSC's producer for the overseas part of the tour, who has been buzzing round the globe for the past six months arranging our hotels and theatres. They tell us the British Airways Flight has been delayed even longer than ours; indeed, it has not yet taken off. Bill and Sylvester were put up at the Heathrow Hilton and will be arriving tomorrow. Romola, who seems to be blessed by the gods (and accepts it as the natural state of affairs), was put on a different flight and has already arrived. A coach is awaiting us and we drive into town along a beautiful, tree-lined road. Every bridge is loaded with bougainvillea.

We are taken to the luxurious Swissôtel Stamford, where the entire company will be staying. It is the tallest hotel in the world outside the United States. From our room on the 55th floor we see the lights of the miraculous city of Singapore spread out beneath us, including the Esplanade, where we will be playing. Its two domes look like silver-encrusted carbuncles. I read in my guidebook that its nickname is 'the Armadillo' because of the thousands of triangular aluminium sunshields, which are set to open or close depending on the angle of the sun. It is mostly made of glass and the sunshields are there to protect it from the heat. It puts the National, Sir Denys Lansden's concrete monstrosity by Waterloo Bridge, to shame. It was built at the cost of £600million – part of the Singapore Government's drive to bring culture to the island city-state.

After a quick drink from our duty free we go back to the lobby to meet Gaurav Kripalani, the artistic director of the Singapore Repertory Theatre (SRT). He is very handsome and looks like a Bollywood star. He has been the driving force that has brought us to Singapore; indeed the small SRT has underwritten our whole visit here. He takes us and half of the company across the road to the Esplanade which, he tells us, like the National in London, contains three auditoriums: a concert hall seating 1,600, the Lyric Theatre (where we will play) which seats 2000, and a smaller, 750-seat venue for theatre or music. On top of that, there are two outdoor performance arenas.

Gaurav takes us into the auditorium of the Lyric which is modelled on a traditional Italian opera house. It is a comfortable red with three tiers towering up above the stalls and could not be more different than the Courtyard. The stage is so much bigger, meaning entrances and exits will have to be retimed and that Gemma will have quite a job adapting the play. The now-familiar set is already in place. Gaurav tells us that because of the distances involved, three separate sets have been built for Singapore, Australia and New Zealand. The company, apart from Bill, Sylvester and Philip, who has been attending his brother's wedding in Montana, reassemble for a meal in the green room. We fall into each other's arms, excited to meet again on the other side of the world. Ian and Frances have come back from their freebie holiday in a luxurious health farm on the nearby island of Bintan, which Frances will now write about for a British

Airways publication. They have spent four days as an unlikely couple in the Honeymoon Suite, being detoxed and having facials and massages. Frances, as ever, is full of amusing stories. They had their own butler who assumed they were in a permanent relationship and insisted on calling her 'Lady Frances' and, having no idea that Ian was gay, was most disappointed to discover they slept in separate four-poster beds. They look positively blooming, compared with the jet-lagged rest of us. Jonathan Hyde's charming wife, Isabel, one of Sylvester's sons, and Russell's delicate Italian partner join Dora as camp followers. Some are more camp than others.

Afterwards, Dora and I slip away to try a Singapore Sling at the famous Long Bar at Raffles Hotel. Very disappointing: overpriced syrup.

Tuesday July 17th

Wonderful night's sleep in a very comfortable bed. The company has the day off, to recover from jet-lag and give the crew time to complete fitting up the set and lighting.

The local paper, *Straits Times,* is delivered to our room. Open to behold headline:

'*All hail the 'King's' Arrival*'

Then:

'*NO NUDITY: McKellen will not shed all here*'
'*Fresh from a four-day retreat at Banyan Tree Bintan resort, British actor Ian McKellen, 68, and Frances Barber, 48, are feeling "fighting-fit" for the Singapore premiere of Shakespeare's* King Lear *and Chekhov's* The Seagull. *Both plays are staged by the prestigious Royal Shakespeare Company and the Singapore Repertory Theatre (SRT).*

Known for playing Gandalf *in* The Lord of the Rings *trilogy and* Magneto *in the* X-Men *films, McKellen looked dapper when* The Straits Times *met him at the ferry terminal last night. While the British run of* Lear *had a brief nude scene, the actor, who plays the title role, will wear underpants here due to an agreement between the RSC and SRT, allowing the play to escape an R18 rating so students can see it. On this, McKellen said: "When you travel to other countries, you respect their laws and traditions. In New Zealand, we won't be allowed to smoke onstage, so that has to be coped with".'*

No mention of this being one of the great *Lears*. As in England, the main interest seems to be in Ian's great cock.

At breakfast we meet Guy Williams, who arrived a few days early to have a holiday with his wife and son. He tells us that the best Chinese restaurants are in the red-light district in Geylang Road. Spend the morning exploring town. Modern Singapore is ever-mindful of the hardship of its past. A sign tells us that this (now elegant) district was where the Samsui women lived in overcrowded squalor. These tragic women slaved as coolies in docks and construction industries up until the 1950s. They worked to send money home to their families in China – most of them died from overwork and never saw their families again. We take a taxi to Orchard Road, the main shopping thoroughfare. Taxis are amazingly cheap: cheaper than a bus in Livingstone's London. Because they are cheap, all 15,000 taxis in Singapore are continuously busy. They don't wait about for hours, they are all clean, well-maintained and metered and offer a far better service than the overpriced and over-vaunted London taxis. Orchard Road is a better-class Oxford Street but there seems to be a surfeit of shopping malls; floor after floor of elegant, expensive shops, waiting for customers. There appear to be no real bargains, unlike in Hong Kong 20 years ago. Dora thinks it is because of the new international copyright laws, which prevent illegal copying of famous brand names.

In the evening we follow Guy's advice and take a cab to Geylang. As with everything else in Singapore, the vice trade is strictly controlled (allegedly for the public good) and Geylang is the legally-permitted red-light district. We pass scores of pretty young girls, standing waiting along the pavements of Geylang Road. The taxi drops us at the strangely-named No Signboard Seafood Restaurant. It is as large as a garage forecourt and is packed with Chinese from all social backgrounds. As we eat our delicious pepper crab surrounded by the local inhabitants, limousines drop off well-heeled Chinese businessmen and their smartly-dressed female companions. The hotel next door has a neon sign advertising rooms for ten Singapore dollars an hour.

We notice how young and pretty the vice girls are. A couple of Australians on the next table tell me they only charge 100 Singapore dollars a night. I remark it sounds like a very good bargain and receive a kick from Dora, who hopes their fate will be happier than that of the Samsui women. We walk back for a mile or so along the crowded Geylang Road, through the girls and their pimps, feeling safer than we would on a Sunday evening in Stratford.

Wednesday July 18th

This morning's *Straits Times* is still abuzz with whether or not Sir Ian will show his genitalia. When a reporter asks him to comment on Singapore's ban on homosexual acts, the old Stonewaller replies that he does feel rather guilty, as it is a law left over from British rule.

In the morning Dora and I go to the Botanic Gardens. The taxi drives us through a beautiful residential district that surpasses Beverly Hills. The colonial types certainly knew how to live. The Botanic Gardens, like practically everything else in Singapore, were first established in 1822 by the ubiquitous Stamford Raffles, to evaluate the cultivation of crops which were of potential economic importance, such as fruit, vegetables, spices and other raw materials. It is now a beautifully-maintained rival of Kew, and has the most wonderful collection of orchids, several acres of rainforest, as well as promoting public education on landscape planting, horticulture and botany.

We walk back along Orchard Road. Being actors, most of the company are left-wing and there have been several comments about Singapore being a police state, reminiscent of 1984. Others complain that the place only seems interested in making money. In fact we have not seen a single policeman. I have never seen such happy, smiling, busy people and such racial harmony of Chinese, European, Indian and Malay, Christian, Muslim, Buddhist and Hindu – and what a pleasure to walk on pristine pavements, bereft of black stains of chewing gum. As we near the hotel in Waterloo Road, a guard stands outside the synagogue. As ever, the Jews seem to be the exception, even though they have been here since 1827.

Thursday July 19th

Arrive at the theatre and find I am sharing a dressing room with Seymour – they have put the two old farts together. It is difficult finding one's way around backstage, as there are very long corridors and the stage is two floors down. Ian has contracted a local complaint, Singapore Ear, and cannot hear in one ear. The locals say it is the humidity; Frances thinks he should have rested more after the detox. Ian goes back to the hotel to sleep and I stand in for him during the second half of the technical rehearsal – very happy to say the lines again. Although I am at Ian's side throughout every performance, it is never the same as speaking the lines myself. In the West End, the understudies have a full rehearsal on stage every week – I have hardly spoken a word of Lear aloud since the understudy run in early May. I look out at the vast auditorium with row upon row of empty seats and wonder if I will be speaking these same lines to a full house this evening. I find myself hoping that I will. But in the evening Ian, though not fully recovered, insists on playing and as Seymour and I lead on the opening procession for our first performance on foreign soil, we are greeted with a loud round of applause. As both Seymour and I have grey hair and beards I'm sure they think one of us is Sir Ian. This is, in fact, a very intelligent, educated audience. They see the points very clearly and we get more laughs than we did at Stratford. They give us a wonderful ovation at the curtain.

Gaurav Kripalani is certainly spoiling us. As well as providing a delicious meal in the green room every night before the show, he has arranged a free meal in a nearby Chinese restaurant as there is no official party tonight. Very tired and very full so I give it a miss.

The day is only marred by the news that John Terry has broken his toe.

Friday July 20th

See a familiar, blonde head and smiling face across the crowded breakfast room: Bill's wife Carolyn has flown out to join him for a few days. Everyone in the company is looking very tired. Perhaps it is still the jet-lag, but the younger members, led by Romola, are holding balcony parties till dawn. I don't know how they manage it as the balconies are only about three feet deep.

Dora and I go to the National Museum of Singapore. It is situated in an old colonial building and has only recently been refurbished. It is full of state of the art audio-visual aids, tracing the history of Singapore down through the ages. It is totally fascinating; in three hours we only scratch the surface. We have lunch in a simple café and have a local dish, laksa, which seems a mixture of paella, seafood linguine and bouillabaisse. Air conditioning is blazing everywhere. There seems little concern about global warming, although the air does seem very clean here.

Ian adopts a new pose at the curtain call: he stands humbly blinking, with hand on heart. We all go to a gala reception at Indo Chine, a luxurious bar-restaurant on the banks of the Singapore River. It is a warm tropical night; hundreds of lights glisten on the sparkling waters as a throng of smartly-dressed people sip champagne under the stars. Kripalani, who continues to make every effort to ensure we have a good time, introduces us to the black-clad Chinese owner, who Dora thinks looks a bit like a gangster. The cream of Singapore society is present, from the imposing and elegant Queen of Malaysia to the down-to-earth British High Commissioner, as well as luminaries from the polo and cricket clubs: it is just like being in a story by Somerset Maugham.

An Indian lady from the Singapore Polo Club asks Bill who he played.

"I was the chap who lost his eyes."

"Oh, you were the king."

"No, I was Gloucester. The king doesn't lose his eyes."

"Really? I'm sure he didn't have any when he carried his daughter on at the end."

See young Peter conversing earnestly with the Queen of Malaysia's daughter and her attractive friend.

Saturday July 21st

Miss Hong Xinyi's review in the *Straits Times* begins:

'There can be little doubt that this is an old-fashioned sort of production. Under Trevor Nunn's direction, the play veers too much at times into hammy hysteria, with plenty of appealing upward gazes that rather belabour the point of the pitiless heavens…'

After that follows a very perceptive reading of the production, picking up on fine points and finally conceding that *'McKellen gives an uncompromising interpretation of this formidable role, one that reveals Lear's kindness and cruelty, to a standing ovation from a full house.'*

Miss Xinyi obviously 'majored' in Shakespeare or drama.

We watch a rehearsal of the National Day Parade from our

balcony. I feel like Gulliver as the regimented, smartly-dressed, Lilliputian figures parade below. On the other side of the wall, totally ignorant of the bustle outside, Romola and Monica sunbathe by the pool.

The Queen of Malaysia has invited the company to her palace in Malaya for tea and a display of native dancing. I ask Peter how he got on last night. He tells me he thinks he is in love with the attractive friend of the Queen's daughter, who is an air hostess.

After another rousing performance, we attend a reception held by Reuters. Dora and I meet a multimillionaire from Fiji, a handsome, dark-skinned gentleman who has flown over in his private jet especially to see the play. I introduce him to Monica, telling him she will be coming to Fiji at the end of August. He says he will not be there then, but offers to make some sightseeing arrangements for her. Monica doesn't seem too interested in his offer.

Sunday July 22nd

The expedition to Malaya has been cancelled. Suspect it is because Ian doesn't want to go and the invitation depends on his attendance. Pity – but it only goes to show the rest of us are not quite the celebrities we thought.

Seagull plays to two, packed houses. Frances says it is the perfect answer to the woman who runs the St James theatre in Wellington.

Russell and his partner accompany Ian on a night out clubbing. Ian, ever ready to promote Gay Rights, wears a pink tee shirt. Apparently when they arrived, the members were hanging from the balconies to welcome him.

Monday July 23rd

Share table at breakfast with Melanie. Dora is getting on very well with her, much better than I've ever managed. Perhaps it has something to do with the fact they are both Jewish and both have a passion for shopping and clothes. The skies here are grey every day – could it be some sort of pollution due to the non-stop air conditioning? Nevertheless, Dora and I head out and pass the elegant, old Victoria Theatre. We walk into the lobby and meet the manager, Mr Gurjeet Singh, who offers to show us around. The original auditorium, with its perfect acoustics, was designed by the ubiquitous Frank Matcham. Mr Singh tells us Sir John Gielgud played Hamlet here in 1946, whilst Japanese war criminals were being tried in the next door building. He takes us into his office and shows us the original poster. The auditorium was gutted and redesigned in the sixties; it is now a characterless brown box, but Mr Singh tells us they still have Matcham's plans and hope to turn it back to its original state. As it is Singapore they probably will.

Our run in Singapore has ended too soon. Ian gives final performance of *Lear* to even greater applause.

Tuesday July 24th

Our flight for Melbourne does not leave until the evening, so Dora and I have Tiffin at Raffles.

The only time there is any hint of any member of the cast being more important than the others is on the flights. It is RSC policy that everyone, from Michael Boyd downwards, travels economy, but senior members – Ian, Frances, Bill, Sylvester, Jonathan Hyde and his wife, Isabel – have paid extra to go business class. They can probably write most of it off against tax. (In fairness, Bill has to have extra room because of his arthritic feet.) The rest of us including (surprisingly) Romola – who, unlike most Hollywood starlets doesn't seem to care for such status symbols – are crammed into steerage on two separate flights. The luckier ones, including me and Dora, go direct; the others have a three-hour stopover in Sydney. Flying long distance is hell, but neither Dora nor I could ever reconcile ourselves, even if we could afford it, to spending thousands to avoid a few hours' discomfort – we'd rather spend the money on an extra holiday.

Can't sleep so finally get to watch the end of *300*, which I enjoy in spite of myself. I then watch one of Romola's films: *Amazing Grace*. A worthy effort with some very good acting from Finney, Gambon and, of course, Romola.

Melbourne

Wednesday July 25th

Arrive at Melbourne Airport before dawn. On the bus to the hotel I am amazed to hear certain members of the company complaining about Trevor and saying that they are fed up with him. Someone even suggests that Trevor has deliberately under cast the play to annoy Ian. Although I believe some of the cast to be quite young and inexperienced, it's ridiculous to think that Trevor would ever deliberately sabotage his own production. Trevor has his faults and fussiness but in my opinion he is still the best. Actors are the worst moaners in the world, but I can't understand how and when this change of attitude happened, only a week or so ago everyone appeared to be so happy. We drive into Melbourne as dawn breaks. It looks slightly shop-soiled after Singapore.

We all have apartments in the Stamford Plaza Hotel on Little Collins Street in the centre of Melbourne. The windows don't open, and overlook the bedrooms on the other side of a dark courtyard. We are spoiled after the views in Singapore and not enamoured by our new surroundings. No balcony parties here: there are no balconies. Dora goes into action and we get a slightly better view. After an English breakfast, we walk through Melbourne. The trams and hills are reminiscent of San Francisco but there is a paucity of fashion-conscious women.

The company assembles at the Arts Centre: a modern monstrosity, surmounted by something which looks a bit like the Eiffel Tower on top of a ballerina's tutu. It contains a huge concert hall and two theatres, all of which have been constructed underground. It is a vast complex, even bigger than Singapore's, with a veritable maze of corridors and tunnels backstage. Will one get lost? We are given a tour of the enormous State Theatre, where we will be playing. The auditorium is bigger than Covent Garden and seats over 2000. It is usually an opera house and *Lear* is only the third play to be performed here since it opened in 1986. We then go to a huge rehearsal room for a company meeting. Gemma says that Trevor is on his way and he will probably call extra rehearsals. This does not go down well; there are glum faces around the room.

Most of us go for welcome drinks with numerous Arts Centre staff in one of the many theatre bars. Excellent Australian wines with no added chemicals, so get a sound night's sleep.

Thursday July 26th

We have a free day. Dora and I walk down Collins Street past smart shops and trendy bars. It is a mixture of any city in Europe or America. The trams are excellent and reliable. We have an alfresco lunch in the rejuvenated docklands – we could be in Wapping.

One of the RSC's wealthy American sponsors, Doug McPherson, is in town and has invited the company to dinner at the Red Emperor restaurant, overlooking the Yarra River. Delightful evening, but the Chinese food cannot match what we had in Singapore. Most of the company attend. Dora and I sit on same table as Richard Clayton, who does his job as company manager quietly and efficiently, and Jeremy Adams, the RSC's tour producer. Jeremy says the wind has changed: Trevor has landed.

Friday July 27th

The Herald Sun, a local Melbourne paper, harps on about the tired old theme:

'King Lear *will grace the Arts Centre stage for just five nights, ending next Saturday. A highlight – or a lowlight, depending on your view – is that McKellen will bare all during the play's tempestuous storm scene.'*

I sometimes wish Ian and Trevor had never decided to follow the nudity trend.

Dora and I plan to go to lunch at a fish restaurant on the beach at St Kilda, that Sylvester had recommended, but at 11.15 a note is slipped under our door: Trevor has called a company rehearsal at 4.45. We decide to go to the National Gallery of Victoria instead. It is an excellent modern gallery with a fine collection of Impressionists, Pre-Raphaelites and the odd Constable and Turner, very well displayed.

I go to the rehearsal room and find everyone there, some not looking very happy as their free day has been cut into. Suddenly there is a flash of faded-blue denim and with a toss of his long greying locks, Trevor bounds into the room. I must say I'm glad to see him back. He says he is going to have to do some re-blocking tomorrow, particularly the opening scene, because the shape of the vast auditorium is different to what we have played in before and many seats will have a blocked view if we play it in the original way; with the three daughters Frances, Monica and Romola all placed downstage of Lear. Trevor says he will also have to change some of the entrances and exits. There are a few unhappy faces at this – I can't understand why.

Back at the hotel I receive an email from Larry Belling saying the Flower Drum on Market Lane is one of the best Chinese restaurants in the world. Dora and I decide to go there as it is my birthday tomorrow. When we arrive the Maître d' regretfully informs us they are fully booked and suggests we come tomorrow. I tell him that will be impossible as I am in *King Lear*. Instantly a look of awe comes over his face: "Ah, *King Lear*!" He rings upstairs and talks rapidly in Chinese, then turns and smiles and says they have managed to find a very nice table for us. We take the lift to the dining room above, to be greeted by the owner himself – I now realise they think I am Sir Ian. For one evening I am treated as a star, as a succession of waiters fuss over us. The food is excellent and at the end I decide to pay cash – so they will not be disappointed when they see the name on the credit card.

Saturday July 28th

My 69th birthday – I jokingly remark to Dora that I have only one of my 'threescore years and ten' left and still haven't made it.

Peter's 'Singapore fling' has followed him to Melbourne for a few days. He tells me he thinks he is in love. What it is to be young! Dora thinks there is also a hint of romance between Gerald and young Zoë; I tell her it's not possible as his new girlfriend will soon be arriving from England.

Trevor proceeds to re-block the first scene. Ian agrees that it is necessary but Romola looks unhappy. Trevor tells her to move to the chair, to become attached to the scene. It is an obvious move but Romola seems reluctant and only moves halfway. Trevor, pushed for time because we are opening tonight, is rather short with her.

Later I find myself sitting next to Romola in the corridor that serves as a green room. "I've never been spoken to like that in my life," she murmurs.

I reflect that she is a very lucky girl indeed if that is the worst she has suffered, but endeavour to change the subject. I have already told her that I had enjoyed *Amazing Grace*, but there was one scene I could not understand. "Do you know why Toby Jones as the Duke of Clarence was sitting in the House of Commons next to Kieran Hinds, playing Lord Tarleton, when Wilberforce made his great speech against slavery? I thought dukes and lords were not allowed in the Commons?"

She doesn't seem very interested. "Of course they were. Pitt was a lord."

I seem to remember from my A level history that William

Pitt the Younger died a commoner, but plough on regardless. "Surely the Duke of Clarence was a son of George III, and members of the Royal Family have not been allowed in the Commons since the Civil War?" I realise that I must sound like a pedantic school teacher.

She gets up and glides away, throwing over her shoulder: "The writer researched everything."

I've become one of those boring old actors I used to avoid in my youth.

First performance of *Lear* in Melbourne. The Aussies greet the opening suspiciously. When Seymour and I lead on the opening procession, there is no warm applause as in Singapore and there are very few laughs in the first few scenes but gradually we feel them being won over by Ian's towering performance. There is a tremendous ovation at the end and slowly Melbourne gets to its feet and stands in tribute: a thing, we are later told, rarely seen. It is a wonderful feeling to stand on stage and be part of it. Almost makes up for losing the Ashes.

As noted previously, the conscientious Richard Clayton has provided every member of the company with a cake at the interval on their birthday. I am a bit miffed that he seems to have forgotten mine. But at the after-show reception after Ian and Steve Bracks, the outgoing Premier of Victoria who yesterday announced his unexpected resignation, have made their congratulatory speeches the lights are dimmed and to the tune of 'Happy Birthday' a chocolate cake is carried in, in my honour. Russell and Naomi each give me a warm kiss.

Sam Neill, my favourite Australian actor, is present. He says he's discovered things tonight about *Lear* he had never dreamed of before. I neglect to ask what but, after discovering he is not in fact an Australian but a Kiwi, we have a long talk about our mutual friend, Julian Fellowes. As ever, where Julian is concerned, there is a story. In 1984, when Sam and Julian were both trying to make their names in Hollywood, staying with

Christopher Cazenove who was out there doing a stint in *Dynasty*, they decided to fly down to Nicaragua to see how the Sandinista revolution was going on – as one would. Sam, moderately left-wing, had started out supporting the Sandinistas and Julian, naturally was rather on the side of Reagan and the Contras, but in the end they both felt the whole lot of them were pretty hopeless. Sam and Julian did everything, from attending rallies and demonstrations, going up into the war zone, and dining with the American Ambassador after being smuggled into the American Embassy in the boot of a limousine. It all sounds like something out of Evelyn Waugh.

Dora has long chat with Tony Lazaros, an Anglo-Indian from Leicester who is now a travel agent in Sydney and has made all the arrangements for our flights in this part of the world. Sydney is not in our schedule but he offers to arrange for her to spend a couple of days in a top hotel there.

Sunday July 29th

The *Dr Who* Club of Victoria has hastily arranged a convention for Sylvester. When he tells them I was in the original series with William Hartnell and also did a series with Tom Baker, they want me to come as well. I will not be able to stay long as, unlike Sylvester, I have to rehearse *Seagull* this afternoon. At 12 noon Dora, Sylvester and I wait in the hotel lobby for a member of the society to drive us to the convention, which will be held in a town hall in one of Melbourne's suburbs. A young man with a very small head arrives and when I tell him my concern about getting back for the rehearsal, he tells us the town hall is only 20 minutes away. We pile into his overheated car and proceed to drive past the university area and along a road full of interesting-looking Italian restaurants. We pass pretty little houses with ornate filigreed canopies and beautiful parks. It is a charming drive until we realise we have been driving for over half an hour. The young man takes us down suburban streets and then back onto the main road. Every time we stop at a traffic light he pores over the A-Z of Melbourne. We think he is taking us on a short cut until I notice that we have passed the Ivanhoe Garage three times. It's a bit like the passing of the currant bun in the maze in *Three Men in a Boat*. It is now 12.45 and the young man eventually admits he is lost. Sylvester and I exchange glances: Dr Who is lost Down Under without his Tardis. After more map reading we turn around and eventually pull up outside the town hall at 12.55, where a very frenetic Peter Rosace, the club's president, is waiting for us.

Sylvester is taken to have lunch whilst Dora and I are led up to a conference hall, where nearly 100 *Dr Who* devotees of all ages and sexes are eagerly awaiting us. I do a question and answer session. They are all so keen, polite, devoted to their passion, and ask me detailed questions on something I did over 40 years ago. I don't tell them that in those days my career was going so well, I considered doing four episodes of *Dr Who* a bit of a comedown. Apart from Peter Purves, I think I am the only surviving member of those William Hartnell episodes. Unfortunately the BBC wiped most of the tapes in those days and there is nothing left apart from the soundtrack and a few photos. I talk about fellow cast members such as Eric Thompson (Emma's father and narrator of the *Magic Roundabout*) and André Morell, a very distinguished actor (and friend of Olivier himself) who got very annoyed one morning when I, a very young actor, had the temerity to open his *Times* to read the football results and didn't fold it back properly. Also I talk of my friend, poor Barry Justice – nephew of James Robertson Justice – who committed suicide when he was barely 30.

Suddenly somebody recognises Dora. She did a few episodes of a long-forgotten series called *Space 99* and questions begin to be fired at her as well. I then do a signing session; books with my face on the cover and photos that I have never seen are produced for me to sign. Nearly everyone present has something. Towards the end of the line, a young blind man holds a BBC audio cassette. He rubs my hand and thanks me for helping his childhood – I cannot help but be moved.

A Somali taxi driver, who goes to England twice a year to watch Manchester United, gets us back to the Arts Centre in 15 minutes.

The opening performance of *Seagull* is rapturously received. At the party afterwards, an Australian journalist says he is surprised how well the small parts are played. I reply that, unlike the English Cricket Team, the RSC bat all the way down to 11.

Monday July 30th

Philip, with typical American get-up-and-go has hired a couple of minibuses and most of the company put down their names to spend the day driving the scenic Great Ocean Road. Dora and I don't fancy waiting around for latecomers so we hire a car and go by ourselves. Ben Delfont, who looks after his stage management team, containing Rhiannon Harper the prettiest girl in the company, with the care and discipline of a seasoned sergeant major, has hired his own minibus and gone off on a separate expedition. It's good to get away from the others for a while and to see English place names on the signposts.

We read reviews whilst having coffee in Torquay. The Melbourne papers are raves. Cameron Woodhead in *The Age* writes:

'Lear is a role that has defeated great actors…but Ian McKellen is at the height of his powers. And he crafts an unforgettable performance that will, in all probability, set a new benchmark for this century, as Scofield's did for the last… As a director of Shakespeare, Nunn's particular genius is that the visual and textual aspects of his imagination are as indispensable to each other as the chambers of the heart…It is a great privilege to have seen the RSC perform King Lear. *With richly interpretive direction, a brilliant cast and a searing performance from Ian*

McKellen in the title role, it is a production that will be talked about for generations to come.'

Kate Herbert in *The Herald Sun* is almost as favourable, although I must admit to a certain degree of schadenfreude when I read:

'Unfortunately, Garai's Cordelia lacks the dignity and weight to balance her sisters' treachery. Cordelia's gaucheness in the opening scene does not elicit sympathy and her later scenes crave a young queen's nobility and grace.'

Alison Croggon's review in Rupert Murdoch's, Sydney-based *The Australian*, which, we are told, is against everything in Melbourne, is not good. She describes Trevor's production of *Lear* as *'a kind of comic opera, complete with Gilbert and Sullivan costumes, overblown set and arch winks at the audience.'* Although she thinks Trevor redeems himself with a superb production of *Seagull*, and I feel the reverse of schadenfreude when she praises Romola's *'thrilling, fearless Nina.'*

We find a quiet fish restaurant near Lorne – see wallabies and some penguins. On the way back we stop at a headland to take in the view of the distant Twelve Apostles: great towering rocks in the ocean. There, beneath us, by the breakers of the Tasman Sea in an otherwise-deserted open air restaurant, we see a flash of familiar white hair: Lear and most of his court are having a late alfresco lunch.

Back at the hotel a girl comes running along the corridor in tears. Dora thinks it is Gerald's girlfriend, who arrived this morning.

Tuesday July 31st

Dora and I eventually get to St Kilda, on the outskirts of Melbourne. It's like a mixture of Miami and Margate and I have one of the best fish meals I've ever had at the unpretentious Clay

Pot – a throwback to the little bistros we had in London in the sixties – whilst an old gramophone plays nostalgic French songs. Afterwards we visit the excellent Jewish Museum and find a quotation from the *Wisdom of Ben Sira*, which could so easily apply to Shakespeare: 'There is none that hath never made an end of learning it, and there is none that will ever find out all its mysteries. For its wisdom is richer than any sea, and its word deeper than any abyss.'

Because of the vast size of the theatre, Trevor has changed several of the entrances and exits. There are two doors on each side of the auditorium which have replaced the easily-accessible vomitaries we had in the Courtyard. The door nearest the stage is a dead end. It leads out into the front concourse and Trevor only uses it if people have to make a quick entrance back onstage through the auditorium. Only the second, further door has a quick passage backstage. When Lear sends me to 'Prepare my horses', I rush down the steps into the auditorium as usual, making for the further door. As I pass the first door, which is manned by a stagehand, it opens. Thinking I must be wrong, I dive through it then realise the stagehand manning it, whilst reading a newspaper has mistaken my exit for a later cue. I curse him silently and desperately ponder how I will get around the back of the stage to lead Ian and Sylvester in through the corresponding door on the other side, where we will wait for Lear's entrance into the 'reason not the need' scene. As I wait for my cue I decide, when I re-enter, to point to the other side of the stage as I say my line, hoping that Ian will realise. This I duly do, but Ian is so used to following me off the side that I come on and he storms off the wrong side – although I do manage to lead him to the second door and we make it backstage. There is great consternation; we now have to get to the first door on the other side, to the box that I carry on, which is vital to the positioning of Lear's next, crucial scene. An Australian stagehand volunteers to lead us up the back way. We have less than ten minutes.

Ian is remarkably calm as we are led down long endless corridors. I now know how he got his nickname: 'Serena'. At last we come to a door but when we open it we find that, to our dismay, we are still on the wrong side of the auditorium. We plunge back up the stairs and come out in the vast foyer. Bystanders turn in amazement at the sight of Lear, Fool, and Gentleman hurrying frantically through their midst. It is the actor's nightmare: the minutes are ticking away to our cue. Down more stairs and then, to our horror, we find ourselves backstage, back where we started. For the second time in two days Sylvester and I are hopelessly lost in Melbourne. But help is at hand. A little, old Aussie speaks up: "There's the small lift. We're not supposed to use it during performances, but that would land you in the right spot." We hurriedly pile into what looks like an old miners' cage and go up five floors. He then leads us gingerly across part of the lighting rig; we can see the audience way beneath us, rapt as they watch Kent being put in the stocks. Down three flights of stairs and there it is: the wonderful sight of my box and a stagehand waiting to open the door for us on our cue.

Ian then gives one of his finest renditions of the scene yet.

Wednesday August 1*st*

Gerald is distraught. He'd invited his new girlfriend to join him out here for a holiday, but things have not worked out and the poor girl is now going back to London only a few days after her arrival. A young heartbroken actress, it's a bit like the plot of *Seagull*: should help him with Trigorin. Dora, as always, was right.

Tomorrow the company have had two invitations. The cast of *Neighbours* have invited us onto their set for a photo and a tour of the studio, and the Melbourne Cricket Club has offered a tour of the MCG. I phone my sons in England and they tell me there is only one possible choice.

Thursday August 2nd

A highlight of the tour. Apart from me, Richard Goulding, Ben Addis, Adam Booth (stolid, sports loving Yorkshireman that he is) and his girlfriend, Lindsay, a properly brought-up girl whose dad is a member of the MCC are the only takers for the tour of the M.C.G. An elegant old gentleman, who looks as though he has stepped out of the Long Room at Lord's, is our guide. He takes us onto the pitch itself and we gaze up at the intimidating stands all around, which can hold up to 100,000 rowdy Aussies. We sit in the box where English batsmen wait to make their lonely way to the wicket, and walk the blue carpet they must follow when they are out. The magnificent ground, where the 1956 Olympics were held, is also used for Australian Rules Football. Richard takes a photo of me sitting, most appropriately, on the substitutes bench.

The *Neighbours* group say they also had a great time. Peter, in the brashness of youth, asked the producers if he could have a job; they have told him to write in with his details. Some of the cast of *Neighbours* are coming to *Seagull* tonight.

Lear's substitute gets a warning call: Ian is ill with a urinary infection. He insists on playing Sorin, but will he be strong enough for Lear tomorrow? Although it would feel a bit like breaking up a holiday I'd love to do it just once, but I know Ian will have to be confined to bed and strapped down to boot to miss it. I take the script home with me, just in case.

Naturally, Ian plays Sorin to perfection.

Gerald is still stricken with guilt. His girlfriend is now staying on in Melbourne with friends and will try to have a holiday.

Friday August 3rd

The company is given a lunch at the Arts Centre, with Melbourne's high and mighty including, it is rumoured, Rupert Murdoch's mother. They are expecting Trevor and Ian to give speeches, but Ian is still not well and needs to conserve his strength for *Lear* this evening and Trevor is spending time with his grown-up Australian daughters who live out here, so Bill Gaunt and Gemma stand in. Although I admire Gemma as an assistant director, she is a little out of her depth. Why did they not ask Jonathan, who was born an Australian or Sylvester, who can be very funny to speak instead? Surely it is the actors they want to see and hear? Bill does better, although one of his jokes is worthy of Dame Edna's alter ego, Les Patterson:

"The last time I was in Australia, I did an Alan Ayckbourn play in the small theatre inside the Sydney Opera House. Your then Prime Minister, Paul Keating, came to the opening night. As it was just before the Olympics I asked him if he was going to invite the Queen to open the Games. He replied: "Over my fucking dead body!"

Melbourne's great and good receives it in stony silence.

Saturday August 4th

Dora decides to accept Tony Lazaros' offer and goes to spend a couple of days in Sydney. Pleasant though it is, I've had enough of Melbourne, especially the lack of air in the Arts Centre.

Ian, still ill, limps through Lear but somehow manages to use the illness to make his performance even more moving. Geoffrey Rush is in the audience. He would make a great Lear, but then so would Sam Neill and so many other mature actors – is that one of the reasons it is a great part – the universality of the role? But what makes a great actor? I remember Richard Burton saying to me as we watched Peter O'Toole loping onto the set of *Becket* after a very heavy lunch: "See that old praying mantis? He's a great actor – he can play a king. Only great actors can play kings. I can play a king, Olivier can play a king. Albert Finney will never be a great actor – he can't play a king." Burton was wrong there: Albert Finney is a great actor.

Come to think of it, Burton has a lot to answer for – he told me to become an actor in the first place. It was at the opening night of *Henry V*, the very first Youth Theatre production at Toynbee Hall in the East End in 1956. We had acquired the costumes that had been used at the Old Vic the previous year. Burton had played Henry in that production and had somehow been persuaded to come along, together with Sir Ralph Richardson. After the show they came into the dressing room we were all sharing. I was playing the comic part of Pistol and could hardly believe my ears when Burton walked up to me and said: "Very good, my boy. You should become a professional actor." I didn't see him again for seven years until I got the part of Brother John in the film *Becket*. I was invited by the legendary producer, Hal Wallis, to a pre-shoot cocktail party in an ultra-elegant house in Brompton Square. I walked nervously into a room crowded with theatrical legends: Sir John Gielgud, Sir Felix Aylmer, Sir Donald Wolfit, Martita Hunt (looking just as fearsome as when she played Miss Havisham in *Great Expectations*), Pamela Brown, Peter O'Toole, Richard Burton and Elizabeth Taylor at the summit of her beauty. The only person I had met before, apart from Sir Donald, was Burton.

I went boldly up to him and said, "Well I took your advice."

He turned from Elizabeth and asked, "What do you mean?"

"Well, don't you remember?" I faltered, "When you came to the first night of the Youth Theatre a few years ago you told me I should become an actor and here I am."

He puffed on his cigarette and surveyed me intently, with half closed eyes: "Oh, yes. I remember you well. You were very, very good." Elizabeth showed interest for the first time at this. She regarded me intently with those violet beautiful eyes, framed by double lashes. I blushed. Burton sipped his vodka before the blow fell: "Yes, you were a very good Henry V."

I shook my head sadly: "No, I was Pistol."

He smiled kindly: "Of course. You were very good too."

Elizabeth's interest had waned.

Sunday August 5th

Final performance in Melbourne: *Seagull* with Bill as Sorin. Frances tells me that Ian remains ill, "Like a wounded lion." Afterwards, at the farewell drinks party, Bill and I meet up with Lewis Fiander, an Australian actor who was a member of Olivier's company in the early days of the National Theatre. Lewis is a great raconteur and tells us some great stories:

On the opening night of Olivier's acclaimed *Othello*, Lewis, who was not in the play went backstage to congratulate his friend, John Stride, who was playing Cassio. At the stage door he was met by a distraught stage manager.

"Who are you going to see?"

"John Stride."

"Forget John Stride. Larry's sitting up there all alone. Go up and congratulate him."

He went up to find Olivier waiting very nervously in his dressing room. He looked up anxiously and enquired in a faltering voice: "Ah, dear boy! Did you enjoy the play?"

All the great actors, Ian included, are chronically insecure.

Also, when Coral Browne, the grand dame of Australian theatre came to do a play at the Vic her dressing room was adjacent to Larry's. One evening as he was applying his make-up, terrified screams emanated from Miss Browne's dressing room. Larry charged in to find out what was the matter.

"RATS! You've got fucking rats in your fucking old theatre!" (They were, in all probability, mice).

"Don't worry, Coral, darling. I'll have traps put down."

"Traps! What fucking use are traps? With what you pay 'em, the actors will eat all the fucking cheese!"

I sense that Lewis is pining for the exciting theatre scene London had in the sixties and seventies. Bill and I assure him it no longer exists – the giants have gone.

Romola announces that tomorrow is her birthday and she will take lunch at the Clay Pot and will be at a certain karaoke bar in the evening. I don't think I will attend either function, although I'm sure Peter, Monica, Philip, John, Ben and nearly all the younger ones will be there. Now the tour is settling into some sort of routine the company seems to be drifting into several groups. Guy, Julian, Adam and Seymour tend to be lone dogs; Russell floats around and goes where any invitation is offered; Naomi seems to be always on her own (I've asked her several times about her boyfriend and she assures me he will be joining her later in the tour – I hope he does – indeed I hope he exists); Gerald is, naturally, preoccupied with his romantic situation. Then there is the older group around Ian – Frances, Bill, Jonathan, Melanie and Sylvester. Klare, the deputy stage manager, has formed another group with Lorna, Claire-Louise and Rachel, the no-nonsense hard-working girls who attend to the make-up, wigs and wardrobe. The four musicians stick together – we rarely see them, playing their relayed music in the depths of the building, although they always turn up for free drinks. I am particularly fond of the cheerful, red-faced percussionist, John Gibson.

Dora returns. She loved Sydney and has had a wonderful time with Tony, who managed to arrange complimentary accommodation for her, in a wonderful hotel on the waterfront with views of the Sydney Opera House. He is her new best friend – they even share the same birthday.

We have dinner at the European restaurant, opposite the floodlit State Parliament.

Monday August 6th

Monday August 6th

Free day. Last day in Melbourne.

Fascinating visit to the Immigration Museum followed by alfresco lunch on the banks of Yarra River.

Early night for a 5.15am start.

Wellington

Tuesday August 7th

Rude and unhelpful staff at Melbourne Airport – the only unpleasantness in our entire time in Australia. One female officiously weighs each bag and makes Monica and others pay excess for theirs being overweight. It seems a bit unfair that the RSC don't pick up the tab because many of the company are not going back to London and have to carry clothes for every season. Gerald's girlfriend has decided not to come. The poor girl has remained in Melbourne and will stay there with friends and try to have a holiday. After an uneventful flight, Seymour and Zoë are fined $200 each for bringing a satsuma and an apple into New Zealand. Ian is at the airport, having flown in from Sydney. He still feels ill and says he has barely slept for five days. He will see a specialist tomorrow. It's only four days till our first performance here; but I know this is the one place where he will definitely not be off. Ian loves this country, having spent all that time here making *Lord of the Rings*, which finally established him as an international star. He sits next to us at the front of the bus, excitedly pointing out the sights as we drive round a huge bay dotted with pretty, white houses. Ian could have taken this tour to practically any country in the world but insisted that it visit New Zealand. He asks Dora and me if we would like to go to dinner at the home of Peter Jackson, the Oscar-winning director of *Lord of the Rings*, on Thursday. We would have loved to but have been invited to stay with the sister of Dora's friend Jocelyn on the South Island. At least we'll get another chance to meet him on a tour of his studio next Monday.

The entire company are booked into the Museum Hotel, an

odd-looking building near the waterfront, which appears to be made of black glass. Dora does her usual when we arrive and we end up with a beautiful apartment. Wellington is a lovely city, with white wooden houses set around a vast, unspoilt bay, reminiscent of Norway. Dora and I find a wonderful fish restaurant called Shed 5. The gay manager takes an instant shine to Dora.

Wednesday August 8th

In the morning we walk around Wellington. The waterfront has been converted into a pedestrianised area with bars and restaurants and the main shopping streets are just a block away. The shops are smarter than in Melbourne and it is generally a more sophisticated city, probably because the seat of government is here. We meet Gerald and Zoë, who seem to have become an item.

In the evening we are invited to a reception with the Prime Minister, Helen Clark, at her official residence, Premier House. A bus takes us to a large, elegant house built on the hill overlooking the city (looking a bit like one of those southern mansions in *Gone with the Wind*) where each of us is personally welcomed by the PM herself. The house is full of interesting people; writers, fashion designers, actors and a few politicians, whilst white-coated waiters glide around with silver trays bearing flutes of champagne. We are given a brief concert from students of a local drama school. After the customary welcoming speeches, Ian comes up and asks if Dora and I would like to attend a private dinner with the Prime Minister and some of her cabinet colleagues. We are delighted to accept and soon join a party walking down a dark street towards the modern parliament building, known as the Beehive. It is amazing how relaxed things are – half the New Zealand government appear to be walking casually with us – with no security in sight. After one of the ministers gives us a short tour of the building, Jonathan and

Isabel, Melanie, Bill, John Heffernan and (to my slight surprise) Peter, are among those who enjoy an excellent meal with superb New Zealand wines. Strangely in this land of macho rugby players, nearly all the cabinet ministers present seem to be gay. They are cultured and charming and, unlike some of the younger members of the company, actually seem to listen to what I say. Dora, who can be a bit of a fag hag, is a big hit.

Thursday August 9th

Dora and I get up early and take the ferry to the South Island. It is a beautiful trip with magnificent scenery. We sail up the Marlborough Sounds with dolphins playing in our wake and disembark at Picton. We could be in the South Seas: it is a pretty little harbour with palm trees. As we walk into the town to meet our hosts, Jenny and Ian Robinson, we pass a war memorial and are shocked to read that, from this little hamlet alone, 31 died in WWI and seven in WWII. Tragically, some family names appear in both wars. We find out later that New Zealand lost more men in proportion to its population than any other nation in WWI.

We meet Jenny and Ian and they drive us to their beautiful house in Blenheim. After a short rest, they take us on a tasting tour of the wineries. They tell us that most of the vines were planted once we, the British, stopped buying their lamb, wool, and dairy products after we had joined the EEC. Ian Robinson used to farm sheep and now he manufactures plastic equipment for mussel farming. They don't say it, but surely Britain showed great ingratitude after the huge sacrifices New Zealand had made in both wars.

Friday August 10th

Jenny takes us to Omaka Aviation Heritage Centre. Extraordinary place. On an old airfield in the middle of nowhere is one of the largest collections of WWI aircraft and memorabilia in the world. It is largely due to Peter Jackson, who has donated his own vast collection and has given his expertise in constructing the huge and lifelike dioramas in which the aircraft are displayed. I have seen nothing like it anywhere in Europe or America. The climax of the museum is the death of the Red Baron. On one wall is a huge cinema screen showing Sopwith Camels closing in on the famous, red, three-winged plane. There is a close-up of one of the pursuing British pilots. Under the helmet and goggles is a familiar face and for a moment or two I think it is me, as years ago I was in the film, *The Red Baron*. I begin to wonder whether I should be getting paid for this but then the camera moves in closer and I realise, it's George bloody Peppard in *The Blue Max*.

The Robinsons then take us to lunch in a winery. It seems like Tuscany – sunshine, vines, fresh wine and delicious food. Is New Zealand the last refuge? The Robinsons then drive us back to the ferry and we arrange to meet up with them next month in New York. We are beginning to feel like jet-setters. As we dock in Wellington, a ferocious southerly wind springs up from the Antarctic and nearly blows Dora off her feet.

Saturday August 11th

The near-hurricane wind rages through the night and continues in the morning. Dora decides she will not go out today.

Go to rehearse in the St James Theatre for tonight's gala performance of *Lear*. Ian, as expected has fully recovered his health. The theatre is in a sleazy quarter of Wellington, next to a girlie bar where naked females swim in huge aquarium. Go to the stage door up an alley between the buildings which reeks of chlorine. I wonder if it's leaking from the aquarium or the waterbeds. The St James was built in 1912 and the vast and gloomy auditorium is clearly in need of a coat of paint. I think of all those young men bound for Gallipoli who must have looked upon this very stage, perhaps watching a final concert before sailing to fight for king and country.

Rachel Seal, our pretty blonde wigs and make-up girl, cuts

my hair. She tells me she is beginning to get fed up with certain people complaining. Like me, she thinks this is a wonderful experience and most of us will probably never be in a success like this again, or have such a fuss made of us.

But I sense something unfriendly about the management here. I suspect it goes back to the letter telling the RSC they did not want that final performance of *Seagull*. No welcome visit to dressing rooms before show, not even the customary, complimentary programme.

At the end of the 'reason not the need' scene – Lear's great scene before Goneril and Regan drive him out into the storm – Ian rages off like Donald Wolfit, crying, "Where was my light?" At the interval he calls me into his dressing room and asks me if I will walk through Lear tomorrow afternoon, so that he can see from the front where it needs to be relit. I say I will do it willingly but don't know why he is so upset, it was one of the best performances he has ever done. He shakes his head, like an upset little boy: "Peter Jackson is out front. It's the most important night of my life, and they cannot see my eyes. Normally you go on stage and are dazzled by the light. In this production you can see the audience watching you. In a theatre this size you need footlights. Olivier could say so much with a little glance of his eye." He demonstrates, doing a very good imitation of the great man. "How can I achieve anything like that with the lighting they have given me?"

At the curtain we receive the most tumultuous ovation we have yet had. Ian bows humbly with his hand on his breast and then gestures as if he were giving Wellington his heart. He loves New Zealand; we are only here because of him.

The reception afterwards in the dress circle bar is the most ill-managed we have had. Ian and most of the men are ready but we are told we must wait until everybody is there because they want us to enter together. Ian says it will take the women another 15 minutes at least to get ready and he has friends at the reception who will not wait. We hang on for another five minutes watching a waiter with a tray of champagne – so near and yet so far. At length, we are reluctantly admitted into a large dark room. Ian rushes over to join Peter Jackson's party. A fat lady from the theatre, who hasn't even bothered to get my name right (I've told her twice it's 'Weston', not 'Western') comes over thinking I'm Bill Gaunt in the gloom. When she realises it's only me she turns and makes off in a different direction. I drink one glass and struggle back through the wind to Dora. Unexpected bonus: Sunderland v Tottenham is live on Sky.

Sunday August 12ᵗʰ

Dora and I meet Ian for lunch at Shed 5. As Ian and I walk to the theatre for the lighting rehearsal I ask:

"Did Peter Jackson enjoy last night?"

"He was knocked out. He'd never seen Shakespeare on stage before."

"What did he think of the lighting?"

"He loved it."

I begin to wonder what we are doing but Ian, like Trevor, is a perfectionist and so I walk through the scenes he is worried about and slight adjustments are made. Ian says he is beginning to have reservations about certain performances. He doesn't mention names.

Later he gives another mint-fresh performance and we receive another great ovation. Afterwards I meet up with Ian Mullins, whom I worked for in the early sixties when he ran Cheltenham and other Reps so ably. He has retired to Christchurch on the South Island but has come to see us as he is a great friend of Bill Gaunt. I am shocked to see how ancient and fragile he looks but realise he must be over 80. Just ten years ahead of me. I hug him as I say goodbye and think this is another acquaintance I will never see again.

Sit up through the night and watch Chelsea beat Birmingham

3-2.

Monday August 13th

Laurie Atkinson's review in the *Dominion Post* is headed:
'A star performance that should have shone brighter.'

He writes that there has never been so much anticipated excitement for a classical theatre company since Laurence Olivier played Richard III in 1948 (I wonder how many Wellingtonians can remember that). He goes on to say that though Ian gives a towering performance he was prevented from shining brighter by the production and a supporting cast that only 'intermittently blazed as brightly.'

Well, Mr Atkinson, unfortunately we are not all Ian McKellens. But at least he says we speak with great clarity, unlike the National's production of *History Boys* last year.

But the article reflects what I am beginning, albeit reluctantly, to feel myself. In my opinion, some of the performances have not developed as they should. Much as I like Sylvester, his Fool still needs more pathos and sense. Philip is a lovely lad, who swordfights like Fairbanks and already has a career in film, but his speaking still needs to be improved. Romola has great confidence but her voice occasionally irritates and she continually bends forward as she speaks. Ben Meyjes is a good young actor but shouts too much, and even Jonathan, accomplished as he is, is beginning to sing some of his speeches. New York will decide how good we really are.

Fascinating morning, we are invited to visit to Peter Jackson's WETA Studios, which are so named after a ferocious New Zealand insect. In what looks like a small and insignificant industrial estate in a quiet suburb of Wellington, some of the biggest movies of the past decade have been created. We are shown round by Peter Jackson's partner, an ex-farmer who was digging ditches less than ten years ago. In every department, skilled artists are working on inspired works of imagination that by the magic of digital filming, beyond my comprehension, will thrill and excite the world. We learn that until Peter Jackson inspired this explosion of filmmaking here, these people had worked as blacksmiths, bricklayers and even operated Ferris wheels – they are all untrained. Painting and model-making were their hobbies, now they are creating a new style of cinematic art, somewhat like the artisans who founded the Elizabethan Theatre: Ben Jonson was a bricklayer, Burbage a carpenter and Shakespeare the son of a butcher.

Towards the end of the tour we find ourselves in a large warehouse containing the models of the sets of *Lord of the Rings*. A small, shy, bearded man watches with a friendly smile. He could be the caretaker but is in fact the great PJ himself. He humbly shakes our hands and thanks us for coming. He then invites us into a beautiful, small replica of a 1930s-style cinema where we watch his latest tests on a new form of 3D. Amazingly realistic – I grab Dora's hand and scream as King Kong bounds towards me.

Tuesday August 14th

Lloyd Dorfman is in town for a few hours, inspecting his Travelex empire. Dora takes him to dinner in Shed 5 before he sees *Seagull*.

Go over the Lear/Fool scenes with Russell. He is in love with Lisa Minnelli and is taking his husband to a concert that Minnelli is giving in New Jersey whilst we are in New York. He tells me that when she did her last concert in London, Ian went round to congratulate her afterwards. She begged Ian to come to her suite at the Savoy the following afternoon and give her some notes. Ian reluctantly agreed but when he arrived at the Savoy he was told by reception that Miss Minnelli was not taking visitors that day. I say it is appalling behaviour. Russell, forgiving soul that he is, replies: "She is always so high after a performance; she doesn't know what she is saying."

Seymour's wife has forwarded him the notice of his fine for illegally importing fruit, which has been sent to his home address in Colchester. Seymour is usually a very sensible chap, but he thinks the RSC should pay his fine. The maximum penalty is $100,000 or five years in jail. Can you imagine being asked,

"What are you in for?"

"A satsuma."

Meet Lloyd after the show. He has not been overly impressed by *Seagull*, but I do not see how the poor chap can judge anything, suffering from acute jet lag. I wouldn't fancy sitting through Chekov after a 24 hour flight. Lloyd is now on the board of the National Theatre as well as being chairman of the new set-up at the Roundhouse. I would think a title cannot be too far away.

Auckland

Wednesday August 15th

Dora and I have decided to forsake the flight to Auckland and drive ourselves up by car. Philip and Jonathan are doing the same and others are intending to hire cars and make excursions from Auckland. We drive north through the mountains, past little wooden farming towns, like something out of the Wild West. We have lunch in Napier, a beautiful art deco town by the sea, built after the devastating earthquake in 1931. From there we drive through extraordinary country to Lake Taupo. Green mountains and hills are dotted with great, ancient, native New Zealand trees, which look as if they have been left over from *Lord of the Rings* and are about to drag their roots from the earth and stagger down towards us, waving their bare, arm-like branches. We arrive at Lake Taupo as dusk falls and book into the Millennium Hotel, situated on the lake itself. Hot, thermal waters pour into the lake beneath our balcony. We swim in the thermal waters of the hotel pool and later head to the bar, as Philip arrives. He informs us that he and Jonathan Hyde have both been fined for speeding by the same traffic cop. I jokingly ask him if he expects the RSC to pay their fines.

Dora and I have a romantic dinner in the hotel restaurant, overlooking the moonlit lake. A CD is playing the great American standards that we love, but we cannot recognise the voice. The phrasing is so clear and the sound so fresh. I think it must be a new, black American female singer. We decide we must buy a copy and ask the waitress who it is. She returns and rather shamefacedly tells us it is Rod Stewart! We will buy it nevertheless. A familiar, bushy moustache comes into the restaurant and sits at the next table. It is Lord Winston and his wife. We exchange pleasantries – he is here to give lectures. He tells us he is looking forward to seeing *Lear* in London.

Thursday August 16th

Drive through fields steaming with thermal springs to Rotarua. Sit in the rain in thermal pools of 42 degrees at the Polynesian Spa. The muscle sprain in my leg, which has caused me pain for the past month, disappears. As we leave we meet Gerald, Zoë, John Heffernan and Ben Addis outside. Romola has arranged an excursion for her gang and they have all driven down from Auckland this morning. Past Hamilton, the drive to Auckland is very dreary. Enter Auckland in traffic jam in the rain.

I suppose we can't be lucky every time. We are all lodged in Oaks Apartments on Hobson Street, next to a Mission for the homeless. The view from the window is of blocks of grey soulless flats – a bit like Eastern Europe. Great steak dinner at Tony's on Wellesley Street. Don't know how Chelsea did yesterday – it's always bloody rugby on New Zealand TV.

Friday August 17th

Sneak out before breakfast to an Internet café. Very relieved: Chelsea has beaten Reading 2-1.

Much has been made of today's visit to Orakei Marae for a Maori welcome. We have been told they will sing to us and will expect us to reply. Our response has been debated again and again over the past weeks. It seems we mustn't sing anything vaguely British which might cause offence. Gemma suggested that we sing a Beatles song: 'All You Need is Love'. I proposed that we let Jonathan's wife, Isabel, a professional opera singer, sing a Scottish ballad. It was shot down by Monica, who said, rather sharply, that Isabel was not a member of the company. Eventually it was agreed we should reply with a Shakespearean sonnet, each line spoken by a different actor. Needless to say, the sonnet chosen was one of the most impenetrable.

Everyone makes a great effort to attend. Gerald and his party leave their beautiful hotel on Lake Taupo at 6am to get there; Frances and Ian fly from Wellington even earlier. Because of the promised press and TV coverage, Frances has paid great attention to her dress and make-up. I'd expected a real native village with the inhabitants in traditional costume, presided over by a venerable elder and, after a moving and lively ceremony, an ethnic feast. A bus drops us in a field by something which resembles a cricket pavilion. About a hundred yards away is a large, wooden building with some totem poles in front, and behind that a brick building, a bit like a church hall. There are some white New Zealanders waiting but nobody bothers to introduce us. There is not a reporter or television camera in sight.

Then a Maori lady comes over and tells us we must wait as the pupils haven't finished their classes. She then attempts to explain some of the Maori culture to us, especially why they rub noses. A tall, thin man wearing a trilby hat, whom I have never seen before but who I am told is the chairman of the Aotea Centre where we are playing, tells us he will speak for us first when the ceremony begins. I begin to have misgivings as he clearly has no idea of voice production – I can barely hear a word he says.

Eventually a young girl comes over and tells us all is ready. We trudge across a muddy field with Ian at our head to a large gate that leads to the wooden building. Outside the wooden building are assembled about a dozen young people of various shapes and sizes, dressed in school uniforms, plus half a dozen middle-aged women and two Maori men. One young man, dressed in traditional attire and holding a stick, comes out of the building. He advances towards us whirling his stick and looking as though he has acute indigestion. He stands in front of Ian, yelling defiance before turning and waggling his grass-skirted bottom. He then makes off towards the building. Ian follows dutifully, with us all behind.

After we have taken off our shoes, we go inside. The traditional-looking painted beams are in fact plastic. We sit facing our hosts. I can see that half of the young people appear not to be Maori. One of the men then proceeds to address us in the Maori tongue. He goes on for about ten minutes in a monotonous voice – nobody attempts to translate for us. It is obvious that he does not know who we are. Eventually our man in the trilby hat gets up and mumbles just as unintelligibly. Then the Maori rumbles on again. Finally Ian gets up and delivers a brief but heartfelt speech about how honoured he is to be here, then the Maoris sing a short chorus. We follow it with our sonnet, which makes no sense at all and must have left them completely mystified.

We are then led to the church hall where we are served tea and ham and tomato sandwiches – not a roasted pig in sight. It is a complete waste of time; nobody really knows who we are or why we are there. We finish our tea and sandwiches and somebody says the bus is not due back for another 40 minutes, so the second Maori man says he will take us on a tour. We go back to the big wooden/plastic building where we hear the nose-rubbing story again. He also tells us his ancestors were cannibals who ate and excreted their enemies, then sent the shit back to their families as a final act of humiliation. Melanie murmurs that her ancestors listened to Bach. The bus eventually arrives and later Dora and I explore Auckland's shops – she is not impressed. Frances Barber is right: it is like Birmingham on a wet Sunday, although Frances is perhaps being unkind to Birmingham. We decide it's better if Dora goes back to London tomorrow; I will not have much spare time here as we have eight performances this week. Moreover, she will be able to see Emil's family before they go to Spain. She phones her new bosom friend Tony, the Sydney travel agent, who manages to get her on a BA flight at no extra cost.

We have a final New Zealand dinner together at Kermadec,

an excellent fish restaurant on the harbour, whilst Ian, Russell, Richard Clayton and Craig Almond, our props man, attend a dinner given in their honour by the Gay Auckland Business Association. I gather it is a sedate affair and no tables are danced upon.

Saturday August 18th

Dora leaves. Sylvester has another *Dr Who* conference tomorrow. The organiser rings me and says he would love me and Bill (who also appeared in the series in the distant past) to attend as well. There will be no fee but the punters will be charged $25 for every photo we sign, of which we will keep $20. "You should come away with at least $1000 each," he assures me. I am highly dubious but accept nonetheless.

We re-rehearse *Lear* all day with Gemma in another gigantic modern arts complex, the Aotea Centre. Great performance by Ian in the huge 2256-seat theatre – a wonderful ovation.

Sunday August 19th

In the morning the organiser, whose name I never caught, takes Bill and me to the *Dr Who* conference which is taking place in another part of the vast Aotea Centre. (Sylvester, the star turn, will be making his entrance later). When we arrive we pass a table stacked with grainy, colour photos of the two of us, which have been taken from the TV screen. It was the series in which I appeared as Biroc – a sort of lion-man – and I am utterly unrecognisable under the make-up. I remember I spent so much time having it put on that I missed all my meal-breaks and ended up with massive overtime, which was more than my original fee. We then go into a large, darkened room where about 80 people of all ages are watching an episode that I was in. We made it in the seventies and I have never seen it. I didn't realise how bad it was, but the aficionados sit watching, rapt.

Afterwards Bill and I do a question and answer session,

which I enjoy. Then the organiser announces that, for an extra fee, the fans can have their photo taken with me and Bill. We go outside to where a big, sweaty New Zealander is waiting with his camera. Two men and a boy take up the option. We then sit and wait by the piles of photos – it is humiliating. I sign three and Bill signs four. We are put out of our misery by the arrival of Sylvester. The organiser slips $150 into each of our hands and thanks us for our time. As an afterthought, he gives us each a pile of the grainy, unsold photos.

The Prime Minister, Helen Clark, enjoyed *Lear* so much last week that she decides to come to *Seagull* as well. At the reception afterwards, I meet the Arts Minister, Alastair Carruthers again. He is full of enthusiasm and tells me how much he enjoyed my performance as Lear's Gentleman, which does wonders for my ego following this morning's humiliation. I also meet Ben Hawthorne, a New Zealand actor who was in my class at RADA 50 years ago. We arrange to have lunch later in the week.

Monday August 20th

Now have Internet in my room. Wake up, am very relieved by Chelsea's draw at Liverpool and chuffed by Manchester United's defeat by City. Were we wrong about Sven? Receive email from Emil telling me Dora has arrived safely.

In contrast to Wellington, Paul Simei-Barton gives us a rave review in *The New Zealand Herald*: declaring Ian's Lear an absolute triumph and praising Trevor's loving attention to detail and brilliant inventive stage-craft:

'Ian McKellen's Lear is an absolute triumph – an enthralling, deeply moving portrayal…. The intense physicality of the performance is astounding, with the 68-year-old McKellen drenched with rain and staggering beneath the weight of Cordelia's body. Even more impressive is the voice that finds rhythm in the most complex speeches and uses rhythm to transmit emotions ranging from comical bemusement to the

animalistic howl of a grief that is utterly beyond words.

Trevor Nunn's direction is not constrained by the need to make grand interpretive statements. Instead there is a loving attention to detail, brilliantly inventive stage-craft and a willingness to embrace the play's many contradictions and enigmas'. Then comes recognition at last: *'One of the great pleasures of a RSC production is the attention that is lavished on the minor parts.'*

Mr Simei-Barton should take over from Nicholas de Jongh immediately. It never fails to astonish me how much critics can differ.

Day off. I miss Dora and realise how much more fun the trip is when she is here. Try to explore Auckland. I have read somewhere it is considered: *'One of the top five cities in the world for quality of life'* – they must be joking. What about the suicide rate? There is no sense of being in a city at all and it is impossible to walk around, because of steep hills and busy multi-lane highways of speeding cars. When you try to cross a road you have to wait several minutes each time for the pedestrian light to go green. Moreover, apart from Queen Street, there is hardly anyone on the streets to ask for directions and unlike Singapore and Melbourne there is not a taxi in sight. I eventually find the Art Gallery and quite enjoy the collection of Victorian paintings. I find a taxi at last and go to Parnell, which is an attractive area of cafes and art galleries. It's a bit like Hampstead, but with white wooden buildings.

Tuesday August 21st

Walk along the waterfront. Stop at a bar for glass of wine and start up conversation with an Irish surgeon who has just come off a flight from London. He is an expert on dental reconstruction and is here to give some lectures. It is a relief to talk to someone new. We get on very well and he insists on buying me lunch. I, in turn, say I will get him a ticket for *Lear* tonight.

The publicity girl had arranged for Romola to do a radio interview at 9am. When Romola asked why she had to do it at such an early hour, she was told that, as her reviews are so mixed, it would be a good opportunity for her to answer some of them – Shannon Huse in today's *New Zealand Herald,* describes Romola's Nina as *'at times annoyingly gauche'*. Romola was not best pleased – I don't blame her.

My surgeon stands me up: he doesn't come for the ticket I leave for him at the box office. I expect jet-lag has caught up with him. A pity – I liked him and I don't even know his name.

Wednesday August 22nd

The latest craze among certain members of the company is bungee jumping off Auckland's Sky Tower, the world's 14th tallest tower. Not only the people you would expect – like Peter, Philip and Gerald – but more senior and responsible ones, such as Melanie and Gemma. Today the madness has increased; Philip and his understudy, Peter, both go skydiving.

In the old days, principal and understudy were not even allowed to travel in the same car in case of an accident. Nobody seems to care these days – am I really such a boring old reactionary? I suppose they did not skydive at exactly the same time.

Both shows continue to be enthusiastically received.

Thursday August 23rd

Had lunch with my old RADA classmate Ben Hawthorne, or Raymond as he is now known out here. He is a big fish in the small New Zealand theatrical pond; he acts, directs and teaches. A sobering thought that we studied *Seagull* together 50 years ago – it seemed such an old play then, but it had been written little more than 50 years before. We talk about long-forgotten fellow students and the few of us that have survived in this merciless profession. One is Sloane Shelton, an American girl I lusted over in my youth who, Ben tells me, is still a working actress in New York and living with a rich lesbian on Long Island. A lesbian? I never even knew about lesbians in 1957. Could be why my gauche advances never got me very far with her. Ben says he is in touch with her and will tell her I am coming. Sloane was called Mimi when I knew her. I'm sure she will get on with Dora; it will be an interesting meeting at least.

Peter is going back to Singapore in the break: his Malaysian girlfriend has booked him into a five star hotel. How is he going to pay for it? Does she think he is already a star? But being an air hostess she's probably got him a special deal.

Friday August 24th

Almost the entire company seems fed-up and bored in this grey city – perhaps this is why they have taken to jumping off buildings. Everything closes at ten: there are no restaurants, not even an Indian, to go to after the show. The exception is Naomi. For some inexplicable reason, she has decided to stay on here during the spare week before we are due in New York. I like her very much but sometimes I think she's as nutty as a fruitcake; still no sign of her boyfriend. There are a lot of hard-up looking Maoris in the streets. New Zealand is not the paradise it first seemed.

Take ferry across the bay to Devonport: a bit sad, like most seaside resorts out of season. Climb Mount Victoria, an extinct volcano, and buy a second-hand book of reminiscences by JB Priestley. Take ferry back and buy myself an expensive lunch on the quay. Superb oysters but very average fish.

Pass Adam in the corridor looking very glum. I'm not exactly sure why. No actor in work has the right to be down in the dumps – unless his football team has lost 0-3. You can be despondent after nine months out of work and umpteen rejections for parts you would have loved to have played, but not on a world tour with the RSC. We are constantly rejected and then when we finally get a part it's odds on, if you're even noticed, the critic will say you weren't any good. Peter Hall once said there were only ninety actors in England that were constantly in work: I suspect that the number is slightly higher than that – but it is still a ridiculous profession.

Nevertheless poor Adam, I expect he misses his girlfriend. I look around my functional hotel room and miss Dora very much. I wonder what we are doing apart when we have so few years left. Old age will get us, as it does everyone.

Saturday August 25th

Enjoying Priestley's reminiscences; they deal mostly with his experiences in WWI and I think could be adapted into an excellent one-man show, with a few speeches added from his plays. Mention it to Ian as it would be ideal for him. He's a northern socialist, albeit from Lancashire not Yorkshire, and is 68 – the same age Priestley was when he wrote it. Am glad to do two shows: matinee of *Seagull* and *Lear* in the evening. At least it's something to do.

As reported, Gerald's girlfriend stayed on in Melbourne with friends. He tells me today that as the seats were already booked, she will be sitting next to him on the flight back to London – he's not looking forward to it. I try to cheer him up. Later, after the show, Julian Harris and Russell have a drink in my room. Julian has been very morose, missing his wife and children. I am surprised to learn that most of the cast strongly disapprove of Gerald's conduct. But what can Gerald do if he doesn't love the girl any more? Things have changed. In 1966, at the Cambridge Theatre, Laurence Harvey would turn the attractive young model he was involved with out of his dressing room as his other lady, the super-rich widow of a Hollywood mogul, arrived at the stage door. It didn't seem to worry the rest of us.

Get up at 3am and check the Internet: Chelsea beat Portsmouth 1-0 and to my pleasant surprise are top of the league.

Sunday August 26th

Last day in Auckland. We do our final performance – a matinee of *Seagull* – and then are given a farewell barbeque party by the Aotea Centre, beside their car park. Concrete walls and supermarket hamburgers and sausages – not the most romantic setting, but they mean well. One leading member of the company announces very loudly, to all and sundry, that he feels very relaxed as he's just finished a large joint. I hope none of the press are present – this is a country that forbids even the representation of smoking tobacco on stage. I've never done drugs, not even cigarettes in the days when every rehearsal room was thick with smoke – Peter Barkworth even used to give us smoking technique lessons at RADA. Wine and women were more my scene. Ian tells me he does not fancy doing a one-man show on Priestley, so I then suggest it to Bill. He is a genuine Yorkshireman, is also the right age and appeared recently in *An Inspector Calls*. He seems quite keen, saying he's thought about it before: Bill never likes to be caught napping. I lend him the book to read whilst he is in America.

Tomorrow the company splits up for a week. Ian has hired a bus and will travel across some of the western states of America. His American friend the photographer, who does his Internet site has arranged everything. This bus is apparently fitted with every modern convenience plus sleeping accommodation. Frances, Jonathan Hyde and his wife Isabel, Melanie, John Heffernan and Bill Gaunt will be going with him. Ian asked me several weeks ago if Dora and I fancied joining them. I declined – we did that part of America a couple of years ago, besides we want to get back to London to see the family before the second half of the tour. Philip and Monica, plus our two delightful hairdressers, Rachel and Lorna, are going to Fiji, although Philip tells me he is planning to go off on his own to a small island where his grandfather was stationed during WWII. Ben Meyjes and his girlfriend, who arrived a few days ago, are touring the South

Island in a camper van, as are Ben Delfont and his stage management team (including, of course, the lovely Rhiannon). Sylvester is going across the USA by train, stopping off in New Orleans on the way. Doubtless he will find some sort of *Doctor Who* convention to attend whilst he is there. Russell is going to New York early, to spend his honeymoon there with his Italian husband; Seymour is going to the Rocky Mountains to spend a second honeymoon with his wife in a log cabin; Gemma is going to Hawaii and Naomi, as reported, cannot for some inexplicable reason tear herself away from the delights of Auckland. Peter is flying back to his Singapore sweetheart. The rest of us are going to spend the week back home in the UK.

There are fond farewells. We have completed half the overseas tour. Singapore, Melbourne and New Zealand (apart from the unfriendly woman in Wellington) have been extremely welcoming and grateful. America, and especially New York, awaits. Will audiences there be harder to please?

Monday August 27th

Get up early – frightened of being left behind. John Gibson, our jovial percussionist, had bought his son a boomerang. It is taken off him at the security check as it is considered a dangerous weapon. John, who has a great sense of humour, wonders if he will get his boomerang back.

Now we regain the hours we lost on our flight out – all 13 of them. Two stops: Sydney and Singapore – three security checks. Gerald watches films non-stop, as his ex-girlfriend sits wanly by his side. Zoë waits a few seats back.

Finish reading *Secret River*, an excellent novel about early Australia that would make a good film.

London

Tuesday August 28ᵗʰ

Arrive at Heathrow's shabby Terminal 4 – Third World
compared to the airport in Singapore. No organisation
whatsoever and for some reason hundreds of British passport
holders are crammed into a corridor, with nobody telling us what
to do. It takes nearly an hour to get through. Wait for luggage
with John Gibson: his boomerang does not come back. Can't
believe BAA is thinking of axing 2000 jobs when they can't even
run the place properly as it is. Dora is waiting and drives me
home.

Wednesday August 29ᵗʰ

David Warner rings and tells me he missed a preview of *Henry
IV*, believing his stage fright had come back. Nevertheless, most
of his notices were favourable – especially from Nicholas de
Jongh. Stage fright is something that can creep up on an actor at
any time: there are stories of the great Olivier himself cowering in
the wings. Ian Holm was hit by it during a performance of *The Ice
Man Cometh* and refused to act on stage for nearly twenty years
before he came back to triumph as Lear. Others have kept it at
bay with the bottle. I must admit that it has never bothered me – I
couldn't understudy Lear if it did.

Watching *Jack and Sarah* on Sky when a familiar voice rasps
out from beneath a woolly hat – it takes me several shots to
realise that the decrepit vagrant is Ian. The film was made in
1995, before he made it big in films, and it shows. There is an
authority which hedges a king and there is also an aura of
confidence that radiates from a star. Excellent though he is, Ian is

given hardly any close-ups. It is a good part, but if he played it now he would steal the film. Richard E. Grant is very good though: he acts with great feeling. I enjoyed the film he wrote and directed last year: *Wah-Wah*. He belies Dame Maggie Smith, who is reputed to have dubbed him 'Richard 'E Can't'. Vaguely remember him playing the insipid juvenile part of Fenton when I took over Falstaff in *The Merry Wives of Windsor* in Regent's Park about 20 years ago. Reflect that he has certainly come on a bit further than me.

Thursday August 30th

Dora and I go to the launch party for Roland Curram's new novel: *The Rose Secateurs*. We have both loved Roly for more than 40 years and admire the way he has coped with the tragedies in his life. Now in his mid-seventies, he has decided he cannot wait for publishers and agents to ponder over his books and has published two by himself. He has arranged for the party to be held on the 10th floor of what used to be the Shell building in the Strand. It has been lavishly refurbished into apartments and suites in the art deco style. The suite where the party is held opens out onto a large balcony directly beneath the great clock, which, someone tells me, is the largest in London – one inch bigger than Big Ben. The view is absolutely superb. Below is the green, tree-lined Embankment, with Cleopatra's Needle thrusting through. The Thames glints in the evening sun and on the opposite bank, the National and the Festival Hall throng with people. Parliament and the Abbey are to the right and St Paul's and the City with Canary Wharf in the distance to the left. London looks beautiful – the old girl can still hold her own with any city in the world and I love her as much as ever.

Great party: champagne and beautiful food and lots of old friends and acquaintances. Buy a signed copy of Roly's book and will read it in America. Also buy a copy of Roly's first novel, *Man on a Beach* for Ian, as it sells very well in Waterstone's homosexual section.

Friday August 31*st*

We feel duty-bound to watch the first part of *The Lord of the Rings* on Sky. Still can't understand how those little models we saw in Wellington look so awe-inspiring on the screen.

Saturday September 1*st*

Ring Gary Taylor, who supplements his actor's wages by running a B&B in Stratford. He tells me the tourists have disappeared and he is empty during what should be the busiest period of the year. The old RST is surrounded by hoardings and is a muddy building site – only the Courtyard is open. I dread to think what the huge viewing-tower, which, Gary tells me, some locals are already calling the Incinerator Chimney, will do to what remains of the charm of the town. I sincerely hope I am proved wrong.

Dora and I go to BAFTA, which has been redecorated and refurbished in our absence. As I drink at the bar I am aware of a familiar beady eye looking down on me: McKellen's photo has been added to the greats. Can't get away from the bugger! See *3.10 to Yuma* – a good, old-fashioned Western with Russell Crowe and the always-watchable Christian Bale.

Sunday September 2*nd*

Go to Dulwich to see the family. Dora and Georgie take the children for a walk whilst Rubin and I watch Chelsea play Aston Villa. Absolute disaster: they lose 2-0. Lampard is injured and the new players, Pizarro (whom we instantly nickname 'Piss-awful' as he's overweight and can't run) and Malouda seem no better than the run-of-the-mill players Liverpool have been buying so profusely in recent seasons. Both Rubin and I are very depressed.

New York

Monday September 3rd

Emil and Lindsay came back from their holiday in Spain late last night. Dora and I decide to drive to their new home in Bracknell, leave the car in their garden and go to Heathrow from there. Emil looks as handsome as ever – I really don't know how I created him. He drives us to the airport with Mia and Fabian. I sit in the back and Mia tightly holds my hand; we have managed to see all the grandchildren.

As we check in, we see Gerald waiting for Zoë: from now on they will be able to sit next to each other. Meet Richard Goulding, whom I am becoming increasingly fond of and his girlfriend Sarah, an aspiring actress. Her mother is a distant cousin of Emma Kitchener-Fellowes and her father is Keeper of the Queen's Pictures. Surprise, surprise, Julian has found her a small part in his new film on Queen Victoria. We have plenty of time so we have a delicious seafood lunch with excellent Chilean Chardonnay at Prunier's – it's the only decent food in the entire airport.

After New Zealand, the seven-hour flight across the Atlantic seems a doddle. How wrong can you be? The plane is hot and seems to have no air. My seat is uncomfortable and the seat in front of me leans much further back than the ones on either side – I feel as if I am in a coffin. Try to watch a Woody Allen film to get in 'a New York state of mind', but cannot concentrate on the tiny screen. Try to sleep but it's impossible: my nose feels as dry as dust. Dora meanwhile is happily watching a film about Mandela and seems to have no sympathy for my suffering. I twice complain to the stewards but each time they assure me there is nothing wrong with the air conditioning. I eventually spend most of the flight hunched up near a cool air vent in the galley.

When we arrive at JFK, it is a repeat performance of our arrival at Heathrow last week. Hundreds of us wait in lines for well over an hour. At least the Chinese immigration officer is pleasant and seems to have heard of the RSC and our performances to come at the Brooklyn Academy of Music (BAM). Take taxi to the hotel which is not, as we thought, by the famous bridge, but situated in downtown Brooklyn. Everyone – apart from Ian, who has rented an apartment in Manhattan – is staying here. Usual hassle over our room; they want to put us in a double-bedded room on the 4th Floor, with no view. Dora does her stuff and we eventually get a better room on the 18th. Fall into bed, exhausted.

Tuesday September 4th

Wake up to a magnificent view over the East River and a warm, sunny day. Summer at last! We have never been to Brooklyn before; it seems to have more space and trees than Manhattan and everything is at half-speed. Walk under the famous bridge. There are new developments on the waterfront; much like London's Docklands, only on a far larger scale. Walk through a beautiful garden of white flowers and find a large barge moored on the river, with the most stunning view of Manhattan. We have stumbled upon the famous River Café and decide to have an early lunch there. Only three tables are occupied and we are given a table right by the water. As we sit down Dora shivers – it is like being in a fridge; the air conditioning is at full blast. She asks the elegant, French Maître d' if it can be turned down. He replies that it cannot be turned down as it is very difficult to control, but offers Dora the loan of a jacket. Dora does not fancy putting a jacket over her very chic dress, so she turns and asks the other diners if they are cold. Americans are usually very polite and are not used to complaining, but they all nod in agreement.

One poor woman, who looks quite blue and is clutching a cup in her hands, says, "All the restaurants are like this. I'm drinking hot water to keep myself warm."

Dora turns to the Maître d': "You see. Nobody wants it. Why is it on? You are only adding to global warming." The Maître d' senses a revolution and retreats. Within minutes the cold air is turned off. We have a wonderful lunch with half a bottle of excellent Côtes du Rhône.

After lunch and an enormous ice cream we climb up to the promenade on Brooklyn Heights. Through the throng of people a familiar, white-bearded figure comes towards us. For a moment I think I am seeing myself reflected in a mirror, but it is Bill with his wife Carolyn who has only just flown in. We greet each other like long-lost friends, even though we have only been apart for a week. Bill has been through great dramas on his bus trip with Ian. On the flight to LA he suddenly had trouble breathing and felt giddy (for a moment my hypochondriac tendency makes me wonder if that was what I had on the plane to New York). He recovered but was then taken ill again more or less as soon as he got onto Ian's famous bus. He was taken to hospital and Melanie, very nobly, stayed with him for a few days in a terrible motel with plastic cups. He is better now but has a suspected urinary infection. I must say that Bill seems to have aged in the past year. He says he has enjoyed reading the Priestley book, but I can't really see him doing it: another of my bright ideas that will never get off the ground. We leave Bill and Carolyn and walk through beautiful brownstone, tree-lined streets – it's so unlike Manhattan. Get back to the hotel determined to keep young for as long as possible – swim 12 lengths of the 40-metre hotel pool.

Email from the RSC, trying to stir up custom for its new production of *Twelfth Night*:

'Oscar-nominated American actor John Lithgow makes his RSC

debut as Malvolio. He is known to UK audiences for his role in 3rd Rock
from the Sun *and is also the voice of the villainous Lord Farquaad in*
Shrek. *The company also includes Jason Merrells* (Waterloo Road,
Cutting it)....*Siobhan Redmond* (Smoking Room, Holby City) *as
Maria and Marjorie Yates* (Screaming) *as Sir Toby Belch.'*

What have things come to when the once-greatest theatrical
company in the world resorts to tempting its patrons with an
American actor who plays the 'voice' in a cartoon and seems to
relish the appearance of soap actors in its ranks. It makes it sound
like a second rate provincial tour. In fact, John Lithgow is a very
distinguished stage actor in the States, but the RSC chooses to
ignore this. There was a time when the mere fact that the RSC
was performing Shakespeare's greatest comedy would be enough;
everyone knew what standard of performance they could expect.
They would not have even considered the prospect of a female
Toby Belch! But today the RSC seems to be appealing to the
lowest common denominator. They will be finding their new
Hamlet on a television talent show next.

Dinner in the open air on Montague Street. Meet Russell,
who always seems to know what's going on and he tells us
Melanie and Frances have fallen out and are not speaking. He
says he doesn't know why.

Wednesday September 5th

Practically the entire, reunited company assembles in the hotel
lobby. Great excitement as people exchange stories of their
various adventures. Noticing Naomi standing alone, I ask if she
had a good time in Auckland. She says she did, having made
friends with one of the dressers at the Aotea Centre. I ask how
her boyfriend is. She says he is coming to New York soon – I
really hope he does.

We all walk to the Harvey Theatre for our first technical
rehearsal, along the Fulton Mall, which apart from a branch of

Macy's is nothing but cheap, cut price shops. I have always dreamed of acting on Broadway sometime in my career – not this time, baby. This is not Broadway but Brixton High Road. At first we cannot find the theatre: there is not a poster or sign in sight. The building is surrounded by scaffolding – is this the new RSC trend? We follow a tunnel under the scaffolding, above which a block of condominiums is being built, and then walk down a side street to find the stage door hidden behind a police barrier. Inside, everything is packed and crowded. We walk up a ramp onto the stage and there before us is an extraordinary sight. It is as if our decaying set blends into the entire auditorium. The whole place looks gutted, devastated. 'Distressed' is apparently the correct term. The upper levels look positively dangerous as the supporting pillars are so 'distressed' that they seem to have no strength. We later learn from Trevor that it was built in 1904, one many theatres situated in Brooklyn at that time; Noel Coward himself acted here. In the thirties it became a cinema but fell into disuse in the sixties. In 1989, the BAM invited Peter Brook to bring over his famous production of *The Mahabharata* from the Théâtre des Bouffes du Nord in Paris. Brook considered that BAM's Opera House was completely unsuitable for his production and only then was this old, empty cinema remembered. Brook took one look at it and declared it was perfect.

The auditorium is banked around the stage and the seats are unpadded benches – at least the discomfort will keep the burghers of Brooklyn awake. Moreover, the auditorium is quite small after the huge modern opera houses we have been playing in: it will be good to play in a more intimate space. Melanie and Frances arrive and fall into each others' arms. I catch Russell's eye – did he over-egg his tattle? But I can never understand actresses most of the time, maybe that's why I married one. There is no sign of Trevor: he will arrive tomorrow. The lighting has been held up and everything is way behind schedule. We cannot rehearse on stage so, as we haven't performed *Lear* for almost two weeks, Gemma says she will take us on a word run of the first half.

Before we begin, Ian calls us together and tells us he has checked reviews of the most recent New York Lears: Kevin Klein and Christopher Plummer – they were both rapturously received. This is a city that knows theatre despite the present state of Broadway, which does not boast a single straight play. The *New York Times* critic can make or break one's career; even though our official press night is not until Tuesday, one never knows when he will drop in and he may well be in tomorrow night. Ian says we must get back to the truth and intimacy we had in the Courtyard before we went into the vast theatres and asks us all to stay on, once we have finished our spoken lines, to support the others. Romola who is only in the opening scene in the first half, leaves as soon as it has finished.

Bus brings us back to the hotel as it will every night.

Thursday September 6th

Trevor arrives and we start the technical. He goes to reposition a chair in the first scene and then stops short. In this capital of capitalism, according to the stage technicians' union rules, nobody can move a chair onstage but them. Our own technical team are not allowed to work physically but instead have to shadow an American counterpart, telling them what to do. I have never seen so many stagehands lolling about in the wings – there is nowhere for the actors to sit. Trevor is pushed for time but has to stop for half an hour so that *The New York Times* can take its own photo of the production. They have been offered the choice of all the production photos but insist on taking their own, otherwise they won't review it. This is the danger of one paper having all the power – we should have called their bluff.

Romola will miss next Thursday's performance of *Lear* to go to the Toronto Film Festival, where her latest film *Atonement* is showing. She has it in her RSC contract that she can miss some performances of *Lear*. I am astounded to hear Zoë complaining that nobody has bothered to tell her she will be playing Cordelia. Don't complain for God's sake! Just be thankful for the chance (on your first ever professional engagement) to play Cordelia in New York opposite one of the world's greatest actors. 'It is such stuff as dreams are made on,' to (almost) quote the Bard.

First performance in New York. Although the critics will be coming later, we are appearing before the most critical audience so far. More tension backstage than usual, especially as we haven't done the play for almost two weeks. Lack of dressing rooms means I'm sharing with Seymour, Guy, Julian and John Heffernan, right at the top of five flights of stairs. Very hot – with five hot sweaty blokes in a very small room I make sure I sit next to the window.

Not Ian's best Lear – perhaps he is a trifle uncertain and nervous after not having done it for so long – but he still gives a magnificent and moving rendering. Sylvester falls flat. Americans, usually, are very keen to laugh at anything, but they don't want to laugh tonight. There is a gap in the walk down at the curtain call. Sylvester is not there – why? He's such a gentle soul he couldn't possibly have taken umbrage. Even so, the New Yorkers give us a very enthusiastic ovation.

At the reception in the 'distressed' bar at the back of the stalls, mainly for BAM principals and supporters, I get fed-up with everybody thinking I'm Gloucester. On at least eight occasions, someone comes up and commiserates with me for the loss of my eyes. They don't even seem to remember the Gentleman at all – except for two attractive model-types. I am gratefully engaging them in perhaps a too-enthused conversation when Dora drags me away. I bump into Sylvester, who explains he went to have a quiet drink at a nearby bar, as he is not in the second half of the play, but misjudged the time for the curtain. Trevor hangs around the periphery of the party. Dignitaries from BAM refrain from even mentioning him in their ponderous speeches, only thanking Michael Boyd for allowing this wonderful production to come here. Can't understand it – surely they know who Trevor is and what he has done? Or don't they even realise he is there?

Friday September 7th

Walk through back streets to the theatre for *Seagull* rehearsal, passing malodorous drains full of fetid water – the place smells like an African township.

Even more stagehands than yesterday. I keep passing new people in the overcrowded corridors and stairwells as I make my way up to the top of the building where most of the cast are crammed into three dressing rooms. I watch a group of union members on the set, putting up the little curtain for Konstantin's makeshift stage. One is on the ladder attaching the curtain to the rings, two more hold the ladder whilst four other men and a woman watch.

At the stage door is a plastic bucket, full of dollar bills. The doorkeeper informs us that it is 'Dollar Friday' – a long-standing tradition in the New York theatre. Every Friday – pay day – each member of the cast and crew puts a dollar bill with their name written on it into the bucket. At the interval, a bill is drawn from the bucket and the person whose name is on the bill keeps the lot. Again there is overpowering evidence of union power, there seems to be well over $100 in the bucket.

Bill was due to play Sorin tonight but is still not feeling well so tonight's audience get the added bonus of Sir Ian McKellen. The Americans love the comedy of *Seagull* and Ian milks it dry. At the interval the dollar draw is made. Needless to say it is won by the aptly-named Edgar, who is head of theatre security. He's a huge man who looks as though he could have gone the distance with Sonny Liston; nobody questions the authenticity of the draw.

The evening seems to go even better than last night's *Lear*. At the curtain call there is a small unfamiliar figure in a Russian peasant costume and beard that I have never noticed before. I look again and recognise Sylvester, the only member of the company not in tonight's play. A true pro, he is making up for the curtain call he missed last night.

Trevor speaks to us over the Tannoy. He is going back tomorrow and as we have two performances there will be no time for a note session, so he will write them down and give them to Gemma to relay to us. His voice lacks its usual warmth – once his 'beloved company', we now seem to be slipping away from him. I sense he feels that certain members of the cast have turned against him. I still cannot understand how this has happened. Does it all go back to the long postponed first night and the never-ending rehearsals that ensued?

As the bus is about to leave, Trevor slips silently aboard. Why does he not go with Ian in his car? There must be so much they could discuss – not only this production but all the other productions, all the friends, the experiences and the triumphs they have shared.

When we get back to the three star Brooklyn Marriott, Trevor goes to his room alone. Why does he stay here? With his money, he could have a suite in the finest hotel in Manhattan. I wish I could tell him how much I admire him, but in all these years I've never been able to.

Saturday September 8*th*

Trevor has gone. We do two shows. With my entrances in both plays it means I climb the 58 steps up to our dressing room 13 times.

In my mind Ian gives the poorest rendering yet of the 'reason not the need' scene. He seems to lack fire, like a champion boxer who suddenly runs out of steam. As we climb the stairs at the interval, he says: "It's a fucking hard part. It looks easy, but it's fucking hard." Needless to say the ovation at the curtain is the most rapturous we have received anywhere. There is an alleged sighting of Paul Newman in the front of house gent's toilet. He does not come round.

Bill is better and does both shows. He tells me that Ian really wanted to do *Seagull* last night, as otherwise he would have had to do the press night next Wednesday cold.

Sunday September 9th

Dora and I walk across the Brooklyn Bridge before the matinee: stunning views in the sunshine. Go back on the subway which is a far less pleasant experience: iron seats, a harsh atmosphere and no colour as, inexplicably in this capital of capitalism, there are no adverts on the stations. We could be in a communist country.

It feels odd performing on a Sunday, but I can't understand why we do not do it more in London. We do a matinee of *Lear*. Ian is back to form and the reception at the curtain surpasses anything we have had before in all our travels. The administrator of the Harvey Theatre comes onto the bus and tells us that, in eight years, she has never seen anything like it. Let's hope the *New York Times* critic feels the same. Even so, I think with all the problems we have been having we have lost sight of the fact that we are in a wonderful production.

Dora and I are having dinner alfresco in Montague Street when Sylvester passes and tells us that Bill has fallen down the escalator leading into the hotel and has been taken to hospital. Poor Bill, he really doesn't seem to be having much luck at the moment.

Monday September 10th

Free day. I phone Bill. Carolyn tells me he spent the night in hospital having tests, but is now sleeping in his room and should be alright for the press night tomorrow. Phone my old RADA classmate, Sloane Shelton, on the number Ben Hawthorne gave me in New Zealand. She is delighted to hear from me and invites

Dora and me to dinner next Sunday.

Dora and I go shopping in Manhattan. Buy two jackets at Macy's for next to nothing.

The company is invited to dinner with BAM benefactors at the Grill Room at World Financial Center, which is adjacent to the site of the Twin Towers. On our way we walk past the huge crater, full of lights and busy with construction. It is unearthly – like a fantasy from *Lord of the Rings*. Someone points out that tonight is the eve of the sixth anniversary of the attack: we pause and contemplate.

We have a wonderful evening in a luxurious restaurant with stunning views of Jersey City. All the company is present, looking very smart, apart from poor Bill and Romola whose boyfriend has arrived from London. We sit at separate tables and dine with wealthy BAM supporters. Ian makes a wonderful speech, stressing the generosity of America in building the old theatre at Stratford and the Swan; he hints they will probably be asked to contribute to the new one. He is a great diplomat; he has charisma and has surely made enough money now from movies. He would be the ideal person to head the RSC and lead it forward to another golden age.

Tuesday September 11*th*

We wake to a torrential downpour, as if the heavens are remembering the anniversary of the atrocity.

Dora and I take a taxi to Grimaldi's, the famous pizza restaurant below Brooklyn Bridge. It is in all the guidebooks (it was patronised by Sinatra) and every evening a long line waits outside for a free table. It is a huge disappointment: the toppings seem to have come out of jars and cans and there is no atmosphere. The waiters are Polish, as they now seem to be all over the world (apart from Singapore). Is there anyone left in Poland?

Go in early for the press night of *Lear*. *The New York Times* critic is in tonight, as are many others – time, perhaps, to find out how good we really are. Trevor has emailed a note to us which has been pinned on the notice board by the stage door. He begins by apologising for only staying two days with us but he has to get back to his production of *Cymbeline* with the Cambridge students. He thanks us all for our hard work and says he has passed some notes to Gemma who will relay them to us. He continues:

> *'Please all try and receive these responses in the context and spirit in which they are given, of great admiration of your work, striving to find ever greater perfection....Enjoy the Big Apple, remembering that it can sometimes be a spicy passion fruit and an old banana.'*

I find it amazing that Sir Trevor Nunn, head of the RSC for 17 years, head of the National for five and creator of some of the finest productions in classical and popular theatre for the past 40 years, should feel it necessary to apologise for wanting to give his actors notes, some of whom, in my opinion, have been performing significantly below par.

The performance goes smoothly, though is not Ian's best. In the first scene, Romola, being a modern young woman chooses to make Cordelia wilful and laughs in Lear's face when he asks how much she loves him. This is a perfectly acceptable way of doing it but, to my mind, it makes her unsympathetic. I begin to wonder if the problem lies in the fact that Trevor cut two small asides from the text in which Cordelia tells the audience that she loves her father. But what do I know? *The New York Times* critic will probably love her. A lot of gay men in the front rows. Usual standing ovation. Susan Sarandon and Tim Robbins come round to congratulate Ian in his small, crowded dressing room which he shares with Bill, Jonathan and Sylvester – a world apart from the luxury, air-conditioned trailer that every minor film star considers his due.

Party laid on for us by BAM at a nearby noisy bar. Dora and I have one glass of very average wine and after three people mistake me for Bill, we go back for a Martini in our hotel room – it was all much more glamorous in Singapore.

From our window we can see two searchlights on the site of the Twin Towers blazing up to heaven, whilst on TV is a documentary on the plight of the rescue workers. Although Congress voted a billion dollars for their injuries and subsequent illnesses and disabilities, only a handful have received anything, whilst millions of dollars have been spent on lawyers and the total annual salaries of the three officials administering the fund apparently amount to more than £1million.

Send Trevor an email via his secretary Morag, saying he can go on giving me notes until the crack of doom – although I don't mention that I am still waiting for the notes he promised me on the understudy run of *Lear*.

Wednesday September 12th

Bump into Frances outside the hotel, on her way back from visiting her boyfriend in Manhattan, who is over here directing a commercial. She is dressed in a black trouser suit, black trilby, black sunglasses and bright red shoes: she looks like an exotic, black bird. Apparently she attracted quite a bit of attention on the subway. You cannot help but like her, she is full of fun and vitality – though Dora gets on better with her than I do.

Dora and I take the ferry past the Statue of Liberty to Ellis Island. Take the audio tour with different voices relating their own experiences: very moving, especially for Dora with her Jewish roots. Dora had complained about Grimaldi's to our hotel doorman, who is Italian. He recommended the Gemma restaurant on the Bowery, where we have a delicious lunch.

Am surprised to learn that some of the younger members of the cast think Romola is a tad arrogant and her performance in both plays is wrong. Yet they always seem to flock around her – probably because she stars in films. I must admit, if I was young I'd probably do the same.

Thursday September 13th

Romola has left for her premiere in Toronto. Practically the entire company, including Ian and Francis, come in to rehearse with Zoë. I am a little surprised that there is no message of thanks or apology from Romola for causing us all this inconvenience, but I suppose I am just old fashioned. It is a costly rehearsal as the stagehands' union will not allow us to work onstage unless a full complement of stage crew is present. Their overtime will allegedly cost the RSC or BAM an extra $4000. Naturally, the English actors get nothing but we are all happy to do it for Zoë and are convinced that she will give a true rendering of the role. Halfway through the rehearsal, Carolyn phones in to say that Bill has been taken ill again so Seymour is on. Seymour was one of the few not to be called, so frantic phone calls are made to bring him in. Poor Ian will now have to perform *Lear* with two of his closest relationships played by understudies. But the enforced changes generate a freshness and energy and Zoë somehow uses her inexperience to make Cordelia vulnerable and sympathetic – we give one of our best performances. Seymour also does well and there is the usual enthusiastic response. Ian looks very happy.

Zoë's parents have flown over from London to see her perform. They are staying at a very luxurious hotel and take her and Gerald out to dinner. Her father is a successful businessman and Zoë is the apple of his eye. I wonder how he feels about her relationship with an actor – ten years her senior?

Fathers are strange creatures. My son Rubin who is besotted with his daughter, Charlotte, recently told me he didn't care who she married as long as she was happy and the chap didn't support Arsenal.

Friday September 14th

Wake to read Ben Brantley's long awaited judgement of both

plays in the complimentary *The New York Times* hanging outside the bedroom door. It is a rave for Ian's Lear, *'the main event'* as he calls it:

'One of the marvels of Mr McKellen's performance is its suggestion that a so-called second childhood can be as rich an educational process as the first. As the harsh and imperious figure that was Lear dissolves, occasionally reasserting itself in choking spasms of rage, Mr McKellen makes sure that we see the wisdom in what the unenlightened might take for mere senility. By tortured degrees, with labyrinthine twists between piercing acuity and anesthetizing vagueness, this Lear arrives, with a clarity that I've never seen before, into a state of cosmic empathy and humility, a pained resignation that comes with facing the nothingness into which all men descend.'

But it is not good for the production as a whole, calling it, '*A popcorn Lear*'. He considers Trevor's interpretation '*spotty*' – whatever that means – and finds much of it '*heightened costume drama sped along with adventure-style movie music, replete with black hearted snarling villains*'.

He more or less dismisses *Seagull*, saying that Trevor has treated it like a roaring twenties theatrical comedy, with Frances Barber as a self-centred actress, '*a cross between Norma Desmond and Elizabeth Taylor*'.

The Daily News is a complete rave but the *Wall Street Journal* prefers *Seagull* to *Lear* and says that Romola's Nina is the star of the show. Michael Croft was right: he always told us when we were in the NYT to take no notice of critics – 'because if you believe 'em when they say you're good, you've also got to believe the buggers when they say you're bad'.

Brunch at Katz's, where Meg Ryan had her famous mock-orgasm in *When Harry Met Sally,* is disappointing: a huge pastrami sandwich but not the expected atmosphere. Perhaps Meg made all that noise because she was suffering from indigestion. Walk through Little Italy, decorated for the Feast of

San Gennaro, expecting to meet the Godfather. Pass scores of wonderful Italian restaurants, spilling out into the street but are too full of pastrami to partake.

As I leave for the theatre, I am much relieved to see Bill sitting downstairs, blaming his indisposition on a bad prawn. I'm not sure if he's telling the truth but I admire his guts and bravery.

In the dressing room Julian, who still spends most of his time offstage on his laptop, has downloaded various blogs on the production. As at Stratford, they are almost universally bad; sounding as if they were composed by frustrated actors and directors or aspiring critics trying out their acerbic wit. Trevor comes out worst, although one says that Romola is more equine than avian in *Seagull*. In the Green Room, I am really shocked to hear a couple of actors saying that they agree with the critics who find Lear too melodramatic and blame the faults in some of the performances on Trevor. Seymour and I do not agree. Guy, as usual, is smoking outside in the street so cannot give the casting vote.

Monica wins the dollar bucket draw, which might go some way to soothing the pain of one blog, which says her Regan was like a gargoyle – but, of course, she is one of those people who claim never to read the notices. I am beginning to think they are very wise. Romola is back and makes a speech over the crackling Tannoy in which I think she thanks Zoë and us for our trouble and invites us all for a drink in a bar in Smith Street. Most of the younger members accept. I prefer to go back to the hotel for another quiet Martini with Dora.

Saturday September 15*th*

Two shows today. Dora and I have brunch in a diner in Montague Street. There is a group of old people, mostly Jews, who seem to meet there regularly. They are like characters from *Seinfeld* or *Cheers*. One of them, called Victor, is particularly endearing. He wears one of the worst wigs I've ever seen but has a great interest in life and a sharp sense of humour:

"The trouble with old people is they're always complaining about their aches and pains. I say to 'em: 'How old are ya? Ninety. Ya must have had a couple of good days.'"

I learn later that he is a great favourite of Ben Delfont and other members of the stage management team. I suggest we club together and get him a ticket for *Lear*.

Frances is off with a glandular infection: Melanie is on. I think that lately, although Frances is superb in *Seagull*, she is getting fed up with *Lear*, and Melanie now plays Goneril with more fire and venom. Ian, like Lear, appears to be increasingly troubled by his onstage daughters. Monica is a very effective actress but lately her performance, in my opinion, seems to be becoming slightly coarse. I sense Ian feels it as well. Likewise Romola takes a lot of pauses in the reconciliation scene which makes it very difficult for Ian to take his time awakening from his madness, because he has to pick up the pace.

It seems crazy after all the note sessions we've had, but I really think we need another one. Part of the magic of theatre is that a performance is always evolving. Each night is slightly different. But any production needs a constant guiding hand else things get slowly out of control.

Sunday September 16th

A busy day. Brunch with Davina and Larry Belling in a fantastic apartment on the 30th Floor of one of the Trump Towers on Central Park South. From the huge windows the 26,000 trees in Central Park are laid like a thick carpet beneath us. Davina, as ever, has landed on her feet; only she could have a friend with such an apartment, who only uses it three days a week and offers Davina the use of it for the other four. *Lear* seems to be the talk of the town. All the other guests, a mix of smart Manhattan showbiz folk, are full of it and many have been lucky enough to get tickets. I am reminded again of the significance of this production: the RSC, in Shakespeare's greatest play, directed by the guy who did *Les Mis'* and *Cats*, and starring Gandalf himself (with a full-frontal to boot).

Have to leave early for the matinee of *Lear*. Frances is back, though I think she'd have been wiser to have rested her throat longer. When Ian, Sylvester and I arrive at Gloucester's house we are surprised when Seymour's Curan comes out to greet us, instead of Bill's Gloucester. Seymour deftly says the lines substituting 'we' for 'I'. We play half the scene, thinking Bill has had another turn and are very relieved when he walks on stage and calmly takes over the lines. We learn later that he had mixed up the scenes in his mind and was waiting to make his entrance on the other side of the stage for the storm, dressed in his waterproofs. Sheer professionalism on Seymour's part.

In the evening Dora and I go to dinner at Sloane Shelton's apartment in the heart of Greenwich Village. Sloane has been a working New York actress for 50 years, which takes some doing, even if much of it was understudying and off-off-off-Broadway. I have not seen her since 1958 when I left RADA to do my National Service. She was then called Mimi and was a vivacious, gamine-like creature. She was the first American girl I had ever met and I thought she was wonderful. A little old lady opens the door, but the sparkle is still in her eyes.

We have an evening full of nostalgia. She remembers me as a big, good-natured cockney boy, full of enthusiasm – I distantly remember that boy as we talk. From her window she says she watched the Twin Towers burn for five weeks. Her apartment was covered with dust – she now has a permanent cough. Bin Laden's victims will continue to multiply over the years. As I'd expected, Dora and Sloane get on very well and I promise to try to get her a ticket for *Lear*.

Monday September 17th

Day off. Schlep all the way to The Metropolitan Museum to find it is closed on Mondays. We meet Gerald who's off to dinner with Zoë's parents in their suite at The Four Seasons. I'm beginning to think they are really in love.

In the evening we are guests of Barbara Carroll and Mark Strook, whom we met at dinner at Sheridan Morley's several years ago. Barbara plays every Monday evening at the Oak Room of the Algonquin Hotel. We sit in a dignified old room, along the walls of which sit dignified old bankers and Wall-Street types dining with their wives and lady companions. They are nearly all older than me and are fans of the sophisticated music and jazz of my youth. Mark was 83 when he first met Barbara but she is the love of his life. Mark, an ex-newspaperman, is witty, generous – a wonderful host. We remember Sheridan with great love and affection and all agree that he would never have settled in New York. Barbara enters, beautiful as ever although she is over 80, begins her act, and is sublime. She is a link to the legends of jazz: Billie Holiday, Dizzy Gillespie and Charlie Parker. Her hands float over the keys and she plays the notes and improvises with the same level of skill with which Ian plays the words and thoughts of Shakespeare. She turns and sings *'I've got a Crush on You'* to Mark with such feeling that tears come to my eyes, proving we are never too late for love. A truly wonderful evening.

Tuesday September 18th

Dora and I have an al fresco lunch at Da Nico, which claims to be Rudy Giuliani's favourite Italian restaurant, on Mulberry Street. We sit and eat a fantastic seafood linguine complete with half a lobster each, drink a delicious Sicilian Pinot Grigio and watch the San Gennaro procession pass by.

When I arrive at the theatre I see that the superfluous New York stage crew have turned the huge container, which has transported our set across the world, into an intimate, little hideaway complete with coloured lights where they can sit, smoke and play cards undisturbed. Melanie is sitting amongst them, complete with customary cigarette. Now at least there will be some vacant chairs in the wings for the actors.

Adam is off, I don't know why. Everyone has become so much a part of the production that the smallest cog is missed. The knights' scene is not the same without Adam's bulk and energy. In the second half I am waiting to come on for the scene on Dover Cliff when I notice there is unusual activity in the prompt corner. Ben Delfont turns and rushes up the stairs towards the dressing rooms. Then I am aware of Rhiannon, the very pretty assistant stage manager who is on the book calling over the Tannoy: "Mr McKellen, Mr McKellen, come to the stage... Mr McKellen you are off... Mr Weston, come to the stage at once!"

I think that something dreadful must have happened to Ian and that the moment of truth has finally arrived. I realise that this is the worst possible moment for an understudy to take over – cold without any time for reflection or revision of the lines, and in the middle of the play to boot. But I am somewhat surprised that I am completely calm and am looking forward to the challenge. Unbeknown to me, Bill and Ben Meyjes have been treading water on stage for the past few minutes. When Ian does not make his expected entrance Ben improvises to Bill: "Sit sir... Sit and rest."

Bill, being an old pro, replies: "Aye, rest I will, but first I'll pray." He then gets down on his knees and prays to heaven. They are put out of their misery by Ben Delfont – who has dashed up to Ian's dressing room and failed to notice him sleeping under a white sheet – coming on stage and announcing that the performance has to be temporarily curtailed for technical reasons.

I am pondering if I should go on dressed as I am as the Gentleman or change into Lear's 'mad' costume when, from the top of two flights of stairs, Ian's mighty voice bellows: "No they cannot take me for coining. I am the king himself." A very apt line, in the circumstances. With that he rushes on to the back of the stage, barely giving Ben Delfont time to exit downstage left.

Peter whispers at my side: "I know exactly how he feels." I put my arm around his shoulder and give him a squeeze. I am relieved but at the same time disappointed not to have given my Lear in New York.

We later discover that Rhiannon had given her usual call for Mr McKellen's dresser to wake him. Ian usually has a sleep in the 40 minutes that Shakespeare provides for rest after the rigours of the storm. This is surely another proof that the actor from Stratford wrote the plays – no aristocrat would have been so thoughtful. But tonight Ian's New York dresser claims he was waiting in the corridor outside the dressing room and did not hear the call. Ian is mortified but the audience is as enthusiastic as ever at the curtain.

Get home to the Internet and am mortified to learn that Chelsea can only draw 1-1 at home to Rosenborg in the Champions League. I don't even know where Rosenborg is. This, after a defeat at Aston Villa and a 0-0 home draw against Blackburn! What is going wrong? It all started when José was forced to have Shevchenko and Ballack – both useless. Because of this tour I haven't been doing my usual runs before the games; am I partly to blame? Must remember to swim 20 lengths before the Manchester United game on Sunday.

Wednesday September 19th

In the morning we visit the National Museum of the American Indian in the grandiose old customs building – we see beautiful artefacts but nothing about their history or fate. We then go to the nearby Museum of Jewish Heritage: as ever, very moving. Surprisingly few visitors in both. Alfresco lunch at Battery Park with one of the best views in the civilised world.

In the evening at the same point of the play as last night, just before Ian's entrance on Dover Cliff, I am sitting in the wings in the chair in which Bill has recently had his eyes gouged out, when Ben Delfont approaches me. "David, I'm glad you're

sitting down..." Again a thousand thoughts race through my
brain. Is Ian really ill tonight? Is this going to be it? Through the
gloom I can see that Ben's face has broken into a sympathetic
smile: "José Mourinho has just resigned as Chelsea Manager."

I can only think of what Napoleon is reported to have said,
after the retreat from Moscow: "Is this the end of all glories?"

Thursday September 20th

Email from Emil; he had just bought the kids a cocker spaniel
puppy and had called him José. What will he call him now? I
suggest Terry. Arrive at the theatre to find Peter playing poker
with the stagehands, outside their hideaway. He sits at the table
with huge stack of chips before him, like the Cincinnati Kid.

John Heffernan tells me that John Lahr has written a four-
page article on Ian in the *New Yorker*, in which Ian is quoted as
calling Trevor a 'fat-arsed bastard'. I immediately go and buy it.
It is in fact a good-humoured piece in which Frances, very
amusingly, describes Trevor directing Ian in the storm (obviously
on a day I wasn't present). Ian asks for more thunder on a
particular line and Trevor says it's only a half-line and he can't
have it. He's given Ian thunder, dogs; every sound effect in the
book – besides, Shakespeare is not a meteorologist. To which she
quotes Ian, jokingly calling Trevor "a fat-arsed bastard". On such
things malicious rumours are spread.

Friday September 21st

Dora and I have morning coffee with Ian and his young painter
protégée, Nick Cuthell in the loft apartment Ian has rented in
Chinatown. Nick is tall and willowy, with the eyes of a fawn. Ian
met him in New Zealand whilst filming *Lord of the Rings*. Nick
has just arrived from Florence where he is studying art and Ian
shows an almost fatherly pride as Nick displays photos of his
beautiful portraits. Nick and Dora hit it off straight away and he
wants to do her portrait as soon as he gets back to London.

Dora fancies a steak as tomorrow, being Jewish, she will fast for Yom Kippur. Ian recommends Frankie and Johnnie's, an old speakeasy in the theatre district which is famous for its steaks. We go and find it deserted – apart from an old waiter called Mario. Nevertheless, he makes us very welcome and gives us an illustrated tour of how the joint worked during the Prohibition, complete with steel door to keep out the cops. He then says he used to baby-sit for a beautiful actress when he worked in London 30 years ago and wonders if she is still alive. He then mentions an actress I had an affair with more than 40 years ago. Dora kicks me under the table and says: "She is still alive; but very old and very fat."

We have two vast steaks which defeat both of us, and Dora longs for a postprandial cigarette. Mario says he doesn't mind, but he will have to close the door in case anyone should come up. With that, the steel door is slammed shut and Dora puffs contentedly away: smoking has become the new Prohibition. The steaks are duly wrapped and we take them with us to break the fast tomorrow.

Pick up a copy of the free paper *Village Voice*. What has poor Trevor ever done to Michael Feingold? He heads his review: 'Nunn and Nothingness', and makes a savage attack on Trevor's productions. The actors fare little better, with some exceptions among the younger ones, and the actresses are fried alive. Ian, after Mr Feingold has dismissed his previous stage work as *'being marred by his tendency to treat every role as the occasion for a show-horse exhibition of technical skill in lieu of a performance'*, is grudgingly allowed that *'he may yet become an actor in his old age'*. Have the packed houses that have been standing and cheering us to the rafters every evening in four continents been faking it like Meg Ryan? I think not.

Our agents have been contacted again about the film. The rumour is that it will be made by HBO and Channel 4. It could mean a nice little pay packet at the end of the job. No extra cash this week though, as the dollar draw is won by the female Assistant Head of Security...

Saturday September 22nd

Wake up very tired, and we have two shows today. Nevertheless I decide I must follow Norman Mailer and go swimming to infuse Chelsea with extra strength before their away game with Manchester United. This makes me even more exhausted and I can hardly make it up the four flights of stairs to the dressing room. All the same, I ascend them 17 more times throughout the day.

According to *Newsweek* tickets for *Lear* are now going for $2000 on the Internet: am therefore amazed to see an old lady asleep in the front row throughout the matinee with her feet resting on the edge of the stage and her chin resting on her bosom. I tell Russell she is my agent.

Sunday September 23rd

Go to brunch with Dora's old acquaintance Rachel Ramati, who has an extremely elegant apartment on the Upper East Side. On the subway we meet Philip on his way to church to hear a particular preacher who he thinks is really inspiring. Philip appears to be a very good person. At first I thought his cheerful bonhomie was typical LA phoniness, but I could be wrong. He can be a charming young man and his presence and good looks (his profile has grown on me) should give him a good career in film and TV. Our fellow guests at Rachel's are all Jews or Israelis. I have always got on with Jews – I suppose that's why I married a one – they all seem to have a thirst for life and knowledge, as well as a great sense of humour. I always say they are the yeast in any society. They have all either seen *Lear* or have tickets for the final week. Jews and gays keep the theatre going here, as in London.

Before the matinee of *Lear* I dash back to our room to check the score. Manchester United 2 – Chelsea 0. I have exhausted myself for nothing – but Chelsea played most of the game with only ten men, and both United goals came in extra time at the end of each half. At least the team have played with spirit (a true fan will grasp at any straw).

After the matinee nearly all the company are taken by bus to a sponsors' dinner at the Paris Commune, a restaurant in the West Village owned by Laurence Isaacson, who is on the RSC Board. Very many wealthy people here and money seems no object. Dora casually mentions that she hasn't got an iPod, whereupon a lady dips a bejewelled hand into her handbag and gives her one of several. Sit next to a charming Wall Street banker who tells me that his son, after taking law degrees at Yale and Cambridge is trying to become an actor in New York. He has just had his first audition for a part off-off-Broadway, which will entail him being stripped naked and anally raped on stage every night. I think he rather envies me when I tell him one of my sons is a partner in a law firm and the other has his own software business. But, who knows – miracles can happen – the lad could end up being a star.

Monday September 24th

Day off. Quiet day in Brooklyn. Check the Internet myself and find a single ticket for *Lear* is being offered for $1000.

In the evening we are given a reception at the Century Association, a New York club very similar to the Garrick – gleaming wooden panelling and old oil paintings. It is co-hosted by Susie Sainsbury and Mickey Wolfson, who has given away millions of dollars endowing museums and the arts. The great and good of New York are in attendance, but I don't recognise any of them. Before we partake of the most lavish buffet I have ever seen, we are forced to endure a recital of American poetry read by six members of the company: Bill, Melanie, Zoë, Russell, Peter and Ben Addis. Someone in some obscure department at

Stratford chose the turgid anthology. It is even worse than the farce we put together at the Maori centre in Auckland (and at least they couldn't understand what we were saying). I can't think why the RSC, asking these patrons for $25million to fund their future work, did not put on something like an anthology of the 'English Actor in New York', starting with Macready's diaries (he caused riots here resulting in fatalities in the 19th Century – it was the subject of an excellent play at the Swan about ten years ago). We could have then continued through Irving, Coward, Olivier, Gielgud and Burton, throwing in Vivien Leigh, Edith Evans, Judi Dench and Maggie Smith. It would have been easy to do and I would have been happy to put it together, but I suppose I am not considered a scholar.

We were treated however, to an inspiring speech by Chris Abele, a 40-year old philanthropist and chief executive of a real estate firm, who has just donated $5million to the fund and is the biggest single donor in the RSC's history. The many reasons he gives for wanting Shakespeare's works to be performed at the highest level I find moving and compelling. Later, Dora and I speak to him at length. He seems to be a truly good man with the finest of intentions. I hope all his money is not going to be wasted on the new theatre and incinerator tower. One earnest lady on the Board at Stratford, who has come over especially for the event enthuses to me about both structures. I tell her I think the tower is completely unnecessary.

"But don't you want Stratford to have a landmark?" is her horrified reply.

"It already has two and they are known throughout the world," I answer, having had another very good Martini. "Shakespeare's birthplace and grave. It also had a fine theatre that has just been gutted, that was graced by Olivier, Burton, Gielgud, Richardson and Laughton, to name but a few."

"Be quiet," she hisses, "the man who is giving the money is standing behind you." One of the advantages of being my age is that you don't have to give a damn.

Tuesday September 25th

We get up early, to be at the Metropolitan Museum at 9am for a special guided tour of the 'Age of Rembrandt' exhibition, which has been laid on especially for the RSC. Surprised so many make it – nearly half the company is there. We are given a fascinating and illuminating tour before the public is admitted. The Metropolitan is vast: a combination of the British Museum, National Gallery and the V&A (though I prefer having the three separate entities).

Ian knows that Lauren Bacall and Vanessa, Lynn and Corin Redgrave are in tonight, Corin seeing it for the second time. Ian gives a strangely erratic performance. He tends to be very nervous when people he admires are out front – they seem to affect him more than the critics. Nevertheless, the entire audience is on its feet at the end. Lauren Bacall is very noticeable, sitting unperturbed in the aisle seat in the third row.

After the show, Ian waits for her at the stage door. Half of the cast cluster around her, although even John Heffernan, who has seen practically everything ever made, admits to never having seen any of her films. Ian is becoming very fond of John – he invites him to a small gathering he's hosting in la Bacall's honour at his apartment.

Wednesday September 26th

Dora and I decide to have lunch in Robert De Niro's restaurant, the Tribeca Grill. When we get there it is closed for a private wine tasting, although we do manage to get a glimpse of the huge paintings by De Niro's father which line the walls. Nevertheless we have a beautiful alfresco lunch at Dekk just around the corner.

When we get back to the hotel, one of the younger members tells Dora that this is the most dysfunctional company he has ever been in. I think I see what he means. Certain members of the

company have completely gone off Trevor, others now question
his production, and Ian has ongoing problems with two of his
onstage daughters. I don't remember being in a situation like this
before. What on earth is going on???

At the theatre I ask Ian if Vanessa Redgrave enjoyed it. He
shakes his head very sadly and said she told him it wasn't really
her cup of tea. Tonight we have Faye Dunaway and Rachel
Weiss out front; it is the week of the grand dame. Ian is very tired
– I'm not surprised; I don't how he keeps going with so little sleep
and rest. He gives another slightly erratic performance, but
nevertheless still finds new and exciting things. He has a great
spasm of anger in the first scene and very nearly strikes Romola.
Frances appears to be tired too. Her Goneril seems to have lost a
little of its energy. I wonder if something is bothering her.

Nobody seems to listen to poor Gemma. She knows her stuff
and is extremely efficient and conscientious, but being assistant
director is a thankless task, you have no real power – perhaps
someone older, with more experience might have wielded more
authority? I was assistant director once, on a British Council tour
of *Macbeth*, as well as playing Macduff. We performed in places
where they didn't usually get Shakespeare. At one matinee,
performed in the small theatre on the promenade in Newquay as
the Atlantic thundered outside, the schoolchildren were making
such a row during the murder that the actor playing Macbeth
stormed off stage and demanded: "Get those little sods quiet, or I
don't continue."

There was nothing for it but for me, Macduff, to wander on
in the middle of the murder (anyone who knew the play must
have thought it a brilliant directorial stroke, a new slant on the
drama). I cleared my throat and said: "I've acted Shakespeare all
over the world – I can honestly say that you are the noisiest
audience I've ever played to. May I suggest that those who are
not interested go outside to the beach and let those who want to
stay and enjoy the play in peace?"

There was a mighty silence. No one went out, and there was
not another sound for the rest of the afternoon. The Porter never
even got a titter when he mentioned 'urine'. We thought that
perhaps they might be dead. Next morning the local paper ran a
headline: 'Actor says Cornish Children are Worst in the World.'
Thankfully, we moved on to Devon before I was lynched.

Trevor cannot see us again until London. Nearly everyone
seems very happy with this. In practically every production I
have been in over the past 46 years, the cast has complained that
the director doesn't see the play enough. There was even the
famous case on *Jim'll Fix It* when an RSC actor asked if Jim
could fix it so that he could see his director, Trevor Nunn. I don't
understand it; Trevor hasn't suddenly become a bad director, and
some performances, in my opinion, are going wrong and
definitely want fixing. Frances needs her fire back as Goneril,
Jonathan needs to stop singing as Kent, Romola needs to be
more sympathetic as Cordelia. And something needs to be done
to sort out the friction between Ian and Monica. None of them
are big problems – they can all easily be fixed with goodwill.
Sylvester, though, is finding his way deeper into the Fool and is
getting more and more laughs.

Have a drink with Michael Cadman after the show. He now
runs the drama department at the O'Neill University of
Connecticut, but I've known him since we were in the Youth
Theatre at the Edinburgh Festival in 1958. There were 27 shows
on the Fringe that year and our director, Michael Croft,
complained to the press that he thought 27 was far too many.
Last year there were more than 2,000.

Thursday September 27th

We're invited to lunch at Bolo, an excellent Spanish Restaurant
by Hope Dillon, a publisher friend of Julian Fellowes. I had
expected someone very hard and snazzy – like one of the
characters in *Sex and the City* – but instead a delightful, little,

middle-aged woman who could be on a day trip from somewhere like Surbiton turns up. We exchange many warm reminiscences of the redoubtable Fellowes. She is desperate to get a ticket for *Lear* and has been unable to procure one – I promise to see what I can do.

Tonight during *Seagull* Frances, all in white and looking beautiful as Arkadina, sits in a chair in the wings as Gerald and Zoë hug and kiss before her. It is very unprofessional, in my youth we only drank beer in the wings. It's alright for Zoë: she has nothing to do but walk on as Arkadina's maid, but Gerald is supposed to be the leading man. I give him the benefit of the doubt and decide he's trying out the Stanislavsky method: Trigorin is a womaniser, Zoë is playing his mistress' maid – what could be more natural than for him to philander with her?

Friday September 28th

Walk through Meatpacking District and Greenwich Village. Bump into a young, Chinese man wearing a Chelsea shirt. I shake his hand and say: "Well done. I'm a season ticket holder at Stamford Bridge." He clearly doesn't speak a word of English and thinks I'm mad.

Lovely lunch by a fountain in the courtyard of Cascata Café Italiano in Bleecker Street. On the next table are a handsome young couple. Dora starts a conversation and asks where they come from. They answer: "Minneapolis." We think it is an amazing coincidence and tell them we will be there next week: they give us a list of things to do.

Tensions are only natural after several months on the road. I gather some of the cast of *Seagull* are concerned that Monica is falling about too much in her drunken state as Masha, but she shows no sign of adjusting her performance and the audience continue to find her very amusing. I know from past experience how hard it is to resist the temptation of a laugh.

The assistant head of security wins the dollar draw again:

that means the security department has won it three times out of four. We discover that they both put in 20 one dollar bills. It is a system that obviously pays off – glad I only did it for the first week. Naomi's boyfriend has turned up at last – I really did doubt his existence. He looks very respectable and middle-class; not at all what I expected. It's good to see her so happy.

Dora goes to see *100 Saints You Should Know*, which is one of the few plays on or off Broadway that looks vaguely interesting. People keep telling us that the season doesn't start until October – in London we have plays opening every week of the year. She quite enjoys it and brings back the programme. Why oh why do American actors and actresses put such daft things in their programme notes, such as, '*she dedicates her performance to her great-grandmother*', '*pet*', a '*person of great faith*', or '*love and luck to Lucy's grandparents*'? It's only a job, for Christ's sake, not an awful Oscar-winning speech!

Saturday September 29th

To paraphrase Gloucester: 'Terry in injury parted and the noble and true-hearted Drogba banished'. Chelsea's woes continue: their ten men can only draw at home to Fulham. They are not even in the top six. In a way I am relieved to be away and not suffering at the Bridge. Phone Rubin, but he has just got back from the game and is too distressed to talk.

My humour is not improved when Melanie comes into the dressing room and asks everyone to contribute $10 towards a farewell gift of booze for the stagehands. I ask her why – we have never done this in any other place, indeed I have never come across the practice before and on top of that they all probably make more than we do. She spends her evenings smoking with them outside the stage door and has become very friendly, but I have had no contact with them at all, apart from the fact they always pull off the fallen curtain in full view of the audience whilst I am emoting in the storm. Melanie probably thinks I am a grumpy old man, but I refuse to contribute.

Ian gives his best performance of Lear this week. Bill's health seems to be improving but now Sylvester is ill. He can hardly walk today with arthritis and is also coughing blood. Ian, as Lear, is becoming increasingly brusque with him onstage. It works in character but I think it might be upsetting Sylvester. At least he has only one more performance to get through and then will have five days' rest. I once thought Russell, his understudy, would be as good, but I was wrong. Sylvester's performance continues to grow even as his health diminishes.

Sunday September 30th

Final performance in New York. Before the show, Ian talks with the people waiting vainly for a ticket in the line outside, some of whom have camped overnight in sleeping bags: it is a lovely gesture.

We give one of our finest performances ever. Like a football team suddenly finding its true form, nearly everyone is on song. Jonathan is back on form and is dramatic and moving again in the first scene, Frances is back to her old fire and Sylvester is a revelation. The Fool that Trevor wanted has finally arrived: his timing is immaculate and every word is crystal clear. Ian gives a staggering, towering performance, finding new pathos and anger. No matter that the critics were not overwhelmingly in our favour. New Yorkers, by repute the most discerning audience in the world, give us an ecstatic farewell – I think we have won on points.

Manage to get a ticket for Sloane. Take her and Dora to after-party in an amazing building, the tallest in Brooklyn, an old bank now owned by the ex-basketball legend, Magic Johnson. It has the dimensions and beauty of an Italian Cathedral, with golden mosaic walls and ceilings, ornate filigreed ironwork, and crystal tabletops, inches thick. Huge gathering, delicious food and excellent wine – almost like being back in Singapore. Have a long talk with Bill, whom I have grown to like and respect more and more as this job has continued. His daughter, Tilly, is a fully-trained, experienced, attractive and talented actress but, like nearly all actresses, struggles to get work. Jonathan Hyde's pretty daughter, just out of drama school was seen at Stratford by Romola's agent who has arranged 23 interviews in Hollywood for her. Bill was going to bring Tilly out to New York but he knew it would break her heart to learn how easy it is for some. I'm so grateful neither of my sons went into this cruel business (although I will never regret that I did).

I must say that Romola's agent sounds a pretty good one.

Monday October 1st

Last day in New York. Dora is very sad, but I'm quite happy to say goodbye to the discomfort of the Harvey Theater at BAM and the depressing walk to it every evening. That's what I like about touring – you're always moving on. Dora and I are invited to lunch at 44 ½ by Ben Widdicombe (no relation to Ann) who we met at the sponsor's party last week. Charming man; an Aussie, educated at Dover College, who writes a humorous gossip column called 'Gatecrasher' in the *Daily News*. Tells us Monica Lewinsky once hit him with her handbag after he described her as *'200 lbs of quivering flesh'*. We had expected him to pump us for gossip about Ian, but he behaves immaculately and is a credit to his Alma Mater.

After packing, Dora and I spend our final evening in New York having cocktails on the terrace of the Ritz-Carlton and watching the sun go down over the Statue of Liberty and Ellis Island. It is utter bliss – such a relief to get away from the company for a while. Afterwards we finally have that dinner at Robert de Niro's Tribeca Grill. There's no sign of the Raging Bull.

Minneapolis

Tuesday October 2nd

Get up early with no time for breakfast to catch flight on budget airline to Minneapolis. Have to admit I don't have a clue where it is. We are only going there because Tyrone Guthrie, the great British director, founded a revolutionary new theatre there in 1963. It became world-renowned and has subsequently been re-built, only reopening last year. At the airport, nobody from BAM has told them we are coming so everyone, including Ian, who, because it is a short flight, is flying tourist class like the rest of us, waits in line whilst a solitary check-in-person weighs every bag. The plane then waits for an hour before getting clearance for take-off – so we have a four-hour flight without food. Someone at BAM could have advised us to get some sandwiches, but I suppose that we are adults and should be perfectly capable of thinking for ourselves.

We arrive in Minneapolis in heavy rain. It is a culture shock after New York. We all check into the Marriott Residence Inn, a glorified motel just down the road from the Guthrie Theater. We all have very comfortable apartments; ours has two bedrooms and comes complete with three TVs – if only there was anything to watch on any of them. As there are no shops nearby, the bus takes us to the nearest supermarket to get supplies. The check-out girls are astounded to see Gandalf wandering around, looking for health food.

Beginning to get tired of touring and of several members of the company – as I'm sure they are of me. Looking forward to getting home. Having replenished our supply of vodka and vermouth, Dora and I decide to postpone exploring the dormant nightlife in the Twin Cities and have an early night.

Wednesday October 3rd

Awake to sunshine, but instead of the stunning vistas of the East River we had in Brooklyn we face a Hopper-like view of a long brick wall. Wander round the deserted streets of downtown Minneapolis. Amazing architecture with huge avenues of modern skyscrapers, five times the area of Canary Wharf. But where are the people? We later learn that they pass from building to building and cross the streets by the overhead, enclosed walkways, built because of the extreme coldness of their winters.

I am taking Dora to lunch at Dakota's, a very smart jazz restaurant on Nicollet Mall that was recommended by the Minneapolitans we met in New York, when there it is (at first I think it is a mirage) – Brit's Pub, with the sign: *'All English Soccer Games Shown Here'*. I go in and the barman tells me that the Champions League match between Valencia and Chelsea will be shown in just over an hour. I cannot persuade Dora to have sausage and mash in the pub, and there is no time for the smart restaurant – we have a rushed meal in a dingy diner. I leave Dora to go shopping and rush back to the pub to watch the game in the company of a Lebanese-Armenian jeweller, an Israeli diamond merchant and an Italian waiter. They all support Chelsea and we end up very close friends. Wonderful game – Chelsea, for the first time this season, have practically their best team out (apart from Lampard) and win 2-1. Have they turned the corner? Dora is not best pleased when I get back to the hotel having had a couple of celebratory drinks with my new friends.

In the evening we are all offered complimentary tickets for *The Home Place* by Brian Friel, which is being performed in the smaller theatre at the Guthrie. There are no other attractions as in New York so most people go. The Guthrie complex looks and feels as if the architect, Jean Nouvel, is merely showing how clever he is: it is a vast, seemingly dysfunctional building and appears to have no soul. There is no sense of coming into a large, welcoming space and unexpectedly meeting friends as you get (for all its faults) at the National. You go up long, dark escalators, disappearing into a void. Many little bars are dotted around the large empty spaces but there's no central point. People seem lost and don't know where to go.

I don't get into many of Friel's plays and am not mad about this one. Some of the company leave at the interval. John Heffernan, who, as noted, sees everything, saw Tom Courtenay in the original production at the Gaiety in Dublin and thinks this is very poor. Dora and I stay to the end, as does Ian. The house is 75% full and I sense they have not enjoyed it very much. I hear one old lady mutter behind me: "Well, I'm really looking forward to *Lear* next week." I hope we do not disappoint her.

Thursday October 4th

Very pleasant walk by the Mississippi. The falls here once powered the flour mills that ground vast quantities of wheat from the prairies. The land originally belonged to the Dakota Indians. There is a great amount of urban regeneration of the huge mills and factories along the banks, which are all being converted into upmarket apartments. But who will live in them? The streets are devoid of people.

In the afternoon Ian and other leading characters, including Frances, Bill, Jonathan and Sylvester, give a press conference at the theatre. The lesser mortals join them for a tour of the building and a welcome from Joe Dowling, the artistic director, whom I'm sure I met several years ago when he was escorting a group of American theatre-goers around England. I remember that he still owes me a fiver and debate whether I should remind him. Several cast members do not turn up: they are right not to, it is a complete waste of time. Joe Dowling makes a short welcoming speech, after which I go up to him and remind him of the time we met nearly 30 years ago. He smiles condescendingly and informs me I am getting him mixed up with *Vincent* Dowling – another Irish director who works in the States, who is 20 years older than he is. Thank God I didn't mention the fiver – I would have felt an even bigger fool.

We are given a long tour of the vast complex by a guy who would certainly not have won tour guide of the year. He tells us that Jean Nouvel and Dowling wanted to make the whole purpose of the building an 'endless bridge' giving a spectacular view over the Mississippi. I would have thought the purpose was a user-friendly theatre. We are told that twice the amount of steel went into the making of the 'endless bridge' than went into the building of the Eiffel Tower. To get this view, the theatres had to be built high – up to nine stories above ground – hence the never-ending escalators, which are among the longest in America. When we eventually see the auditorium of the Guthrie, our guide proudly announces that the patrons can tell no difference from the original; Ian asks what was wrong with the old one. We are given the usual answer: not enough space for administration and education. I think the real reason is the same as at Stratford: people wanting to leave their mark. In Stratford they will have an ugly, unnecessary tower; in Minneapolis, an 'endless bridge'. Change for the sake of change.

Dora and I eventually have dinner at the recommended Dakota Jazz Club listening to the *East Coasters* – a mega-talented five piece band. Two great steaks, a bottle of wine, and wonderful entertainment, all for $80. Fantastic value.

Friday October 5th

Back to *Lear*. Am starting to think the tour has gone on too long. You can have too much of a good thing, and anywhere in the world would be an anticlimax after New York. The whole of Minneapolis seems like a Hopper painting: empty streets and buildings in long, geometric lines. I sense most of the cast want to go home. Peter and the other young blades hang around the solitary pool table as there seems little else to do.

The Guthrie, which from the outside looks like a huge, black, shiny nuclear reactor is like a huge warren backstage. It takes far longer and more energy than ever to get from exit to entrance. Nevertheless, we give one of our best performances. Ian attacks the role with extra vigour and is superb, but comes off from 'reason not the need' murmuring: "What can I do? What can I do?" I suppose he means Monica, although she seems no different than usual. Why not call a company meeting and clear the air? Gemma, industrious though she is, is not strong enough – it's up to Ian. He is the one person they respect – but I suppose all his energy goes in playing Lear. At least now there is space in the wings, as the overmanned New York crew has gone. Our own RSC staff manage, as before, with a handful of locals.

The Guthrie audience is very alert and appreciative (I can understand their appreciation after having seen *Home Place*). We are given our usual thunderous, standing ovation, although the main concern of the company seems to be breakfast. We have been docked $7 from our per diems because the Residence Inn, where we are staying, provides a complimentary breakfast. It does not amount to much and Dora and I have not even bothered to go downstairs for it. Bill and Seymour asked Guy, as Equity Rep to complain to Richard Clayton. Apparently Richard said: "Well, you get waffles."

Guy replied: "Waffles! This is an English company. An English actor does not consider that he has had breakfast until he has eaten bacon and eggs!" The situation is as yet unresolved.

Saturday October 6th

Unbelievably hot and humid. We are well into October and apparently they get to 20 degrees below freezing in winter. Dora and I sit by the river and watch little lines of people pass by wearing crash helmets, perched apprehensively on electric Segways, like characters from *Dr Seuss*:

On the banks of old Mississippi
The Segwayers pass by
With helmet on head
And goggle on eye.
They stand upon wheels
With their feet off the ground
A sillier sight could never be found.

The inadequacies of the building become more apparent. Millions have been spent on the bridge – Bill asks why they couldn't have built the theatre closer to the Mississippi. Despite the architect's fixation with windows and views, there are no windows in the dressing rooms, not even a comfortable chair although in an overdose of political correctness every dressing room has been provided with a disabled toilet. (A play is yet to be written or conceived with 20 disabled characters – besides as the lifts do not work during performances, how would they get up to the stage?) Mr Nouvel, who apparently is Brad Pitt's favourite architect (he named a child after him) also appears to have forgotten to provide a proper green room or staff canteen.

Dora goes to see a visiting company perform *The Pillowman* in the studio theatre on the 9th Floor. The escalators stop at the 5th floor, where the entrances to the other two theatres are. After that, the only way up for the 400-strong studio audience is by two lifts which hold eight or ten people each. There are long lines of people waiting to get into them and it is even worse after the performance. What would they do in case of fire? Dora finds a flight of emergency stairs and leads a group down; every door is locked until they get to the 5th floor. There they join the throng coming out of the other two theatres, who are all now trying to get onto the escalators – absolute chaos. Apparently the original plan was to build all three theatres side by side, on the large plot which had been acquired, but the Board and Jean Nouvel, whose first major project this was, thought otherwise.

A party is given in our honour in the rehearsal room. The American cast of the Friel play are also present. We are given two tickets each which will allow us two drinks. After so many glamorous parties, this seems like something you would expect after a school play. In any case, we are partied-out, receptioned-out, dinnered-out. Apart from Peter, who is deeply engaged in conversation with the pretty, young actress who overacted as the maid in *Home Place*.

Sunday October 7th

I am glad that Rohan Preston, in his very favourable review in the local paper, picks out '*Sylvester McCoy's great comic timing*' – he has finally got it right.

I have been reading John Huston's very amusing autobiography, which I bought for $1 in a second-hand bookshop in Brooklyn. There is a very illuminating passage where he quotes his father, the great American actor, Walter Huston:

'*Only through playing to a live audience, and playing a part time after time, whittling it, shaping it, smoothing it, can perfection be attained. In motion pictures all too often, an actor is given so little time to prepare for a part that he must resort to tricks. Tricks to a good actor are a cheap device…he may fool others with them, but he can't fool himself.*'

John Huston continues:

'*I think it goes further than that. Leonardo da Vinci said that an artist should "paint as if in the presence of God." I think that's what a true actor does – subconsciously. He is playing God… a surrogate God… a live audience… faceless, numberless, therefore infinite. He can play this "God" and win instant approval – as he merits it. I suspect that's what actors really mean when they say they prefer the theatre to film-making, where there is no applause, only the approval of the director.*'

Tonight – like so many nights – Ian is God.

Monday October 8th

A free day in Minneapolis – to quote Dickens: '*What larks!*' The weather has changed dramatically; yesterday we were sweltering in the 80s, today it is freezing cold with a wind blowing down from Canada. Dora and I wander through empty streets and malls and bump into the solitary figure of Jonathan Hyde. Isabel, his lovely wife, must have known something and has missed out this leg of the tour. Jonathan says he finds Minneapolis a charming city – I don't know what he's been smoking.

After all the magnificent meals we have had on tour, the food here is terrible. Everything is tasteless and soaked in cheese. Seymour went to a restaurant yesterday and the only thing on the menu that didn't have cheese on it was the ice cream. Philip, our all-American boy, says it is because we are in the middle of the cheese belt of the USA.

Yesterday Dora was crossing the Third Avenue Bridge over the St Anthony Falls when she saw an overweight young man climb over the balustrade, as if to throw himself into the torrent below. She and a young girl ran over to him, pleading with him to stop. The young girl held his hands and gently stroked them, whilst Dora attracted traffic and called for the police. Two police cars soon arrived and closed the bridge whilst the young girl continued stroking the would-be suicide's hands. Four huge cops stood waiting until suddenly the man, who seemed to be under the influence of both drink and drugs, pulled free his hands as if to throw himself down. In that moment, the four cops threw themselves at him and caught his hands just in time. They hauled him back over the balustrade, handcuffed him and waited for an ambulance to arrive. Dora is convinced that he was suffering from 'Minneapolis Syndrome'. It is the only place, apart from Singapore, where there are no Poles. They must know something.

Tuesday October 9th

Yesterday, as we did not perform, I had a Margarita at lunch, a glass of wine in the afternoon, a Martini at sundown, a beer and chaser with an awful dinner and finally vodka on the rocks before I went to bed. I had heart palpitations throughout the night and have decided to go on the wagon.

Three weeks today we will be home. Meet Julian at breakfast, looking like a big woeful spaniel – homesick for his wife and children. He is convinced that this, the last lap of the tour when everyone is tired, is when everything finally falls apart. Ian spends his days in his apartment at the hotel, only venturing across the bridge to the supermarket for his daily supplies. Frances has asked to be in a dressing room on her own – she is frantically writing her report on the health resort where she and Ian were detoxed before Singapore. The deal was that they stayed free if she gave them some good publicity, but she has been so busy that she hasn't had time. Now they've given her a strict deadline.

Most of us are suffering from the Minneapolis Blues. Naomi spends a lot of the play sitting in the wings, she doesn't like the atmosphere in the dressing room and feels she is being ignored. Poor old Bill soldiers on magnificently although he is dying to get back to his beloved spaniels and garden in Chiswick. Gerald and Zoë are snug in their little nest. Guy, in desperate boredom, is trying to organise a company Segway outing but doesn't seem to be getting many takers. He has lost the breakfast battle: Equity informed him that the RSC are only bound to give us $68 per diem – the $75 we got in New York was a generous gesture on their part – waffles will have to be acceptable. Russell pumps iron frantically at the YMCA, Melanie shops like mad and Peter plays pool whilst the other younger members slump dispiritedly around the small hotel lounge. Dora has retired to bed with a good book. Only Philip seems happy – I suppose his home in Wyoming must be a bit like this, with scenery. Am quite relieved when Gemma announces an understudy word run of *Lear* for tomorrow. It will be something to do – and we need it.

Performances continue as normal. They stand for *Lear* every night we do it, but we are in sore need of some direction. I, for one, am looking forward to having Trevor back again, even if the others aren't.

This time next week we will be in LA.

Wednesday October 10th

I am being swamped with emails trying to sell me Viagra. Going over Lear's last lines for the word run, I discover a new reading that could make good advertising copy for a Viagra commercial:

(Shot of old man looking down sadly at himself in bathroom room mirror.)
    'No, no life?
    Why should a dog, a horse, a rat have life
    And thou no breath at all?
    Thou'lt come no more,
    Never, never, never, never, never.'

Perhaps not – this is what being in Minneapolis does to you.

There is a crazy rumour going round that Trevor applied for the job of artistic director here in the eighties and was turned down. I can't believe it.

Walk to word run with Gerald. He has been looking up his various notices for *Seagull* on Google. They go from one extreme to another; one says his Trigorin looks like Rasputin, another says Cat Stevens. We decide you just can't take critics seriously *'if you believe them when they say you're good, you must believe 'em when they say you're bad'*. But we do – we do – we do.

Ask Gerald where Zoë is and he tells me she has been excused the word run, as she has a girlfriend staying with her for a few days. I am gob smacked: the whole purpose of Zoë coming on this tour is to provide adequate cover for Cordelia and Nina. True, she performed Cordelia very well last week in New York, but she needs all the practice she can get, and it is much easier for the other understudies, especially me, to have a proper actress feeding them their cues, instead of a stage manager on the book. Am relieved to find that I still know Lear – am practically word perfect, as are most of the others, though Julian has become a little uncertain with some of his lines as Kent. I suppose it's slightly different for him as he plays the good part of Albany every night.

The word is that *Lear* has sold out its entire London run. Still no confirmation of the film, although it is rumoured that HBO will see *Lear* next week in LA and finally decide.

There is a special post-show discussion after *Seagull*, where the audience get to quiz the actors on their performance. I always find them very tedious and usually get asked things like: "What was your most embarrassing moment on stage?" I don't attend – what could anyone possibly want to ask the non-speaking Butler? – but hear that Jonathan Hyde declares it should be easy for a Minneapolis audience to understand the dilemma of Chekhov's characters – they too live in the middle of a vast country, miles and miles from anywhere. I'm not sure how they'll have taken that.

Thursday October 11th

See on the Internet that Kenneth Branagh will direct Jude Law as Hamlet next year. After much debate, I decide to write to Branagh offering my services. I've never worked with him, but he was very friendly when we were in separate plays at the National a couple of years ago. But do I really want to be in another Shakespeare play, one in which, in my youth, I played Laertes to Richard Chamberlain and Horatio to Michael York? The best I can hope for now is perhaps the Ghost or Marcellus and to understudy Polonius. I will be 70 next year: do I really want to go through the palaver again? But what else can I do? Sit at home and read? Play with the grandchildren? I am an actor – as long as I can stand up and remember the lines, I will continue trying to act. I therefore write Branagh the all-too familiar asking-for-work letter. Dora and I go to post it in Minneapolis' amazing giant Post Office, which looks as if it has come straight out of Hitler's Reich.

On the way back we meet Klare and Charles, part of our excellent stage management team – they are always cheerful and seem to actually enjoy their jobs (unlike many of the actors). They don't know what to do, so we tell them to go and have a look at the Post Office. They laugh – it must be a pretty rum place if a visit to the Post Office is a point of interest.

At the theatre an admirer has sent Ian (who is a semi-vegetarian) 100 hamburgers. Why? Ian gives them to Richard Clayton, to give out around the dressing rooms. I am highly suspicious – perhaps it is not really a fan, perhaps it is a homophobic who wants to get rid of Ian. You hear about such people in the Midwest. Richard assures me that Ian can vouch for the donor. I take a small bite of the greasy, foul-tasting thing and am still not convinced. The dressing room litter baskets are overflowing with discarded hamburgers at the end of the evening.

Friday October 12th

See in *USA Today* that Branagh and Law won't be doing Hamlet until 2009. Feel an utter fool – Branagh will think I'm either desperate or a nutcase to be writing so early.

Dora bought a mobile phone with 100 minutes on it for $40 in New York. It has now run out and we spent a long time yesterday unsuccessfully trying to get it topped up. I suggest we just buy a new one in LA for $40 but Dora, as ever, has a will of her own. She rings a number on a card and is told that the only place to do it in Minneapolis is 3426 Nicollet Ave. We begin to walk along Nicollet Mall, the main drag. Dora is wearing her new mock-leopard coat and looks extremely wealthy. We get to the end of the shopping precinct and I realise we have only got to 340; I point this out to Dora but she says she needs a walk. And walk we do; first through the Black area, then the Mexican, then the Vietnamese and finally the Somali – each area more run down than the last. I did not know this, but there are 30,000 Somali refugees in Minneapolis. Then the road comes to a dead end at 2046. I stop an old lady on her bicycle and she tells me the road continues if you take a right, then a left, go two blocks and then take another right. We go into little streets and pass the Somali Centre – it looks like a refugee camp, people are sprawled in the streets looking very unhappy. By now my temper has gone: I tell Dora I've had enough. I'd get in the next taxi we see, but in this godforsaken district we haven't seen a taxi since we began our trek – I'm certain we're going to get mugged. Dora suddenly sees what she thinks is a blue and white taxi and steps into the road to stop it. To my horror, I see she has stopped a police car. A big policeman gets out and asks, "What's the problem?" Dora explains that she thought he was a taxi; this doesn't seem to amuse him. He asks where we want to go. Dora tells him 3426 Nicollet, he nods and says "get in". As I struggle to get into the back, he puts his hand protectively over my head. I notice that the windows are barred and there are no handles on the inside of the doors. I point out there's not much room – he replies that his passengers are usually lying down.

I am convinced that he has arrested us on some by-law which makes it a felony to stop a police car, and am therefore very relieved when we pull up outside 3426 and the astonished Moroccan owner watches two potential customers crawl out of the back. The cop says he's off to a domestic violence case but will pick us up on the way back, if we are still there. Dora gets her phone reinstated and the Moroccan calls a cab, which takes us to the amazing Minneapolis Institute of Art. It must be one of the great museums of the world; a superb collection in a magnificent building in a rundown suburb.

In the end, perhaps due to the paucity of rival attractions, 19 of the company go on Guy's Segway expedition. Both Ian and Frances fall off, but no knees or other limbs are injured.

Saturday October 13th

I have yet to find food here that isn't tasteless, and the wine is terrible. At least it makes it easier to stay on the wagon.

I think Jonathan Hyde is feeling the pinch after all his business class flights and expensive New York restaurants. He now keeps the bread and cheese I give him in *Lear*, and eats it later.

Sunday October 14th

The day starts amusingly, when the old saga of Ian's mighty cock raises its head again. 'The Dish' – the gossip column of the *Star Tribune*, written by someone called C.J – is headlined:

'Advice Sir Ian's Lear ignoreth: Have more than thou showest.'

'Sir Ian McKellen put his manhood on display at the Guthrie. Not everybody was glad to see him.

"It was the most exhibitionist piece of theatre," said Anne Tennant, a regular on FM107, who normally discusses trends in celebrity plastic surgery. "He's on the thrust stage," she said. "He's right there in the faces of the local blue bloods with famous names who sit in the front row of every opening night. He is probably the greatest Shakespearean actor we've got and he completely derailed the climax of King Lear *by exposing himself. And not only does he expose himself but when he pulls his shift up, he does a 360."*

Now that's staging.

"It was five minutes of Sir Richard in your face. As he's rotating, I realize with shock that he is considerably better endowed than anybody I've ever met in my bedroom career. I turned to the fellow who took me

*and my eyes are HUGE. My date gave me a look that said: If you dare
say anything, I'll never invite you out again...*

*No, he wasn't even relaxed. He was nowhere near relaxed. He was
happy to see the audience. Now, whether or not we were so happy to see
that much of him... at that moment we're supposed to be considering that
Lear has lost sovereignty over not just his kingdom but over his mind,
what we had was the sovereignty of Sir Richard."*

Sir Richard was not the name she used on the radio station.'

I suppose she said, 'Dick'. King Dick III was another of Ian's
great roles. I think he quietly revels in all of this.

At the final Minneapolis performance of *Lear* this afternoon,
everything falls apart. Ian begins in fine form, angrier than usual,
finding new meanings, roaming around the stage like a hungry
old wolf. He continues in that vein in his big rant into the 'reason
not the need' scene, using his anger to keep his performance fresh
and real. He begins by pushing me aside when I go to help him
get up from his knees; I react in character, I turn upstage and give
Bill, as Gloucester, a shrug of despair. I don't mind at all: it gives
the moment spontaneity and freshness. Practically the entire
company are on stage when Monica enters as Regan. She
addresses Lear in the condescending manner she has adopted.
Ian, as Lear, berates her even more furiously than usual. He
positively snarls. I naturally watch his every move and swear he
never does more than slightly push her. A few lines later, when
she finally refuses Lear a single knight, Ian waves his hand back
and forth contemptuously before her face. I think it is a
wonderfully inventive moment and consider doing it the next
time I rehearse the scene.

I exit with Lear and then rush back onstage to do my scene
with Kent. When I come off I see Philip, the committed, smiling
Christian, storming down the corridor with an unfamiliar scowl
on his face. I ask what the matter is, but he stalks past me in a
furious temper. I then see Ben Meyjes in earnest conversation

with Guy, our Equity rep. While Ian is still onstage, completing the last three scenes of the first act, some younger members of the company complain to the management about Ian's conduct. I bump into Frances, incandescent with rage – she says she will back Ian all the way. I go to the dressing room Ian shares with Bill. Sir Ian McKellen is standing there alone and distraught – Bill is still onstage having his eyes plucked out. His agonised screams echo down the Tannoy. Ian looks at me, like a hurt little boy with tears in his eyes; "The whole company is against me. They say I have behaved badly." I assure him of my unswerving support. I go to my own dressing room on the floor below and am shocked to find that practically everyone thinks Ian is in the wrong. I ask what Ian has done? He was struggling to give another magnificent performance; he is a great actor and must be given some latitude. They seem unimpressed and say that being a great actor is no excuse, and Ian should behave with due respect to others. I have to leave the room – I cannot speak, I am so angry. When I was young we looked up to Olivier, Gielgud and Richardson as gods and would never dream of questioning anything they did on stage. It should be the same here with Ian. I have worked with Kirk Douglas, Richard Harris, Richard Burton and Peter O'Toole, among others – they all behaved badly at times, but they were stars and perhaps that is what makes stars exciting and different. They've always pushed and shoved for predominance – I've even witnessed one renowned actress making sure she upstaged her own children. Where is the excitement and drama that makes theatre, if we all behave like politically correct ninnies?

I feel a bit like Gary Cooper in *High Noon* as I walk about backstage looking for someone to share my anger with. I know Bill and Jonathan will be 100% behind Ian, but they are on the floor above. Sylvester is onstage being hung. Guy, who usually displays common sense, is, as usual, somewhere outside smoking. I go into the scene dock and meet Russell. I ask him what he thinks of the situation – he shrugs his massive shoulders with tears in his eyes and says how much he hates unpleasantness. What's the use of all that muscle if you're such a wimp? I leave him immediately and go for a pee. A young actor comes in and stands beside me. I ask his opinion. He says Monica has the perfect right to do her performance as she sees it – *Et tu, Brute?* I go out into the corridor and bump into Ian, who is wandering around looking very lost. He asks me where the girls' dressing room is, I point it out. He knocks and goes in, I presume to apologise. For a moment I think perhaps I am wrong and the others are indeed right – but then again what does Ian have to apologise for? I saw what he did – it was just a push. Nobody would be here without Ian; he has carried some very average performances on his shoulders across the world. Many of the cast have probably earned, in proportion, more this year than they will for the rest of their careers. But times are changing in the theatre as elsewhere – old customs and standards no longer apply. I feel like a dinosaur.

Ian goes on for the second half and is as moving and brilliant as ever – at the curtain the entire house gives him a thunderous standing ovation. I look down the line and wonder how many think this acclaim is for them.

Dora comes to the theatre for final drinks, but I am so upset I insist on going back to the hotel. Later Dora rings Frances, who tells her that Ian is terribly distressed. Frances also says that HBO are still not sure about doing the film and Ian has been thinking of putting £1million of his own money in. There is no chance of that now. I cannot believe what I am hearing: the whole thing is unravelling like a Shakespearean tragedy. We started off with the best director and best Shakespearean actor in the world but it appears to be all falling apart at the seams. Where did it all go wrong? Haven't had a drink all week but am so upset I have a large Martini and then Dora and I share a bottle of Pinot Noir.

Terrible night – can't sleep a wink.

Monday October 15th

Another free day in Minneapolis. Why couldn't we have flown to LA today and have had an extra free day there? Dora and I keep to ourselves. The only recreation on offer is shopping. The younger members slouch about the lounge. Peter and Ben Addis play pool – I'm not sure what they think about it all; I'd rather not be disappointed again so don't mention it. I don't think big Adam cares one way or another, Gerald only seems to care about Zoë, but I know Naomi will definitely side with Ian. There is no sign of the poor, distressed, old knight. I decide not to phone him, I am sure he'd rather be left alone. I wouldn't be surprised if he's already in LA. Still feel very despondent about it all.

Los Angeles

Tuesday October 16th

Can't wait to leave Minneapolis. The bus is about to go and there
is no sign of Ian or Frances. I am certain they are already in LA,
when Ian rushes down with his bags: his alarm had not gone off.
He takes the bus' mike and apologises profusely for being late. As
he sits next to Dora in the front seat he says, *sotto voce*: "Got to be
very careful with this company," then sits gazing intently out of
the window throughout the drive to the airport. Usual confusion
on arrival: the people from the Guthrie said they had arranged a
group check-in for us, but nothing seems to have been done.
Gemma, nominally in charge, like the Grand Old Duke of York
leads us all up to the second floor and then back again. The plane
is delayed an hour. Ian wanders round the lounge making great
efforts to be friendly with everyone, especially Monica and
Romola. He is still very upset. He even allows Dora to show him
photos of the grandchildren and helps me with the *USA Today*
crossword.

More chaos at LA Airport: Ian has lost his wallet on the
flight and UCLA have only sent two small buses to pick up the
lot of us. We leave and then have to go back because we have
managed to leave Ian behind. There is no room for the luggage –
people sit with it on their laps or else it is piled in the aisles. Some
of the younger ones are not with us as they have hired cars and
gone to Las Vegas for two days. An amazing metamorphosis
comes over Philip as soon as he reaches this strange city. He goes
from smiling, American country boy to something like a frantic
character from *The Player*. He sits at the front of the bus, with a
fixed grin on his face, making loud calls on his cell phone to

various agents sounding, to my cynical old ear, completely phoney. Peter, who never likes to be in the shade, dials his agent in London but appears to have woken him up in the middle of the night. The UCLA have seen fit to put us in The Hotel Angeleno, which is the equivalent of being put in a hotel on a roundabout in the middle of Spaghetti Junction. Frances has been there a day already and is waiting, in tears. The noise and pollution are unbearable, meaning it is impossible even to open a window. The full extent of LA.'s pollution problem is obvious from our balcony: multi lanes of unceasing traffic stream past, 24 hours a day, whilst busy slip roads loop around the hotel. The smog hangs over the city like a shroud and the palm trees, not native to California, are dying; someone has read they will all be dead in two years – I am even more down in the dumps and fear for the future of our civilisation. On top of that we cannot walk anywhere as we are surrounded by expressways and speeding cars. We will have to hire cars, take taxis or wait for the courtesy bus to take us to shops or restaurants.

Within an hour Ian, Frances, Sylvester, Jonathan, and surprisingly Peter, have moved out and taken rooms in a hotel in Westwood, near the theatre, at $400 a night. I let Dora loose and we end up being given a suite on the 15th floor, probably intended for Ian, but we still cannot open the window. Take taxi with insane driver to Westwood and have an excellent dinner at Tanino, which we remember from previous visits. Ian, Frances, Jonathan, Sylvester and Peter come in. Frances, who has regained her normal bubbling vitality, laughs, saying that Dora and I always seem to know the best places. She urges us to join them at their new hotel, but we decide to stay at the Angeleno – what is the point of spending $4,000? We would rather spend it on a holiday in a place of our choosing – although any further trips abroad are now very far from my mind as all I want to do is get back to London. We miss our family, our friends and our home. Dora, who has hated LA since she was here as a starlet in the sixties, decides she'll go back early.

Wednesday October 17th

Day off. Hire a car which will cost $500 with insurance. On top
of that I have to pay $10 a day to park at the hotel and $7 at the
theatre. I am becoming more and more disillusioned with UCLA,
who have made all the arrangements here. Apparently they have
got a good deal with this hotel, which is ideal for travellers
spending one night whilst driving along the freeway, but not for a
company of actors performing *King Lear* for two weeks. Bill
Gaunt is the latest to move out. He can't sleep and the pollution
has given him a sore throat.

We drive to Santa Monica; Dora is happy to see people
walking on the streets again. On the pier I see a young black guy
with, as usual, the crutch of his jeans around his knees and a
back-to-front baseball cap on his head. But there is something
different about him: he is wearing a Chelsea shirt with Drogba's
name on the back. I go up to him and say: "Who let the Drog
out?" He looks perplexed. I explain that's what we yell at
Stamford Bridge whenever Drogba gets the ball.

He gives a huge smile: "That's real cool, man." Then he gives
me a high five, "You're a real cool old fella." Dora doesn't
understand a single word of what we're talking about.

Guardian reports tickets going for $3000. Even the head of
Warner Brothers cannot get a ticket.

Thursday October 18th

Brunch in Santa Monica watching the strange people pass by.
Old men with ponytails, faded flower power females, left over
from the sixties. Nearly every other girl's a would-be actress, as
are all the waitresses – they give an audition every time they tell
you the daily specials. I could not live here. Then up to Rodeo
Drive: exactly the same designer shops as Sloane Street. Michael
York once told me LA is an awful place to visit but a great place

to live. I wholeheartedly agree with the first part anyway.

Friday October 19th

UCLA has a huge campus. Royce Hall, where we are performing, is not a theatre but a vast assembly hall with lots of cream walls and dark brown wood – back to doing a school play. Why are we doing it here? Set looks ridiculous and the hall is so wide that it is overlapped by a dreary, blank wall. Because of the thrust stage, a quarter of the seats cannot be sold. There are no proper dressing rooms and we have to make our entrances down corridors opening on to empty classrooms. Everyone is tired and dispirited, though a truce seems to have been established between Ian and Monica.

After rehearsal I walk around the campus before the show. It is a beautiful evening and new students show their parents around. Almost expect to bump into Robert Redford and Barbra Streisand in *The Way We Were*.

Ian, despite it all, is on top form and at the curtain we are given the usual tremendous reception. There are drinks afterwards in what is probably the staff common room. Naomi, of all people gets on very well with Gene Kelly's widow, who looks a bit like Annie Lennox. She invites the company for drinks at her house after the show one night next week. By now I have had enough of social gatherings and decide to go back to the hotel on the first bus. On my way out I pass a mega-tanned George Hamilton, his face stretched into a seemingly permanent grin. "Well done," he says. I'm sure he thinks I'm Bill Gaunt and curtly nod my thanks.

As I get to the bottom of the stairs, I hear someone say; "Did you see Warren Beatty?" So Warren Beatty thinks I'm Bill Gaunt and I think he's George Hamilton. Who has the better deal?

Go back to hotel in courtesy bus and find I'm sitting next to Romola; realise I haven't spoken a word to her since Melbourne. She cannot understand why we are playing in such a vast space and not in a proper theatre in San Francisco. I want to hold my tongue but can't help myself saying: "Trevor insisted on playing in LA because he wanted the young people to be seen."

Saturday October 20th

Back to *Seagull*. I have many entrances and exits, and am not on stage all that long, but from what I can see, we are no longer an ensemble, but every man for himself. I Spend every moment I can in my dressing room, engrossed in a good book.

Michael York is out front. He has been a friend for nearly 50 years, since the early days of the National Youth Theatre and I later played Horatio to his Hamlet. After the show, he hugs me on his way to see Ian and says, "Well done." I feel embarrassed and humiliated as I haven't said a word all night.

Sunday October 21st

Wake up with dark clouds of smoke in the sky from the fires all around: California is burning. With people's homes and livelihoods in danger, the ongoing deaths in Iraq and the general awful state of the world, the petty squabbles that have engrossed us for the past weeks seem trivial and terribly unimportant. Nevertheless, when I find the *Los Angeles Times* outside my door, I turn first to Charles McNulty's well-written review of *Lear*. Like in most of the recent reviews, he is critical of Trevor's '*broad and brittle*' staging and says Ian's Lear, '*which gusts across the stage like an angry wind*', is more Donald Wolfit than Laurence Olivier. I wonder if he ever saw Wolfit's Lear – it was considered his finest role – Olivier's television Lear was fragile and disappointing. McNulty praises Ian's technical virtuosity, the surprising inflections he puts on familiar lines, and the way he uses props to punctuate a moment:

   '*Take the handkerchief McKellen resorts to when in the grip of strong emotion. He tears at it, mops his brow and blows his nose like an elephant with a miserable head cold. This little piece of cloth is wielded with such flamboyant expertise that it wouldn't seem amiss if its credits were listed in the program alongside the rest of the cast.'*

The great thing about Ian, I notice again and again, is that every evening he serves up something different. We can go weeks with the hanky firmly in his pocket.

All three sisters fare badly. Frances and Monica he dismisses as pantomime ugly sisters, which is unjust, but says Romola's *'aggressive pertness'* in the first act *'is virtually impossible to reconcile with her character's beatific reappearance at the end of the play.'* It's what I've been thinking for months.

He goes on to criticise *'the ensemble's creaky histrionics'* and says Trevor has chosen a more melodramatic approach than is customary today. He is right to a point, but the huge hall here is unsuitable for subtle acting and the staging is the most unsatisfactory of the entire tour. He ends: *'Truth be told, the only time the characters seem to be directly communicating is when they're plunging a sword into a side or plucking out eyes.'* You'd think he'd been spending his time backstage! What we need is a severe note session with the director.

The metamorphosis of Philip grows apace. Last night Jonathan Hyde was backing his car, containing Ian, Frances and Sylvester out of the parking area behind the stage door, when a furious Philip bangs on the top and yells: "You just hit my car!" Ian winds down his window and says, very meekly: "I don't think so. We didn't feel a thing."

An inspection was made but there were no visible marks.

Monday October 22nd

Last free day of the tour. Dora and I drive to Santa Barbara to stay with a nephew of the Earl of Gosford, who lives alone on a huge ranch, together with 300 cattle, five horses, one pig, two dogs and a cockatoo called Bird. Needless to say, we met him many years ago at Julian Fellowes' Christmas dinner. It was where the title of *Gosford Park* came from. We travel through burning countryside; the smoke is in the atmosphere, pervading everything – it seems like the end of the world. I feel very tired and down in the dumps. When we arrive at the ranch, our host, Alex Fleming, tells us they are suffering from a terrible drought: there is no grass left. He drives us round his vast estate in a very battered pick-up truck whilst we stand in the back, throwing out bales of hay for the hungry cattle. It's the nearest I'll ever get to being in a Western. We have a restful evening, eating steaks cooked over an open fire, then we sit in the wooden ranch house, the walls of which are hung with portraits of Alex's noble forebears intermixed with the stuffed heads of various animals he has shot throughout the world. It is strange and eerie: I would like to say he resembled an eccentric character from Wodehouse, but Alex is very quiet and reserved. I think he cannot decide whether he is an English aristocrat or American rancher.

Tuesday October 23rd

Leave early as I am afraid the roads may be closed by the fires. Get back and read Charles McNulty's review of *Seagull* on Internet. He seems to prefer it to *Lear*, Ian's performance notwithstanding. Though he thinks *'most of the cast members are strolling about as though it's a sunny day in West Sussex.'* Would that we were! McNulty must have a thing about actresses because he says that the women are again the weak link and thinks Frances is an acquired taste. I do not agree. Her performance maybe suffering because of the general friction and lack of control, but she is a very fine actress. Romola fares even worse:

'Garai wears Nina's naiveté on her sleeve, has a pleading quality that's a real scene spoiler. While her radiant loveliness would explain why all the men are falling in love with her, her dewy-eyed gaze and squeal of a voice should have sobered them up by now.'

I'm in my dressing room five minutes after the half when

Seymour enters and says, "Ian's not in yet." Could this be my moment at last? And in Hollywood to boot? I take my script and begin to look at the first scene. Every word is seared in my brain, but it is different saying it on a vast auditorium with actors throwing cues at you. Understudies in the West End rehearse every week; we haven't had a proper understudy rehearsal since Stratford, six months ago. This would be the worst-case scenario, having to go on without any warning. But in my heart I know Ian would never miss a performance – acting is his lifeblood. At the quarter, Gemma comes down and tells me to keep cool, and says they are desperately trying to contact Ian. I am only a few minutes away from being officially notified that I am on, when Ian rushes in. He had fallen asleep at the hotel and they had forgotten to wake him, on top of that he couldn't get a taxi. He apologises to me. I tell him there is no need. Even so, I would love a crack at playing it just once – I'm glad they've fixed another understudy run in London on December 11th.

Ian comes off after 'reason not the need', saying, "She's taunting me – on purpose." It is hard to tell; Monica taunts him in character. We receive a letter saying that Richard Price, who has filmed several of Trevor's past productions, is still trying to raise the money for the film. Ian says they only need £1.3million – it doesn't seem much these days, particularly when a pair of tickets for the final performance of *Lear* here on Sunday is being offered on the Internet for $6000.

Accenture, our sponsors, are entertaining their guests tonight. For some reason the caterers bring into the green room all the discarded food on silver foil trays, as if they think we are hungry down-and-outs. Bill Gaunt expects to find a cigarette butt amongst it. The food remains untouched.

Wednesday October 24th

Dora heads back to London and I miss her straight away. I don't think I would have got through Minneapolis without her. I have lunch with Ed Wilson, ex-director of the National Youth Theatre, who now lives out here and is recovering from cancer, and May Routh, the widow of my dear friend Brian Eatwell who died in February. It is strange, but now whenever I meet with my old friends, death seems always to be lurking nearby. Nevertheless, we have a jolly lunch in Tanino and I have managed to get May two restricted view tickets for *Lear* on Friday. Ian is in the restaurant and embraces Ed. They are old friends: it was Ed who persuaded Ian to become Vice-President of the NYT.

When I get to the theatre I am flabbergasted to learn that the understudy word run for *Seagull* tomorrow, which has nothing to do with me, has been cancelled because some of the cast don't want to do it and Zoë has an interview with an agent. What do they think they are on this tour for? It is Zoë's first job; if Romola were to lose her voice tomorrow night Zoë would be on stage playing one of the most difficult of all young female parts, opposite Sir Ian McKellen and in Hollywood to boot! Does she think she's so good that she doesn't have to practise? I gave her the benefit of the doubt when she didn't turn up for the *Lear* word run the other week in Minneapolis because she had a friend in town, even though in my opinion it still showed complete disrespect for her fellow actors. The agent interview is a mere formality and could easily have been changed; agents eat up young talent and spit it out. Poor Peter went to see one yesterday, who asked him how old he was. He smiled brightly and said, "24."

"You look like 30," was her dismissive reply.

Obviously Melanie, who has played both her understudies many times whilst Frances was injured, doesn't need to rehearse, but I would have thought she would have done it for the others, who haven't had the experience of playing the roles. Will nobody get a grip? Feel as if I have a lot to get off my chest, but as I no longer have Dora to complain to, I ring Ian McShane, who is rehearsing Pinter's *Homecoming* in New York, and give him a brief run-down on the state of things. He lends a sympathetic ear.

Naomi's new-found friend, Mrs Gene Kelly, has invited all the company for food and drinks at her home after the show. At the beginning of the tour I would have accepted like a shot but we won't get there until after midnight and I am very tired. Go back to hotel in courtesy bus with Romola and Monica – not a lot is said.

Thursday October 25th

Quiet day – am missing Dora. I realise at times like this how lucky I have been to have had a partner through life.

It transpires that Zoë had three interviews today. I realise that I judged her too harshly, especially as John Heffernan, who understudies the huge part of Konstantin, didn't want to do the line run either. However, it's still not good enough; it should have been compulsory or rearranged.

Have a quiet chat with Peter, who can be quite lovable. He has decided there is no future in his affair with Miss Malaysia.

Friday October 26th

Steve Leigh Morris describes us rather quaintly in the *LA Weekly* as '*a flotilla called The Pride of England, led by Captain Sir Ian McKellen,* but then goes on to liken Trevor's staging as '*being locked into an aesthetic prevalent between 1930 and 1960,*' and compares the RSC to the Moscow Art Theatre which clung on too long to the style of an era until it became an anachronism.

This is unfair and untrue. I saw the Moscow Arts perform in London in the early sixties: they were still doing the original productions with the same actors, growing old in the parts. This never happens at the RSC, where new directors and actors come in every year. And the RSC, for all its faults, is always experimenting; sometimes successfully, as with Rupert Goold's polar *Tempest* last year, sometimes disastrously as with this year's

Twelfth Night, with half the men's parts played by women for no apparent reason. Trevor also is always open to the latest technical aids. Witness his use of back projection as scenery in *The Stoppard Trilogy* and the use of audiovisual in his modern dress *Richard II* with Kevin Spacey that I did with him at the Old Vic. It is much easier to be progressive in small, intimate theatres. The *Macbeth* Trevor did with Ian and Judi Dench (still widely considered to be the best rendering of the play) was a small, experimental production. We are having to perform *Lear* in huge auditoriums; subtlety would be swallowed up in the void.

Take courtesy bus to Santa Monica and find an English bar that will be showing the Chelsea game at 7 tomorrow morning. Resolve to get up at 6.30 and get a taxi down.

At the theatre I am greatly surprised to find Zoë studying a script for a part in a horror film, for which she is being seen on Monday. Though a very attractive young girl, she has almost no professional experience, and it is not even as if they specially wanted an English girl – she is up for an American part – but good luck to her. Zoë definitely has perseverance, she may go far.

Many theatre actors based over here are in tonight. Ian is magnificent. Afterwards Ed Wilson, May Routh and many others come round and say how wonderful they think the whole production is. With all the unpleasantness and dissent I think we have forgotten that we have played *Lear* to packed houses on four continents, with universal standing ovations almost every night.

Saturday October 27*th*

Wake up at 5.45 and immediately decide to go back to sleep for another half-hour, before taking the taxi down to Santa Monica. Wake up again at 7.30 – it will be nearly half time. Turn on the Internet to check the score: Chelsea are already winning 2-0. Decide to conserve my energy and follow the game on my laptop in bed. 6-0 – I feel elated. Was the 'Special One' so special?

Gerald has been signed up by a manager – we don't get them

in England, only agents (which are bad enough). I think managers here sign every young talent they can in the hope of hitting the jackpot. Nevertheless, Gerald is going up for a couple of things next week, so he and Zoë are both staying on and have hired a convertible like a young Hollywood couple. I think Gerald could make it over here; with his dark good looks he could play any number of Latin types – I only wish him well. He is at heart a very nice man. It also proves Trevor was right in wanting the younger ones to be seen in LA – I hope Romola now sees it as worthwhile. Zoë, Ben Meyjes, Richard, Gerald, Philip and even Peter have all had meetings out here. Whether work will follow is a different matter.

No one is interested in an old actor though; my film career finished in 1967. Hal Wallis offered me a seven-year contract when I finished filming *Becket* in 1963, and my then agent told me to turn it down as she thought it would limit other offers. When the 'other offers' stopped coming in, I often regretted it. Dora, though, says it was the cleverest thing I've ever done: if I'd gone to Hollywood in 1963, with the drugs, sex and booze scene as it was then, I'd be long dead by now. When I think of the fate of my contemporaries, David Hemmings and Oliver Reed, she may well be right. Ian McShane and Michael York didn't do bad though.

Ian was very excited before the matinee, as Christopher Lee, whom Ian worked with on *Lord of the Rings* and admires tremendously (declaring that it is a travesty that he has not received a knighthood), had left a message on his voicemail requesting two tickets for this afternoon. Ian has left him two of his own tickets at the box office and has left a voice message on the number Lee gave him, telling him to come round after. I look forward to meeting Dracula. I've worked with three great icons of horror: Vincent Price, Peter Cushing and Lon Chaney, Jr and had a talk about cricket once with Boris Karloff in a lift in Notting Hill. Lee will complete the set.

At the end of the show there is the usual line of the great and good waiting to see Ian in the very cluttered dressing room he shares with Bill Gaunt. It stretches into the green room, where several of us are eating our sandwiches as we do not have time between the shows for a proper meal. Tom Hanks, who radiates stardom, is there with his wife and family, and takes the trouble to thank every one of us. Eva Marie Saint, with the same hairstyle she wore in *On the Waterfront* (a film that helped change my life), waits patiently in line. Next to her is a very odd looking couple: a seedy looking man in his fifties and a woman with very badly dyed red hair. When they get into the dressing room Ian has no idea who they are. The man tells Ian that he couldn't get a ticket so he rang him up impersonating Christopher Lee's dark, English voice. He then has the gall to ask Ian to sign several photos and books for him which Ian, being kind and polite, does. I'd have told the sod to piss off!

Sunday October 28th

Final performances of the tour: matinee of *Seagull* then *Lear*. There is an email from Trevor on the notice board, saying how proud he is of us and that he is looking forward to working with us again on the final lap in London. We are told that Denzel Washington, Danny de Vito, Sharon Stone, Jamie Lee Curtis, Orlando Bloom, and Mrs Jack Lemmon are all coming tonight.

Ian is in great form. All is going well until the awakening scene with Cordelia in last act. For weeks, I have sensed that Ian has been exasperated because Romola goes so slowly and looks out front for much of the scene, not at him. Tonight, as Lear, he gently puts his hand to her cheek and turns her face to his: I find it an affecting moment. I go to change so don't witness it, but apparently when they leave the stage Romola made it extremely clear that she didn't want Ian to do that to her again. It is very tense as he carries her on in the final scene and she doesn't look like a happy bunny at the curtain. It seems a fitting end to a tour that is gradually descending into chaos.

Afterwards at the final drinks party in the green room have a long chat with Mrs Jack Lemmon, a warm, motherly woman. I'm sure she thinks I'm Bill Gaunt but this time I don't care. I tell her I have spent my life watching her husband and always loved him – both our eyes fill with tears. I tell her about our hotel; she can't understand why UCLA have put us in such a terrible location. She says if she had known she would have arranged for us all to stay at various friends' guest houses on the beach. In general, there is little jollity around – most people have had enough of the tour and each other. It is very sad that we end like this, though there is still the London run and possibly the film to come. There's life in this epic yet. I wonder how it will end?

Monday October 29th

Some of the younger ones are staying on for few days to drive up the coast to San Francisco, Romola has already left for Tokyo for the premiere of *Atonement*, but most of us are flying to London on three separate flights. Nearly everyone wants to get home. As we drive to LAX in a minibus, Frances cries: "Not another f'ing sunny day." I too am missing '*autumn mists and mellow fruitfulness*', and have had enough of smog and wild fire smoke.

Very comfortable flight as I am lucky enough to have an empty seat next to me – nearly as good as the pods Ian and the other big spenders are tucked up inside in business class. Feel so nostalgic for England that I watch Branagh's *Henry V* for about the fourth time. It really is excellent – nearly as good as Olivier's in its way. Great watching so many of my old friends and colleagues: Michael Williams, Geoffrey Hutchings, Alec McCowen, Charlie Kay, Ian Holm, and Robert Stephens – only wished I could have taken part. Then watch *Vanity Fair*, mainly because I want to see how Julian Fellowes' script treats the novel. A disappointing film: Reese Witherspoon is not my idea of Becky Sharp. I'd forgotten Romola was in it. Bob Hoskins, Eileen

Atkins and James Purefoy are very good though.

London

Tuesday October 30th

Land in London, on a perfect autumn day. Dora meets me and although the M4 is very busy the traffic seems manageable after LA. Lovely to drive through Kensington, past old houses with people walking in the streets – am so glad to be back.

Spend a quiet day recovering, which is not helped by the after-effects of a flu jab.

Wednesday October 31st

Have dinner with Julian and Emma Fellowes at the Chelsea Brasserie and I really feel I am home. Receive first BAFTA film of the season: *Man in the Chair*. Christopher Plummer gives an outstanding performance. Why is it that older characters always seem the most fascinating?

Friday November 2nd

Get a visit from Fabian, our youngest grandchild, and we meet Spider, née Jose, his completely un-housetrained cocker spaniel puppy. I end up feeling more jet-lagged than ever.

Saturday November 3rd

Both boys and their families come for a welcome home lunch: I feel like a patriarch. Am so busy I almost fail to notice that Chelsea have beaten Wigan 2-0.

Sunday November 4th

Drive through a beautiful, autumnal London to John Fraser's

launch of his new novel *The Wild Beast May Break Them*. Simon
Callow and Vernon Dobcheff have already heard rumours of the
dissent on the tour. I fill in what may well be a few slightly biased
details and, being of my generation, they are subsequently
shocked.

Monday November 5ᵗʰ

Meet Roly Curram at BAFTA and see *American Gangster*. Our
new Bosch fridge has broken down and I think I had a dodgy
piece of bacon for breakfast, as I begin to suffer the effects of
food-poisoning halfway through. It is a very long, very graphic
film and every jab of the heroin needle – plus the cooking smells
wafting in from the restaurant – increases my nausea; I only just
make it to the end. Drive back through St James's Square and
along Pall Mall – the clubs blaze with light, chandeliers, stuccoed
ceilings, huge oil paintings of ex-members – then into the Mall
and before us the golden statue on top of the Victoria' Memorial
outside Buckingham Palace sparkles against the night sky. I
would rather be here than any other place on earth.

Tuesday November 6ᵗʰ

We spend a civilised and stimulating evening with literary agent
Andrew Lownie and his wife Angela. He is a remarkably well-
informed man – I'd forgotten there were more fascinating topics
than the theatre.

Wednesday November 7ᵗʰ

Go to see Chu Ombala, a dear friend (even though he is a fanatic
Spurs fan), in the first preview of Kwame Kwei-Armah's new
play, *Statement of Regret* at the Cottesloe. Realise how few plays
I've seen this year. Forgotten what a pleasure it is to go into the
Long Bar at the National with live music playing and see friends
and acquaintances around – how unlike the cold, car showroom

feel of the Guthrie. Play is excellent: completely fresh in its topicality and wonderfully acted by a talented black cast. Afterwards have drinks with them all in the green room. They are all so keen and friendly, a world away from the current state of the *Lear* company. It is amazing how quickly gossip spreads in the small world of the theatre: they have also heard about our troubles.

Thursday November 8th

Have lunch with a dozen of my oldest and dearest friends from Alleyn's School, all devoted followers of our English master Michael Croft, whom we helped found the National Youth Theatre more than 50 years ago. Only a couple from today's gathering – Richard Hampton and myself – became actors. Brian Croft became lighting designer for the Rolling Stones, Michael Hastings was one of the original Angry Men at the Royal Court, but most of them have gone through life having been enriched by the experience of working together on those plays so long ago. I contrast the philosophy that Michael Croft preached: loyalty to each other, the production and the play, with the events of the past weeks. I wonder how many of the *Lear* company I will want to socialise with in future years? On the other hand, I expect there are very few of them that will want to meet up with me.

See Patricia Hodge in *The Country Wife* at the Haymarket. Theatre and play are in complete contrast to *Statement of Regret* but equally enjoyable. Again one continues to be amazed at the diversity and huge pool of talent in the London Theatre, which must be unique in the world. David Haig is as emotionally committed to Pinchwife as Ian is to Lear, and I manage to understand the plot for the first time – even though I once played Pinchwife myself years ago! As Horner, Toby Stephens out-swashbuckles Errol Flynn. Afterwards we drink champagne with Patricia in Buckstone's historic haunted dressing room.

Friday November 9th

Go to Dulwich and watch five-year-old Jake play football. Even though he has the full kit, he's not quite ready for Chelsea yet.

Sunday November 11th

We go to Davina and Larry Belling's 40th wedding anniversary at Shoreditch House, the spanking new exclusive club in what was once one of the poorest areas of the East End. It is a wonderful, elegant affair in a huge, glass-sided room by a heated swimming pool, with magnificent views over the City. Many people have flown over from LA and New York. Meet a dowager with whom I think I attempted some sort of sexual congress in 1957.

In the evening we watch TV: David Haig is excellent again in a play about Kipling, which reminds me of a story my old friend Julian Holloway once told me. When his father, Stanley Holloway, was dying, Julian sat beside him and said: "Well, Dad, you've had a great life. Huge success on stage and in film and then, at the end, the biggest success of all in *My Fair Lady*. You can't have any regrets."

The old actor opened one eye and said: "Yes, I've got one."

"What was that Dad?" asked Julian, very concerned.

"That bugger, James Hayter, got the Mr Kipling cakes advert instead of me!"

Not looking forward to going back to rehearsal tomorrow – yet another venue. I'm sure Trevor has heard all about the troubles in Minneapolis. How will he handle it? What will happen when 'the King' meets up with his 'daughters' again?

Monday November 12th

Go to *Lear* rehearsals at the New London Theatre. Backstage smells of damp and stale vegetables, but the newly refurbished auditorium is a great space, ideal for both plays. We all mingle on stage; everybody seems glad to see each other again. To my surprise I am kissed by every female member of the company, apart from Romola. I am standing looking out into the blackness when I feel a grip around my shoulder: I am being 'Treved'. He is back, his hair is longer than ever and he has put on even more weight. The dashing, young D'Artagnan I first knew has moved through scholarly Aramis and worldly Athos to become a beaming, portly Porthos.

I find myself saying, "I've missed you."

"I've missed you all" is his wily reply. He goes around and dutifully hugs everyone. His production of *Rock 'N'Roll* has just opened in New York to excellent reviews, but unfortunately our hard-working former colleagues, the New York Stagehands' Union have called a strike. Broadway – apart from the Disney shows, who have made a separate deal – is dark and Trevor does not know how long his actors can wait: it may have to close. Fortune continues to shine on Julian Fellowes, though. *Mary Poppins* audiences had been falling off but now it is playing to capacity again, as there is hardly anything else to see. Julian's royalties will continue to flow.

Trevor then addresses us all and with great tact says that he will look at things that may have changed and be an honest broker. Ian tells me he and Romola have resolved their differences. She seems very quiet and goes where Trevor tells her without a murmur. I ask Ian if Monica has apologised. He says; "Of course not".

Am sharing a small dressing room with Guy and Seymour, to whom I always seem to be intrinsically bound. Guy remained in LA and stayed with Anthony Hopkins, who he became friendly with when they worked at the National years ago. He flew back to London with Sir Anthony on Paramount's private plane and had his own twin-bedded room. He lay in bed, sipping champagne, and looking through a big window watched the Aurora Borealis. At Heathrow there was no Immigration or Customs to go through and a fleet of seven silver cars were waiting on the tarmac to take the seven passengers on board wherever they were bound. He says Hopkins never travels by public airlines any more.

Claire-Louise Hardie, or CL, our hard-working wardrobe mistress tells me that Patrick Stewart was off for two performances as Macbeth last week with laryngitis. Her boyfriend, Robert Horwell, an excellent actor who I worked with at the National several years ago, is his understudy. He is also playing the important part of Ross. When the audience were told that Stewart would not be appearing there was a near-riot; many demanded their money back. The management refused, saying they had bought tickets to see the production, not the star. Apparently some people walked up Charing Cross Road giving their tickets away. I know Robert will have given a good account of the role, but in our celebrity-crazed age the punters are not interested in seeing a good stage performance from an unknown – they only want to see the face they have seen on screen. It would be even worse if I had to go on for Ian: I realise the role of understudy is even more thankless than I thought. Am very cheesed off. Walk through the buzz of Christmas-lit Covent Garden during the meal break and *'note the qualities of people.'*

Tuesday November 13th

Long day: 12 hours of technical rehearsal. Even after ten months, Trevor is full of fresh invention. He gives new little moves and discovers underlying moments. He gently coaxes Monica into adjusting her performance in the first half of the 'reason not the need' scene. He likewise tells Romola she must look at Ian after he wakes up. She complies without a murmur and immediately, to my mind, the scene becomes more moving.

Wednesday November 14th

Still rehearsing. Jonathan Hyde seems to question everything Trevor says. Eventually Trevor loses his temper and asks him if he wants to direct the play. Trevor appears to have a shorter fuse than normal. Ian, by contrast, is very quiet and says hardly anything. I wish the two of them would stand together; it would solve many problems.

Backstage I am disturbed to hear complaints that Trevor will not allow any invention but his own. I have never found this before, quite the opposite. He usually welcomes fresh bits of business – anything to give more texture and reality, as long as it helps his vision of the play. Anyway, I usually assume that perhaps he knows more about the play than I do.

Thursday November 15th

During the past weeks of the tour, Guy has invented a bit of business in which he plays Russian Roulette with Kent whilst Kent is in the stocks. At notes Trevor tells him to cut it. Guy begins to argue and Trevor, quite rightly, says no. Things are clearly not sorting themselves out as smoothly as I hoped. Trevor tells me that the Gentleman is becoming older than Lear in certain scenes (quite right, I am a year older, but I am always grateful for a note); at least it shows he has noticed me. I adapt accordingly.

Our first performance on our last lap of the tour and the London audience seems very hard to please. As I sit at the back of the stage in the first scene I can see glowering faces in the front row. They look more European than English. Unlike the Americans, they are not eager to laugh. Trevor's notes have improved several performances, especially Frances who is now back to form, but it is not one of our very best. Good reception at the curtain, although only a few of the younger people get to their feet. Maybe Dustin Hoffman was right after all.

Friday November 16th

Dora brings Mia to see *Romeo and Juliet* at Covent Garden. Since we've been away, it is no longer possible to put coins in parking meters and I cannot work out the complicated credit card procedure in the dark. The only alternative is to try to do it by text or punching numerous digits into my mobile phone. Give up and tell Dora to wait on a single yellow line until 6.30.

Lear goes much better tonight and as one the English rise to their feet. In fact, they call us back for an extra call – something we have only done a handful of times throughout the year.

Go back to car to meet Dora and Mia and find a £60 parking fine stuck to the windscreen. Dora had left the car three minutes early, at 6.27. It is hardly going to encourage people to go to the theatre – does Westminster City Council realise how much money the hard-pressed theatres generate? The restaurants, shops and bars all depend on the theatre trade – not to mention the general tourist industry. All they seem interested in is grabbing money at the slightest opportunity.

Saturday November 17th

Tonight is the 100th performance of *Lear*. There is a letter on everyone's dressing table. I expect it to be a congratulatory note on reaching such a landmark – it turns out to be a confidential letter from Trevor thanking us for our hard work but addressing the recent friction. I read it and am genuinely touched by Trevor's humility and am therefore amazed to find some people sneering at it derogatorily. I am lost for words: this really has become the most dysfunctional company I've ever been part of.

I listen to Bill's words as Gloucester over the Tannoy, tonight they seem to have added meaning: '*Love cools, friendship falls off…We have seen the best of our time: machinations, hollowness, and all ruinous disorders follow us disquietly to our graves. 'Tis strange.*'

Nevertheless, Ian leads us in a great show and Susie Sainsbury provides the cast with champagne for the 100th performance. I leave mine untouched. Like Marlene Dietrich: I want to be alone.

Sunday November 18th

Feel very down in the dumps. After much soul-searching, I decide to write Trevor a letter of support. I read it and wonder if he will just think I am an old sycophantic flatterer, desperate to be given another job. But I really mean it – and I don't really care if I never work again.

I spend all night debating whether I should send it.

Monday November 19th

Back to *Seagull*. After even more soul-searching, I finally hand my letter to Trevor to the stage doorkeeper (a lovely black guy who often has the only smiling face in the entire building). We spend another three days re-rehearsing. Trevor makes the speaking cast do one run-through very quietly, without any projection – trying to get back to the truth. As I have so little to do, I retreat to my dressing room whenever possible and engross myself in John Fraser's novel.

Wednesday November 21st

Pass Trevor in the corridor. He nods but doesn't mention my letter – does he think I am a crawler?

The big England game is on and there is not a television set in the entire theatre. Listen to the debacle in my overheated, cell-like dressing room during the dress rehearsal. At the interval I go into the auditorium where Trevor is sitting alone at his production desk and tell him we are 2-0 down. His face wrinkles as if in pain. He also is an ardent follower of football (he supported his local club, Ipswich Town, as a boy and worshipped the great Alf Ramsey). England manage to equalise, but eventually lose 2-3 to Croatia. We are out of the European Championships and McClaren must go.

Thursday November 22nd

Seagull opens but notes and rehearsals continue. The more subtle playing that Trevor has been encouraging (such as not going for deliberate laughs) improves things, but I sense the cast still do not act together: it is more a series of performances seeking the limelight. It is very well-received but, despite Frances' vibrant Arkadina, to my mind it is now little better than a good Rep production. I keep my thoughts to myself.

Saturday November 24th

We are doing the long-awaited, public understudy run of *Lear* on December 11th. Gemma puts up a long rehearsal schedule. As excited as I am to attempt Lear one more time, I think that maybe word runs would be enough. The rest of the cast are split: Russell wants to rehearse as much as possible, but Melanie (who in fairness has played Goneril so many times) doesn't want to rehearse at all. John Heffernan, Julian and Seymour are also reluctant, particularly as they will have rehearsals for the understudy run of *Seagull* as well. What is wrong with everybody? Why are they not thrilled to have the chance of being seen performing great roles on a London stage?

Monday November 26th

People are now sleeping outside the theatre overnight to be first in line for returns for *Lear*.

We have our final press nights this week – *Seagull* on Tuesday and *Lear* on Wednesday. The National has broken the agreement and has arranged for Katie Mitchell's *Trojan Women* to open on Wednesday as well – Trevor is convinced most of the press will go to that as it is a brand new production. He therefore thinks some of the critics will sneak into *Lear* tonight. He holds yet another note session wearing the tightest and most ragged pair of old jeans. When someone remarks on them he explains they are his lucky jeans, which he always wears on first nights. I nod sympathetically and state that I have a pair of lucky blue underpants I always wear when I go to watch Chelsea – Trevor sniffs.

Still no definite news about the film – I think we can forget it.

Trevor's notes have had their effect: the performance goes well, but I feel it is not one of Ian's best.

Tuesday November 27th

Final press night of *Seagull*. It seems very strange having a first night after 11 months. Cards and flowers arrive at the stage door; dressing-room visits from a somewhat charisma-lacking Michael Boyd, wishing us good luck; family and friends, agents and critics are all out front. Ian has generously given this first night to Bill, who plays Sorin very well and in fact gets as many if not more laughs than Ian in the early part of the play. Overall, it goes reasonably well, but the excitement of *Lear* is missing and it is not a sophisticated first night audience. There seem to be large numbers of American students. Has the RSC papered it? A party has been laid on in the theatre bar but Dora and I go to Joe Allen's with Hugh Futcher, who accompanied Dora to the play. They both saw the play back in its early stages at Stratford and still thought Frances was superb, but were disappointed with the production as a whole. They felt it had lost something in the vast theatres on its long journey round the world. Am surprised to see Nicholas de Jongh, sitting with a lady at a corner table. Why is he not writing his review? Assume that as he did it at Stratford, one of the minor critics from the *Standard* is covering it tonight. Hugh is auditioning for a six-month minor tour of *The Dresser*, with three weeks' rehearsal in Sheffield. He suggests I apply for the Albert Finney role of the old actor manager. It is a part I would love to play (I would do it in a pub theatre in London for nothing), but to quote Jack Nicholson; '*I would rather stick needles in my eyes than face another six months on the road*'.

Wednesday November 28ᵗʰ

De Jongh has reviewed *Seagull* after all and still insists that
Romola is the glory of the production, which he thinks has lost its
way since Stratford. When did he find the time to write it?
Quentin Letts (why does *The Mail* employ its parliamentary
correspondent as theatre critic?) finds *Seagull* long and tedious
and mounts a seemingly-personal attack on poor old Bill in the
minor part of Sorin.

The supposed press night of *Lear* is one of Ian's very best.
Even after 104 performances I am moved to tears three times on
Lear's journey. As we come off stage at the curtain, Ian mutters,
"Pity we didn't do it like that on Monday, when the press were
really in."

Thursday November 29ᵗʰ

Benedict Nightingale gives *Lear* five stars in *The Times*:

> '*This is a superlative performance from McKellen that has lost
> nothing with its transfer from Stratford to London. Its centre is Lear's
> question: "Is there any cause in nature that makes these hard hearts?" At
> the time the white bearded king is putting a stool on trial in the belief that
> it is his daughter Goneril. But McKellen delivers the line gently, quietly,
> and lingers over the word "hearts" in a wondering, interrogative way, as
> if belatedly discovering that such an organ exists – and exists in him.*
>
> *Above all, McKellen manages to exude vindictive fury while finding
> in himself a concern, a care, a love that's evident when he kisses Sylvester
> McCoy's bumbling old Fool, or cradles William Gaunt's sobbing
> Gloucester, or, now radiating a touching simplicity, is reconciled with
> Romola Garai's sturdy Cordelia. And the scene with her corpse is
> hauntingly true, with Lear's fatalistic repetitions of "never" resounding
> like the muffled bells at a funeral.*'

Guy goes to a funeral in Devon and gets stuck in a traffic jam
on the M4 and fails to get back to the theatre on time. Big Adam

takes over Cornwall and does very well – am pleased he seems to be happy again.

Friday November 30th

Drag myself in to rehearse understudies and find Peter is not there – it seems he hadn't read the board. Zoë, apparently, doesn't want to do two understudy performances and so there will be no understudy run of *Seagull*. I can't believe that she would forgo a chance to play Nina, which should be every young actress's dream. Melanie doesn't want to rehearse at all, but magnanimously says she will turn up on the day. I wonder if she would behave the same way if she had not had the chance to play her roles so many times because of Frances' accident? Nevertheless it feels good to act Lear's lines again.

Seymour is off with a bad back, but as it's *Seagull*, nobody really misses him.

Emil comes up from Byfleet to play football and so we have Mia, Fabian and the still unhousetrained Spider overnight – just what we need with a big party on Sunday.

Saturday December 1st

It's catching: Russell is off tonight with gout. Gout! How can you have gout with a body like Adonis?

Talk to Ian in his dressing room. He is upset that so many people are off sick. He tells me when he was playing Richard III in Washington, they had to bring him in a wheelchair to the wings, but as soon as he walked on stage the part took over and he no longer felt ill. David Suchet is the same – I heard that when he was playing Salieri at the Old Vic he had such terrible stomach problems that he had to sit on a bucket in the wings every time he came offstage, but never missed an entrance. I know Ian will never be off – unless he is trapped in the tube or knocked down by a bus. As we get ever nearer to the end of the run, I find my desire to play Lear, just once, before a full house, increasing. But

I know this will never happen: I will have to be content with the final understudy run on December 11th.

Sunday December 2nd

Today is Dora's annual 'December Bagel Brunch'. Get up early and pick up the specially ordered mini-bagels from Brick Lane. Nearly all our favourite friends attend: Julian and Emma Fellowes, Patricia Hodge, Roly Curram, the Dorfmans, Martin Jarvis and Rosalind Ayres, Davina and Larry Belling, David Warner, Nobby Clark, Henry Goodman, Olly Cotton, Wayne Eagling, Bill Gaunt and Carolyn and our Singapore producer Gaurav Kripalani, who has just flown in. Ian arrives after appearing on Michael Parkinson's final radio show. Frances was supposed to accompany him, but is not feeling well. Ian, though, is in top form. He and David Warner are among the last to leave: Lear and Falstaff sit on the sofa and contemplate life with the RSC: Nobby captures the moment on camera.

Monday December 3rd

My favourite time of the year: every day, BAFTA members receive invitations to screenings or are sent DVDs of movies to judge. Watch *Michael Clayton* this afternoon – definitely one for the shortlist.

It is becoming an epidemic: now Philip and Frances are off. Peter seizes his chance like an eager puppy and does very well. Over half of the understudies have now been on – but Ian will never be off. Dora thought he looked fittest of all at the party on Sunday. Eileen Atkins and Patrick Stewart are in tonight. I wonder what Ian thinks about the *Evening Standard* describing Stewart as '*probably our finest Shakespearian*'? There is yet another reception after *Lear* organised by Susie Sainsbury, for major donors to the RSC at the Theatre Royal Drury Lane. Can't face it.

Tuesday December 4th

Learn that Jeffrey Archer was at the reception last night looking for me. I phone him and he asks: "Where were you? Kept thinking I saw you, but every time it turned out to be the man playing Gloucester."

Spend afternoon watching *Eastern Promises*.

Frances is off and will be for the rest of the week. Melanie will take over both her parts. I can't blame her now for not wanting to rehearse.

Wednesday December 5th

Richard Goulding has already got a job after this: a very good part in the new Ronald Harwood play that is being done at Watford – lucky boy. Guy went to see Declan Donnellan about a European tour of *Troilus & Cressida* with his world-renowned company, *Cheek by Jowl*. Donnellan told him he had just been interviewed by a very young man from the Arts Council regarding future funding. The young man had had the temerity to tell Donnellan to send him some of his reviews, and to ask what he was planning to do towards Muslim understanding. The world is going mad – but perhaps it was ever thus. I remember a story of the formidable Martita Hunt once being asked by an American director what she had done. She replied: "You mean this morning?" (I myself was standing next to her on the set of *Becket,* when the 2nd assistant informed her that her car would pick her up the following morning at 7.30. She replied: "Young man, my bowels do not move before 9." Apart from perhaps Dame Maggie Smith, they don't make them like that any more.)

Thursday December 6th

We do a full understudy rehearsal of *Lear*. Everyone turns up, apart from Melanie who now, of course, has more than enough on her plate. Goes quite well and am relieved I still know it, as do most of the others. Really looking forward to next Tuesday – it will be my final chance of playing *Lear*. I've managed to get quite a large number of people to come and witness it, including friends who didn't get to see it in Stratford, some elderly cousins, and more than a hundred present members of the National Youth Theatre. Even my agent has roused herself and has persuaded the casting director of the Donmar to come along. It may be a way of getting into Jude Law's *Hamlet*.

Very tired, after doing Lear in the afternoon and the Gentleman in the evening. Peter spends a lot of time spewing into a bucket in the wings – will he be the next to be off?

Friday December 7th

Seymour and Richard are off for *Seagull* tonight. Richard Clayton, our company manager, has been off all week with flu; Ben Delfont, our stage manager, has been off for half the week. Who is running the shop? There is a very slap-happy atmosphere. Ian continues to carry the company, no matter who is off.

Saturday December 8th

Seymour, John Heffernan and Frances are off for the *Seagull* matinee and Romola doesn't feel well so is off for *Lear* in the evening. We have six people on who are not in their original parts: Richard is the King of France, Ben Addis is Oswald, Melanie continues as Goneril, Zoë as Cordelia, Naomi as the Countrywoman and Gemma, our ever industrious and conscientious assistant director, has to appear as the non-speaking Lady in Waiting. Gerald jokes: "Six people are off and I still don't have a bloody line."

Ian gives another great performance – it doesn't seem to matter who he delivers his lines to. Bill (now fully recovered), Jonathan and Sylvester are a solid basis around him – and perhaps, in a small way, so am I – and every one of us is over 60. I am staggered at the apparent lack of stamina in the young; I have only been off for one performance throughout my whole 47-year career. That was the night I broke my wrist playing Hotspur at the Ludlow Festival in 1970 and had to go to have it set in London. I came back the next night and played the rest of the run with my arm in plaster and a sling. That's what I was brought up to believe: you have a responsibility to the audience, who have spent hard-earned money to see the best you can offer. Besides, I would never want my understudy to go on, in case he was better than me!

Seymour comes in to do *Lear* in the evening. He has seemed to be morose all week, on the days he has been here, and leaves the dressing room muttering something like: "It's too much, they're all tired. There won't be any understudy runs next week." What does he mean? We are only doing eight shows a week; the same as any show in the West End. Moreover, most of us do hardly anything in *Seagull*. I now have over 100 people coming. I go down to see if there is any notice on the board, but the schedule remains as it was. Does Seymour know something I don't?

Sunday December 9*th*

Spend Sunday going over Lear – probably for the final time – but there is a niggling doubt at the back of my mind. Surely Seymour was just pissed off. If he had known anything he would have told me properly – or someone in authority would have said something?

Monday December 10*th*

To put my mind at rest I ring Gemma and ask her if the understudy run is still on for tomorrow – she says of course it is. Feel very relieved.

As I'm crossing the road to go into the theatre to do my Butler in *Seagull*, Ian appears and suggests we have a cup of tea in the café opposite. He does not know when Frances will be back.

After chatting about mutual acquaintances, the way old actors do, we cross over to the stage door at 6.28 to find Ben Delfont putting us in the book for being three minutes late. I think it's a bit rich – Ben was not even here for much of last week. Ben tells me that Julian is off tonight and to go up to the stage as there is a meeting for all of the understudies. I go up and find them all sitting in the stalls as the resurrected Richard Clayton addresses them. He begins by saying in a faltering voice that, as so many people have been ill and others are tired and no longer want to do it, he has decided to cancel the understudy run. I explode: "Why have you left this to the last minute? How can I inform all the kids from the NYT that are coming tomorrow?"

I look towards Gemma but she lowers her head. I feel like someone who has trained for months for the marathon being pulled up at the start, and this time I am really ready. I know it is the only chance I will ever have of doing Lear again. A red mist descends upon me: I turn to Melanie, who is the only person who has reason to plead tiredness, and John Heffernan, who has said he does not want to risk getting wet by playing Edgar, and let fly. I tell them I am sick of being with so many lazy, self-centred people. Russell and Peter are desperate for work after this and have been relying on the run to help them get it. Russell hasn't even got an agent. I remember Seymour's comments on Saturday night and say: "You obviously knew this was being discussed; why didn't you have the decency to tell me properly on Saturday night? I would have had time to cancel the people coming and not spent yesterday working on it!"

I storm off to my dressing room. Russell is desperate and still tries to persuade them. The ubiquitous Gemma could easily do Goneril if Melanie is too tired, and Guy has already offered to read Kent if Julian is still ill tomorrow, and if John Heffernan is afraid of getting wet, there is no need for the rain to be turned on. How can he consider himself a serious actor when he turns down the chance to play a part like Edgar before an audience? I still have the first night cards from Stratford around my dressing table mirror. John's card and words are in front of me: '*I really hope we get the chance to do the play again. Your performance deserves to be seen*'. I find the irony hard to believe. Even though Peter, Russell, Ben Addis and Naomi still want to do it, our management opts for the easy way out and cancels, even though the RSC will have to pay all the technicians and stagehands for the extra performance, as it has been cancelled without 24 hours' notice.

I sit and fume before I begin to wonder if I am over-reacting. Am I being pathetic? Getting so het up over saying a few lines of Shakespeare to a hundred or so people? I am grateful when Naomi comes in to my dressing room and says she agrees with everything I said. Then Ian comes in and says how sorry he is. I tell him I am worried about all the NYT kids coming to London tomorrow, who I won't be able to get in touch with. He then suggests that he comes in, even though he is playing Lear that evening, and we'll put something together for them. It is typical of this kind, generous man. Peter, Russell and even Zoë, perhaps shocked by my outburst, also offer to take part.

I spend the evening calling all the people I can reach, telling them not to come.

Tuesday December 11th

I arrive at the theatre early and take Dora up to my dressing room to collect my script. She is appalled by the filth and smell. Richard Clayton unexpectedly appears and Dora demands to know why he allows actors to work in such conditions? He has done his job well and efficiently throughout the year but seems to have had enough. He departs hastily, exclaiming: "I can't take this!"

Even though the theatre has been informed that the audience are not to be turned away, when I get to the front of house at 12.45, I am told that the understudy run has been cancelled. I stand in the lobby and point the kids, plus a few people who I had forgotten were coming, up the stairs. At 1pm I stand on stage and face an audience of well over 100; Ian has not arrived and I'm not sure if he has remembered. I've rung his mobile but can't get through. I begin addressing the kids, explaining why they won't be seeing a full performance of *King Lear*. I then launch into the beliefs that were drummed into us by Michael Croft when we first founded the Youth Theatre in 1956. I glance out of the corner of my eye and am touched to see that five of the original founder members are sitting in the front row. I say that Michael Croft believed in loyalty to the play, the production, your fellow actors and your audience, and that if you don't have these qualities you shouldn't be in this profession. The curtain stirs and Sir Ian walks through it dressed in a baseball cap and carrying a vegetarian sandwich.

For the next two hours, the audience is treated to a master class in Shakespearean acting as Ian goes through the play, quite brilliantly, assisted by Russell, Peter and Zoë. He tells them why he does it differently every night – that nothing is the same, that each time we boil an egg, we do it differently; he never stops searching the text for meaning and truth. The first scene is about an old father giving away his favourite daughter on her wedding day. How many fathers have said to their daughters in the car on the way to church: "Do you still love me most?" He also tells them he wears two wedding rings as Lear, because in his mind Cordelia is the daughter of his second wife who died giving birth to her. I link the scenes and keep them amused with some of my favourite anecdotes. It is a huge success and we get a wonderful response at the end: but it is not the same as playing Lear.

Seymour arrives in the dressing room in the evening and says he is expecting me to apologise.

I say: "What have I to apologise for?"

We ignore each other like two grumpy old men for the rest of the evening.

Wednesday December 12th

Tony French's daughter rings to tell me he died in the night. Am so glad I made the journey to Worksop in the summer.

Matinee of *Lear* followed by *Seagull*: a long, awkward day. Melanie comes into our dressing room to make her tea with our kettle. I am astonished to find myself saying: "I'd have thought that, with all the extra money you're getting from these understudy performances that are tiring you out so much, you could afford to buy your own bloody kettle."

Seymour continues to ignore me, even though he sits next to me for much of the day. I learn that the dressers knew on Saturday night the understudy run would be cancelled – the actors were saying that they didn't want to do it. I am angry again: it seems so disrespectful that nobody bothered to inform me.

This job has definitely gone on too long, but there is talk of the film once more. The stage management have been re-checked for their availability for the two weeks after January 15th. Apparently the producers only need another £250,000.

Saturday December 15th

Neil Kinnock (surprised there is only a small laugh on the 'scurvy politician' line), Sting and Martin Jarvis all come for the matinee, plus the multilingual Vernon Dobcheff: the only actor to be out of work in four countries. Vernon asks me if I'd persuaded Trevor to combine several parts into the Gentleman as I never seemed to be off the stage.

Sunday December 16th

Take two grandchildren and a neurotic dog to a Christmas fair in Hyde Park. Visit Father Christmas, whose face beneath the whiskers seems rather familiar. I wonder if he's some poor sod of an actor I once worked with. Reminds me of another Olivier story Lewis Feander told me back in Australia:

At the first Christmas at the Old Vic, Lewis was put in charge
of the organising the actors' children's party. He realised they had
nobody to play Father Christmas.

He knocked at Olivier's door as he was making up for *Othello*.

"Come in! Dear boy, what can I do for you?"

"Well, Sir Laurence, I am organising the Christmas party..."

"Of course dear boy, shall I write you a cheque?"

"No Sir Laurence. We have enough money, but there is a
role that must be filled."

He paused whilst powdering his brow. "A role? What role?"

"Father Christmas."

"Saint Nicholas? The role demands a beard?"

"Yes, Sir Laurence."

"And a robe? A red robe?"

"Yes, Sir Laurence."

"And boots? I suppose I could wear my Vanya boots?"

"Yes, Sir Laurence."

"And a nose? Saint Nicholas would have a prominent, red
nose."

"I suppose so, Sir Laurence."

"Very well, I will accept."

A few days later, Lewis met Joan Plowright in the corridor:
"What have you done? He wakes up in the middle of the night,
crying 'Ho! Ho! Ho!'" On the day of the party, a grotesque, bent
figure arrived with a hugely deformed red nose, crying, "Ho! Ho!
Ho!" in the voice of Richard III. The children were too terrified
to go up for their presents.

Monday December 17*th*

Frances is back and there is immediately more life back on stage.
Michael Boyd is coming into the theatre tomorrow to listen to
what people have to say about their time with the RSC. After
much soul-searching, I put my name down for an appointment.

Tuesday December 18th

Michael Boyd is a good listener. I tell him, perhaps somewhat pompously, that in my entire career I have never been in such a company. They seemed to turn against Ian and Trevor, be off sick at the drop of a hat and then some of them decided they didn't want to do the understudy run, the night before we are due to do it. In my opinion, they appear to have no respect for the production, the director or their fellow actors. He asks me to tell him what happened in Minneapolis, and I give him the entire story as I saw it: that Ian did indeed push an actress on stage but it was not vicious and was all part of his performance. I cannot understand why anyone should have objected. Boyd says he is very sorry about the understudy run and is going to make sure that another date is fixed for it – I tell him I don't expect the others will want to do it, and I'm not all that keen now to do it myself.

I decide I have misjudged him. He is a decent man and has done a good job, turning the RSC around after Adrian Noble (but I still don't agree with the incinerator tower at Stratford).

Wednesday December 19th

Watch *Atonement* for BAFTA awards: one of the best this year. Romola is very effective in it. Fascinating shot of her washing a pile of bedpans.

At the theatre Richard Clayton calls a meeting of all 13 understudies, to decide whether we should attempt another run on January 4th. I speak first and say I don't want to do it. I am completely certain I could play Lear if Ian is off in the remaining few weeks – which he will never be unless he is knocked down by a bus – and I don't want to go through all the heartache and hassle of rehearsing and getting an audience together again. I'm not sure I could face the disappointment of another cancellation, besides, there is no chance of any agents or casting directors coming to see it, because it is in the middle of the Christmas break and they won't be back in their offices until the following Monday.

Russell pleads desperately that we do it: he still hasn't got an agent. Richard Clayton suggests that perhaps we can do it in the penultimate week, on January 11th. Then Seymour, who I'm sure had been expecting me to want to do it, pipes up with what sounds like a carefully prepared speech. "I went round last night and people were saying they didn't want to come to this meeting. Some were thinking of wearing protective vests: they were afraid of being bullied into agreeing to do another run. We should have a secret ballot without pressure. I have prepared voting slips."

I say it is a brilliant idea, take a slip and clearly write 'No'. When Richard counts the votes, I am completely gob smacked that they are 10-3 in favour of doing it. I suspect it is the fact that they all feel sorry for Russell. I don't know whether I'm pleased or not. I don't fancy the sweat of preparing for it all over again, but on the other hand I will get one final attempt at Lear.

Thursday December 20th

My agent rings: the film offer has come through at last. One week of rehearsal, two weeks filming for a fee of £2,500 and no residual rights or payments for the first seven years. On top of that, I have to make my own way to Slough each morning, where a minibus will pick us up and take us to Pinewood. We are also asked to forgo the European Treaty on maximum working hours. The leading characters will be on a different deal. I didn't expect Hollywood money but this is ridiculous – we decide that I will definitely not accept on those terms. The filming will go on to till seven o'clock at night and there is no way I am going to make my own way home then. I won't be back until about nine and then have to get up at five the next morning. We say no and await further developments – but the producers have left everything so late; everything will close down until after the New Year from tomorrow.

I do not enjoy going to the theatre in the evening any more. All through the years I have looked forward to joking and sharing gossip and old anecdotes with my fellow actors. I cannot believe it – what has happened to me? Is it time to call it a day?

Evening Standard charity auction closed this evening: two tickets for Ian McKellen's *Lear* go for £300, whilst two tickets to see Ewan McGregor in *Othello's* sold-out, twelve-week run at the Donmar go for £1,020. Have we passed our sell-by date?

Everyone in the company receives a Christmas present from Ian: a big box containing a bottle of dessert wine and a gourmet sticky toffee pudding.

Friday December 21st

Throughout the day, my agent is unable to contact the producer of the film, who appears to work out of a mobile phone.

In the evening, as I walk through Covent Garden, I spy a grey-painted living statue of Gandalf, with a bowl of coins at his feet. I wouldn't have thought Ian needed to do that – the rumour is that he is getting £20million for the new *Hobbit* film.

For the first time in weeks, Melanie makes an effort to talk to me; I decide to bury the hatchet and we resume relations by discussing the fortunes of Tottenham Hotspur. Nobody mentions the money or the dreadful deal we have been offered. Naomi's agent has heard a rumour that Channel 4 has pulled out – I am very relieved: it will save a lot of hassle. I don't want to do it on the terms offered, but I don't want to let down Ian or Trevor. The latest rumour is they are both doing it for free.

Saturday December 22nd

By pure coincidence, I receive a cheque for £249 from the BBC for world sales on the DVD of Michael Hordern's *Lear,* in which I played the Duke of Burgundy over 20 years ago. I am more certain than ever that we are being offered a ridiculous deal. I have always made it a principle never to discuss money or contracts with my fellow actors – it only leads to discontent and envy – but decide I must talk it over with Guy as he is the Equity Rep. He knows no more than me and we decide to call a company meeting after the matinee.

I am surprised that nobody seems to know much about the details of the deal. We agree that we must ask for transport and that food must be provided, as we may well be on the set for over ten hours. Everyone must negotiate their own deal as far as money goes.

As I expected, John Heffernan has landed on his feet. The RSC has offered him Laertes in Dr Who's *Hamlet*, but he has accepted instead the juvenile part in Nicholas Hytner's new production of *Major Barbara* at the National.

A message comes over the Tannoy that there are some Christmas goodies from Trevor in the green room. I go up expecting a Fortnum's hamper, but discover a rather small box of mince pies. So glad we've got four nights off over Christmas, am beginning to feel as if I am running on empty.

Christmas Day

Dora and I spend Christmas with Emil, his family and still un-housetrained dog in their new, yet-to-be modernised house in Binfield and realise how lucky we are. Get a glimpse of my young self in *The Heroes of Telemark*, which is shown practically every Christmas and for which, unlike Hollywood actors, we poor English saps do not get a penny. The producers of the film were never happy with the title and whilst we were on location in Norway offered £100, a decent sum in 1964, for a better one. My unsuccessful suggestion was *Carry on Kirk*. Throughout the four months we spent making that film Kirk Douglas and Richard Harris didn't get on. Douglas, then approaching 50, was getting near the end of his career as a macho Hollywood leading man, and regarded the up and coming Harris with suspicion. Harris had a very combative nature – he told me tales of his previous quarrels with other co-stars such as Charlton Heston and Marlon Brando. Brando even wore cotton wool in ears when they did a scene so that Harris's voice wouldn't contaminate his performance.

Douglas and Harris first met when we were filming on a boat in Weymouth harbour, which was standing in for Norway. I was standing between them. Douglas gave Harris the hard stare and said: "Are you go gonna be as difficult as they say you are?"

Harris returned his stare and replied: "Are you gonna be as big a **** as they say you are?"

From that point each tried to be a bigger Hero of Telemark than the other – their stunt doubles hardly had a day off. There were seven more of us on that raid, but we hardly got a look in. Another rejected title was: *The Insignificant Seven.* One day Kirk looked at me and said: "I've been watching you. You're a good actor. We should build up your part in this picture: you should get killed!"

And killed I was, even though my character was supposed to go through to the end of the film. Kirk had two good little scenes though: one going back under German fire to make sure I was dead, and another telling Harris I'd been shot.

Boxing Day

Get back in time to go to Stamford Bridge for my first Chelsea game of the season: a 4-4 draw with Aston Villa. Couldn't have picked a more exciting one – although Grant cannot change the course of a game with his substitutions as Mourinho could.

Thursday December 27th

Back to the theatre. I ask Ian if he had a good Christmas: he shrugs and says it was OK. I wish he could find a permanent partner. He has the world at his feet, friends and worshippers galore, but I think he is often lonely.

Friday December 28th

Still plugging away at the BAFTA films. There seem fewer remarkable films than last year. The Supporting Actress category (why do all these female actors suddenly revert back to being actresses at award times?) is particularly thin. I think Romola may well get a nomination for *Atonement.*

Hear that Seymour's wife has been unwell. This explains his tetchiness. I feel petty and small and speak to him for the first time in weeks, to say how sorry I am.

Saturday December 29th

The final performance of the year. Wonderful news: Ian is named a 'Companion of Honour' in the New Year honours list 'for services to Drama and Equality'. It's second only to the Garter and even Scofield – who steadfastly refused a knighthood – accepted it. Nobody deserves it more than Ian; throughout this year he has been an 'honourable companion' in every sense – my personal admiration of him has grown tenfold. Throughout all the troubles he has kept his dignity and has constantly striven to achieve perfection in his performance. I read somewhere that he believes that if the audience could only see the story the way Shakespeare wrote it, their lives may be changed for the better: not a bad ambition. At the curtain call, all the cast join the audience in applauding him: it is the perfect climax to 2007.

Monday December 31st

Dora and I follow our custom and spend New Year's Eve reflecting at home with a bottle of champagne, being thankful for the good life and health that we share. There certainly is a lot to reflect upon.

2008

Tuesday January 1*st*

The New Year starts badly. Bit on an almond last night and split open one of my few remaining back teeth. Now there is a jagged edge on which my tongue rubs every time I speak, and I can't see the dentist until tomorrow. It will be the most expensive nut I've ever cracked.

Take Dora to Heathrow: she's going to Israel for ten days to visit friends. It's not much fun for her in the evenings when I am working every night.

Better atmosphere in the dressing room. Seymour is now speaking to me. Decide he's not such a bad old stick really. Everybody seems to assume we are doing the film, but I have reluctantly decided that I won't do it unless I am picked by car and get at least £3,500. I will be on-call all the time and I know I make a contribution towards every scene I'm in.

Wednesday January 2*nd*

Get up early and go to dentist, who takes out the remains of my tooth.

Am very lonely and depressed at home without the noise and energy of Dora. Furious with my agent: I've paid her 12.5 % all year, for a job I got myself and now she says she will be too busy to see me do Lear next week. I lose my temper and tell her to be there, though what good she will do is a matter for debate. On top of that, when I tell her of my concerns about the film she says: "Oh, I didn't think you were going to do it." I sense it's time for a change, but I can't face up to the hassle of looking for a new one. As the old actor said, 'Swapping agents, at this point in your career, is like swapping deckchairs on the Titanic.'

At the theatre I hear: "Happy New Year, David", and catch a fleeting glimpse of a fit-looking Trevor getting in to the lift, presumably off to see Ian. Better relations continue to be evident backstage – could be because we are no longer confined to each other's company. In London we all have friends and lives outside of our tight little circle. Or is it simply the New Year? The reallocated understudy run is now accepted by all; I feel much more positive about it now – it will be good to have one final stab at playing the old King. Go over my Lear lines with Russell, Julian, John Heffernan and Naomi.

Thursday January 3rd

Trevor has called a meeting to discuss the film for 5pm tomorrow. It all seems a *fait accompli*. Ian tells me Trevor is horrified that we are not going to get transport to Pinewood – he is sure something will be done about it.

As I am eating a lonely supper of Shredded Wheat, one of the front teeth on my plate breaks off. I'm falling apart.

Friday January 4th

Groundhog Day: once more we sit in the stalls listening to Trevor. He tells us that it has been so hard to raise the money for the film, as nobody wants to film stage adaptations any more. I ask why, when there are now so many channels crying out for new programmes. He replies that television executives are reluctant to commission Shakespeare because it always gets poor ratings and they are scared of losing their jobs. *Lear* will only be filmed because it will be shown on Channel 4 here and the public service channel, Thirteen, in America. To raise the money all the TV and video rights have been sold for seven years. We tell him we are not happy and he promises to take it up with the producers. He is also going to have to cut the text by 250 lines, to fit the play into two and a half hours. I fear the Gentleman will become even more insignificant.

Dora rings me – the weather is bad and she wants to see my Lear so she is coming back tomorrow night. I'm very pleased.

Saturday January 5th

Receive email from BAFTA announcing the results of the first round of voting. As I expected Romola has got through to the shortlist, together with Vanessa Redgrave and the young girl who plays her when she is a child. It must be the first time in award history that three actresses have been short-listed for the same character. *Atonement* seems to be the favoured film as far as BAFTA is concerned. For some inexplicable reason Brenda Blethyn has also been short-listed for best supporting actress even though she has only a couple of lines. Strange coincidence: Brenda played Cordelia when I played Burgundy in that television *Lear* all those years ago.

Dora is home when I get back. Only one more week to go.

Sunday January 6th

Spend the day going through Lear for positively the last, last time.

Monday January 7th

Rehearse with Gemma who, in spite of all the setbacks and slights, has never lost her enthusiasm and never fails to give encouragement. She could be a good director one day, but the odds against finding success directing are a hundred times higher than acting. Tonight I watch Ian even more closely than usual. Can't get as enthusiastic about it as I did last year in Stratford, but am still looking forward to having a final fling. The casting director from the Donmar cannot make it and my agent, true to form, has failed to procure any other casting directors and is only popping in for an hour or so. She claims to have so much work, but not a lot of it appears to be falling in my direction. Other directors and casting agents that were coming in December are also unavailable. However I will have 20 or so old friends, a couple of aged cousins, my eldest son's in-laws, and Dora. It's pathetic really – but I still want to give it my best shot.

Tuesday January 8th

Play Lear again at last. It feels even better than the first time at Stratford – I know it like the back of my hand. His words, passion and pain flow through me: throughout the year Lear has seeped into my soul. It is not as difficult a part as Hamlet or Iago as there is no real verbal dexterity and wit, you just have to feel the truth of the situation and express the anguish and fury. A great part really does take you over completely, you forget being tired and can soar to peaks you didn't know you had within you. As I expire, on: "See there... see there..." I realise that I have now, finally, played Lear, and am so glad that we did this run after all. Good turnout from my loyal old friends, plus Ian, Michael Boyd and a couple of unexpected casting agents. My agent, who managed to turn up for the first half thinks I'm wonderful: as good as Gambon and Jacobi, and far better looking. Can I really trust my fate to such judgement? Perhaps I should seriously think about swapping deckchairs. But I know I did it as well as I could and would not have let anyone down if Ian had ever been off. Ian hugs me and says he almost envies me having Zoë and Naomi as my daughters. Meet up with Simon Ward, Richard Hampton and many other old cronies in the pub across the way: life feels good again.

Wednesday January 9th

Back to my dumb Butler in *Seagull*. So looking forward to having my evenings free and restarting a social life. I seem to spend the whole afternoon waiting to go to the theatre and the smelly, stuffy dressing room.

Guy tells me Romola has two new films, including a major role in Richard Eyre's new film: *The Other Man*, with Antonio Banderas and Liam Neeson.

Thursday January 10th

We have a meeting with three overweight DVD producers. They try to be accommodating and have made some concessions; we will get transport and UK residuals but not US for seven years. There may also be extra money from a second showing on Channel 4. Trevor is not present as he is in Coventry, where he began his career, directing his wife Imogen in a stage adaptation of Bergman's *Wild Strawberries*. At the same time, he is preparing *Gone with the Wind* – he never stops.

Friday January 11th

Arrive in the dressing room and see a red and white, official RSC bag on every place. I lift mine up and feel it is very heavy. I imagine it might be a bottle of scotch or champagne. I am disappointed and astonished to discover a dirty, dusty old brick, together with a note from Michael Boyd:

> *'We'd like to give you a small piece of the Royal Shakespeare Theatre to take away with you as you near the finish this week. Thank you for a gorgeous season of work. Come back soon.'*

I am very pleased that he has written at the bottom: *'PS Congratulations on your Lear.'* I don't know whether to be disappointed or flattered that my brick is heavier and dirtier than Guy's or Seymour's. I phone Dora and tell her I have been given a dusty old brick; she tells me not to dare to bring it home. After offering it to all and sundry I duly deposit it in the waste basket.

Russell, who is getting ever more desperate as the job comes to an end, tells me he has phoned my agent and asked her to take him on. She told him to send her his CV – it must be pretty thin.

He then asks me to put in a good word for him. I say I will, although if she does take him, he's such a schmoozer, I know she'll spend longer on the phone to him than any of her other clients.

It is announced that the film is definitely on. They have agreed to provide transport and food, and give us a share of the UK rights – not much advance on the money though. Final day of the run tomorrow. We will say goodbye to *Seagull* forever tonight and do *Lear* for the final time on stage tomorrow.

Saturday January 12th

Haven't felt so demob happy since the end of my National Service in 1960. We have done 135 *Lears* and 102 *Seagulls* in ten theatres across four continents. I've managed to get to the end once more without missing a performance and have covered McKellen for positively the last time. On top of that, Chelsea beat Spurs 2-0.

Gerald, though he plays the lead in *Seagull*, has no lines at all in *Lear* and has decided that it will be bad for his image if he does the film. I wonder if he will regret missing out on the two and a half grand in a few weeks' time. As soon as the curtain comes down, he shaves off his luxuriant black beard and reveals a rather pointed chin. Zoë has never seen him without his beard – will she still fancy him? I hug him tightly and wish him the best of luck in Hollywood – he'll need it. Ben Addis, who just goes through life very quietly and efficiently (with his women as well as his career) has got a part in the new play about Harold Macmillan at the National and, like Richard, won't be available for all the filming. Trevor is going to bring some extra people in.

Can't face end-of-run party in the White Hart at the top end of Drury Lane – I don't think many of the others are going either. It all seems a bit mundane in comparison to some of the places we've been to in the past year and besides, it's not goodbye – we still have three weeks together on the film.

In spite of everything I'm so glad I did this job. When I began my career at Leatherhead in 1960, an old actor called Cyril Wheeler advised me never to turn down a job. He said when he looked back, there were so many jobs he'd regretted turning down and very few that he'd regretted accepting. It's so true. You always get something out of every experience and there has been an abundance of good things on this tour, not least seeing so much of the world with Dora, and getting to know and admire Ian, but apart from Bill, who will always be my friend, I don't think I have formed any other lasting friendships.

I go home to cherish Chelsea's victory on *Match of the Day*.

Sunday January 13th

Charlotte and Jake spent the night with us as Rubin and Georgie had to go to a big party. When Rubin arrives to pick them up I tell him the story of Boyd's brick and show him the card, stating its authenticity. Ever the lawyer, he says I was fool to throw the brick away as it could have fetched hundreds on eBay. I blame it on Dora; she tells me to ask for another brick and say I left the first one on a bus.

Wayne Eagling arranges a box for us at the Coliseum. We see a beautiful production of *Swan Lake*. I know nothing about ballet but even I can see the immaculate standard of the corps de ballet. Dora says that the English National Ballet are now as good as Covent Garden and she should know, having been a solo dancer with the Vienna Opera. Wayne tells us that he has had to weed out so many of the young English dancers because, like our footballers, they lack the dedication and skills of the foreigners. Very depressing, but there is a wonderful atmosphere in the huge and beautiful Matcham theatre: so many pretty young girls in their best frocks with their proud mothers and grandmothers. There are even a few boys. Afterwards Wayne and his wife Monique come back with us and Dora gives our first dinner party in months. It feels great to be free and socialising again.

Tuesday January 15th

Dora and I go to the Mellon Exhibition at the RA. Can't read notes beside the pictures: they have been deliberately put low for the people in wheelchairs. There is not a single wheelchair in the building. I ask an attendant why they cannot at least have two sets of information by every picture, with one at the eye-level of the 99.9% of the public that have paid to see the exhibition. I am told to write a formal complaint – which, being an increasingly irascible old reactionary, I do.

Wednesday January 16th

Groundhog Day returns yet again. We are in a beautiful arts centre in an area of north Hammersmith I never knew existed, re-blocking Act I Scene II of *Lear*. Everybody is present, apart from Melanie and Romola, who apparently is in Vietnam. Trevor assures us it was a long-standing commitment. Ian asks who will tell her of the changes we are making. Trevor replies he will, but she has told him not to worry, as she knows a great deal about film acting. Trevor does not look as fit as I thought – I wonder if he pushes himself too hard.

Frances tells us she saw a clean-shaven chap smoking a cigarette by the stage door on Saturday night. As she passed him, he said, "Good night, Frances." She nodded, thinking it was a member of the audience, before realising it was a beardless Gerald, with whom she has played 102 passionate love scenes over the course of the year.

Pleased to hear that Frances and Bill have also discarded their bricks – perhaps they weren't valuable after all.

Thursday January 17th

The list of BAFTA nominations has come through; Romola has missed out. I know it is mean and petty of me, but I cannot help but be relieved.

Russell has got an agent so I no longer feel guilty for not recommending him more strongly to mine – I probably did him a favour. Melanie won't be at rehearsals: she has gone to Paris. No idea why.

Friday January 18th

Philip rings Peter and tells him he is opting out because he has a horror film in Prague. At the rehearsal he tells Trevor he will only do the *Lear* film if the schedule is rearranged around him; Trevor is furious. Philip leaves rehearsals and Peter, hoping that the part will be his, is on tenterhooks all day, declaring: "I've told my agent to tell them to make up their minds soon, I won't put up with this uncertainty." I tell him to be quiet and to thank his lucky stars if he does get to play the part, which would be a marvellous break for him. But there is no justice in this business. Nothing is resolved as rehearsals end. I wonder if Peter will get lucky.

Saturday January 19th

Meet Peter in street looking very disconsolate. He tells me he met Philip last night in their local gym, who greeted him with: "You've got to play hard to get." Trevor has given in, and Philip has got all that he wanted. Peter is naturally very disappointed, but perhaps Philip is right. You have to be ruthless to get on in this business. It could be the reason I never really made it. I was rehearsing an obscure play by Byron at the Young Vic in the early eighties when out of the blue I was offered the role of the father in the Kentucky Chicken advert. It only required two days filming but the fanatical young director at the Young Vic refused to release me. I should just have taken the two days off but my agent at the time was one of the old school and insisted that I stuck by my contract – pointing out it wouldn't do to fall out with the director as he was bound for big things. So I didn't do the advert, that went on over several campaigns and would probably have earned me a small fortune. The play was a flop and the brilliant young director sunk without trace, but on second thoughts, I don't suppose the role of the father in the Kentucky Chicken advert would have led me back to Hollywood.

Three young actors have come in to take over Gerald's bits and some of Richard and Bens' lines – they won't be available all the time as they have started rehearsing their new plays. It is refreshing to have new, keen people around who seem grateful to be working.

Sunday January 20th

Trevor gets excellent reviews for *Scenes from a Marriage* in *Sunday Times* and *Mail on Sunday*. I suspect it will transfer.

Receive an email from Martin Jarvis in LA. Martin has perfected the art of email: his are always profoundly witty and literary. He has just landed a marvellous job – recording the entire Bible as the voice of God over the course of the next few years. It is a star-studded cast, including Jon Voight as Abraham, Richard Dreyfuss as Moses, Malcolm McDowell as Solomon and Michael York as the Narrator:

'Terence Stamp 'let go'. Me engaged! On Tues have a photo call with not only Shelley Berman but also Stan Freberg…!? Surely this must be a dream I once had involving the wireless and Norwood Sunday lunchtimes years ago…Only person I have seen at the studio so far is M. York. Clearly the Americans feel the tale is best told by a Bromley boy and that, naturally, God was an Englishman.'

Monday January 21st

Polish driver picks me up at 6.30 to drive me to Pinewood. I hardly recognise it from the time I did all those movies there in the early sixties; worthy British productions with the likes of Dirk Bogarde and Nigel Patrick, horror films with Vincent Price and Lon Chaney, epics such as *Heroes of Telemark* with Richard Harris and Kirk Douglas, and even the Disney version of *Dick Turpin*, when I played my only title role and thought I was on my way to being a star. Memories come flooding back – the thrill of having my name on the back of my chair, my stand-in bring me my tea, lunches in the oak-panelled dining room, alongside Anthony Quinn, Yul Brynner and Tony Curtis (it was a great status symbol to eat there, as small parts and extras had their own canteens). I come back to my present humble reality and am pleased to be sharing a very comfortable dressing room with Jonathan Hyde and a large bowl of fruit. Jonathan is being put up in a luxury hotel nearby and his agent has obviously negotiated a good deal.

We do the short first scene with four cameras rolling and complete it within an hour – there is no time to waste as Trevor has to shoot fifteen minutes a day. As ever with filming, you are no longer really in control of your performance. The director can use whichever take or angle he wants, whereas on stage the actor can ensure that he is seen and heard. The rest of the day is spent shooting around Philip, which does not concern me and I am back home by 11.30.

Tuesday January 22nd

Romanian driver picks me up at 6.15. He tells me he has only been here for five weeks. I ask him how on earth he finds his way around – he points proudly at his satnav. It must be a more reliable one than mine. Even though it takes us up a narrow country lane and through a flooded ford, we get to Pinewood by 7.30. Find I am no longer in the comfortable dressing room with Jonathan Hyde but in a very stark one, sharing again with my old mate Seymour. There is no sofa or dressing table, just two chairs and a bowl of fruit on a small table. All there is for me to do is sit and wait in the dressing room, apart from a cursory look-in from make-up, until 9.15. It was ever thus with filming: everyone is terrified that you won't be on the set on time, so each assistant puts your call earlier than necessary to cover themselves.

We shoot the first big scene, where Lear divides his kingdom. Everyone seems to be playing it so quietly for the cameras that there appears to be none of the excitement or drive there was every time we did it in the theatre. Ian's speeches are broken up in stops and starts – I wonder if they will be as powerful when the different takes are knitted together. Filming is often tedious, particularly in this case when we have played this material so many times.

Romola has returned, looking very cool. I suppose all this is very small beer when you are about to start filming with the likes of Banderas and Neeson. She does indeed know a lot about filming but, in my humble opinion, still manages to play her first scene wrong. She still laughs irritatingly when Ian asks her how much she loves him (I know Ian has asked her not to laugh on numerous occasions but she still persists). Why doesn't Trevor tell her? Or is Romola right? Have I been wrong all this time? She is playing Cordelia as young girls behave today – self-confident and not in awe of authority and age. It is only natural that old fogies like me would find it irritating.

What has happened to the gargantuan meals of location catering? A terrible lunch is served on set in a plastic box: fish fingers and canned peas. Not many bottoms will get fat on this. Once more, I wistfully recall the old, oak-panelled dining room and the lunches alongside the stars.

I have been provided with a desk on which I write down Lear's edicts. Am very surprised and chuffed when Trevor gives me my own close-up – but is it destined for the cutting-room floor?

Finish filming at 7pm; Angolan driver gets me home at 8.15. Very tired.

Thursday January 24th

Afghan driver picks me up. We talk about *The Kite Runner*; he has read the book and seen the film. His own story is in many ways similar: his father was a general with the old regime, who was executed after one of the struggles for power. His mother sold their big house in Kabul with 16 rooms for £1,000 to get out via Pakistan with him and his two brothers, and eventually stay with their grandparents here. One of his brothers is now a doctor, the other's training to be an accountant. Do I believe him? I think I do.

Nick Hytner is refusing to let John Heffernan have any time off from his rehearsal calls for *Major Barbara*. It seems very petty as they will have two months to rehearse and John is hardly playing a leading role. Trevor therefore has to shoot around John as well as Philip, which means we do the long scene at Goneril's house, but leave out John's two entrances – it takes more time and it will be difficult to recapture the tempo of the scene when we do them out of context tomorrow. It is also a further strain on Ian. I don't know how he manages to get through these terribly long days without proper breaks, stand-ins or without even a chair to sit in. He bears it all with incredible patience.

I overhear one of the crew telling Frances how a certain knighted actor berated him when he omitted to call him 'Sir'. I contrast this with the humility and gentleness of Ian and wonder how this company would have coped if they had really been faced with a paranoid star.

The sets seem very blank – just plain castle walls – apparently this is what Trevor wants. He's told the designer to get rid of all the extra dressing that had been brought in, such as burning flambeaux and carts. I notice that many of the crew are foreign; how many of the English are actually working? Where are they? A black, cockney, Arsenal supporter drives me home: nice to talk football and have something in common.

Friday January 25th

Another incredibly long and tiring day. The Angolan driver, who

I discover lives round the corner from me, picks me up at 7.30. At 9am we do the John Heffernan inserts and then the crucial 'reason not the need' scene. Trevor shoots it in four long chunks on four cameras, and watches it all played back to him on four separate screens. Ian decides to go full blast and gives superb take after take. He uses his eyes more than he did on stage: at times in his despair his eyeballs disappear into his brow. He told me once that Ian Holm deliberately gives a completely different performance on every take, leaving it to the director to decide which one to use. McKellen goes slightly down that road and, as ever, each route he offers leads to the heart of Lear. Trevor appears to be happier than he has been for much of the year and is very excited with what Ian is doing. For me, the most pleasing sight of the day is of Ian and Trevor walking off the set with their arms around each other's shoulders, caught up in mutual enthusiasm like the two Cambridge students they once were.

At five, after we have been on our feet all day, except for an hour at lunch (which today has been provided by proper location caterers: fried scampi and cold chips – a definite improvement, though 'in the country of the blind the one-eyed man is king'), Ian is very tired and finally asks if he can have a chair. Around the edge of the studio, in semi-darkness, we can see some members of the crew, whose functions are far from obvious, sitting chatting very comfortably. Our first assistant director Suzanna, a friendly lady of indeterminate age who would make a good primary school teacher, finds a plastic garden-type chair and Ian flops into it. Within a minute or two he is called back on set and when he returns he finds another member of the crew sitting in his chair. He then suggests, very politely, that if his name were to be put on a chair it might be reserved especially for him. *SIR IAN MCKELLEN* is duly stuck on the back with gaffer tape.

After four hours I am also getting very tired with lugging on the heavy wooden box, which I have carried on and off stage on four continents, upstairs and down, carefully avoiding the backs of heads and clambering over sprawling feet. I point out that it is my job to carry it on in the scene but not to take it back out of shot when the director calls 'Cut'. I feel very satisfied when one of the chaps who has seen sitting at the back all day (and wearing an Arsenal shirt), is summoned to carry my box off the set. I am even more pleased, when we eventually get to the end of the scene and I follow Lear out into the storm, to realise I will never, ever, have to carry that bloody box again. So, this long engagement is really drawing to its close... I feel the first flush of anxiety that comes to any unemployed actor: will I ever work again?

The Angolan driver, who seems to have adopted me, gets me home at 8.15, where I find two grandchildren waiting for me to read them a story. Very pleased to have three days off.

Tuesday January 29th

A Somali driver takes me to Pinewood by the most circuitous route imaginable: via the Chelsea Embankment, King's Road, Fulham Broadway, Lillie Road, the M4, then across country from Langley. It takes almost two hours – much longer than it should, but I learn a great deal about my driver. He has been here ten years and has great hopes for his three children; two boys who are junior footballers with QPR and Brentford, and a girl who hopes to be a model. Even though he lives near Slough, he is terrified for their safety. One son was attacked on the top of a bus by three Afghan boys, after his mobile phone. Every driver seems to be a decent chap, only wanting work and genuinely liking this country: "Here you have good system. You get fed up with Blair – he goes. Next year you get fed up with Brown – he goes. In Africa – they never go." But how many more immigrants can we take?

The studio has now been transformed into a windswept heath with marshy peat and clumps of bushes in front of a great cyclorama. It looks very impressive. One of the criticisms of the stage set was that with the castle wall always in place, you never really believed that Lear was out in the storm; there can be no doubt now. We do the great scene of Lear meeting the blinded Gloucester, which the call sheet blandly describes as: *'Two old men'* When I come running on and discover Lear, I promptly trip over a bush and go arse over tit. Trevor laughs.

In the afternoon we move on to Lear's awakening with Cordelia. Ian asks if his wheelchair can be put at an angle so that he can actually see people when he opens his eyes. Romola is unhappy with her position and does not like Russell, as the Doctor, putting his smelling salts under Ian's nose whilst she is speaking, but Trevor sorts things out very gently. One of the newcomers, asks me what on earth is wrong with this company – why do some of them slag off Trevor? When he worked with Trevor before all the company loved him. He also confides he cannot believe how bad Philip is, although I suspect his judgement may be coloured by the fact that he originally auditioned for the part himself. Actors are never generous towards those who get the part they coveted – I never forgave David Hemmings for getting the part of Modred in Camelot. We both tested for it.

It's getting like the end of term. People are leaving gradually as they finish shooting their scenes. Say fond goodbyes to Naomi and Ben Addis. Melanie, Guy and Heffernan have also gone.

Wednesday January 30th

Driven in by a Romanian who has only been here for five weeks. He was recruited by the firm in Bucharest. They told him they needed drivers and that they would provide the car. It must be a scam: a sort of sweatshop of cheap drivers who are sent onto our streets, armed only with a satnav. I wouldn't like the job; I had no idea how terrible the traffic is throughout the entire day. I am only scheduled for one scene and am back home before lunch.

Very pleased as I am going with Rubin to see Chelsea play Reading this evening.

At 3.30 I am phoned by the studio to say that they want me back. Trevor has had to let Philip fly back early to his horror film in Prague and he will have nothing to shoot in the last hour: he's decided he can do one of the small scenes I have with Jonathan Hyde. A Hungarian driver ploughs me back through thick traffic. He waits whilst I do the scene and then takes me on to Stamford Bridge. I arrive at half time and have missed the only goal of a very boring match. Still it is nice to be with Rubin – I've spent so little time with him this past year.

Thursday January 31st

Nelson, my Angolan neighbour, drives me to the studio. Today Trevor will shoot the three scenes in the storm. My small scene with Jonathan is the first on the schedule. We act under a real torrent of cold rain – warm electric fires and blankets are provided. I am finished within an hour, but poor Ian and Sylvester will be soaked all day.

Monica has small part in a film in Warsaw and will be flying back, as will Philip from Prague, for the final scene on Saturday. Then *Lear* will irrevocably be put to rest.

Dora and I go to cinema for the first time in months to see *In the Valley of Elah*. It is the best American film I've seen this year. In my opinion, Tommy Lee Jones gives a far deeper performance than Daniel Day-Lewis in *There Will Be Blood,* and it has an ending, which *No Country for Old Men* most certainly does not.

Friday February 1st

Interesting article in today's paper which quotes the Association of Graduate Recruiters:

'*Those born after 1982 are seen by employers as unrealistic, self-centred, fickle and greedy, with a massively over-inflated opinion of their own abilities. They expect everything to fall into their laps and, chances are, they will be cruelly disappointed.'*

Sounds like some people I know.

Saturday February 2nd

The last day. I am driven by the younger brother of the Afghan driver, who is studying accountancy. He tells me the identical story of their father being a general in the old regime so it must be true. He asks me how much I am being paid for doing this film; I ask him how much he thinks.

"Oh, about £20,000."

I tell him it is closer to two and a half. He cannot believe it. He can earn more than £2,000 a month minicab driving.

Trevor takes a long time doing Lear's final scene. He shoots it in one long take with four cameras. Ian manages to find a completely new voice to the one he has used on stage – it is soft, loving and frail; his face is full of love. We complete the third take and seem to wait in tableau for eternity before Trevor calls "Cut." He leaps over to Ian and embraces him: "If we did it 20 more times, we'd never get a better one than that."

"Please let me go again."

Trevor reluctantly goes back behind the cameras. He still has to shoot half of the big scene before the battle after this because Philip, as noted, was in Prague on the day it was scheduled. Ian goes back to his start position and picks up Romola. Trevor calls: "Action".

Ian staggers forward, trips on a tuft of grass – perhaps the same tuft of grass that I stumbled over the other day – and drops Romola's shapely bottom onto the peaty ground. Romola graciously accepts Ian's profuse apology. Then Ian does another heartbreaking take. We freeze, as before, until Trevor calls: "Cut". He rushes over and once more embraces Ian, but says he is still going to use the first one. Ian has finished *Lear*: the crew applauds.

I go up to Trevor to say goodbye – he 'Trevs' me, as he did on the first day.

"Dear David, thank you. I'm sure we'll see each other again very soon."

Does he mean it? Do I really want to do another play for him? Of course I do – I'd be off again like a shot if he asked me. I exchange a cordial handshake with Jonathan Hyde and we each wish each other well.

I go upstairs and change, before going into Ian's dressing room to say goodbye. He is sitting slumped on a sofa, stripped to the waist like a boxer after the most gruelling fight. He thanks me for my support and for being a true friend; he sensed that I was thrilled to uncover the play each time we did it. He apologises for never being off and hopes I am not too disappointed that I never played Lear, apart from in the two understudy runs. I lie and say, "Of course not." We embrace and he says he expects to see me and Dora soon.

Gemma is in the corridor; I kiss her goodbye. There is no one else around. Frances and Peter, the only other cast members called today and to whom I would have liked to say goodbye, are on set shooting the remaining scene. Russell and Sylvester departed days ago as did Bill, whom I'm sure I will see again very soon.

As I go out of the door the television is tuned to Sky Sports News. Anelka has just scored, to put Chelsea 1-0 against Portsmouth. I get into a car driven by one of the Romanians and excitedly turn on my little radio, looking forward to a satisfying drive home, relishing in the promise of yet another Chelsea victory. As we drive out of Pinewood's gates, Portsmouth equalise…

Afterward

Friday 11th January 2008

David – Dear David

Last Tuesday morning I left home with the trite delight in my heart of 'going to see a mate in a show'! Little did I know that I was setting out on a journey that was leading me towards something not dissimilar to St Paul's trip on the road to Damascus. I was, by the end of the play, to have, simply put, an Epiphany!

The 'Luvvie' chatter and laughter engendered by the meeting of Friends-From-Ago and Friends-From-the-Here-And-Now belied the experience-by-proxy of the human tragedy that we were about to undergo – the Tragedy of Lear. We'd hardly managed, amidst all the brouhaha, to take in the sweeping, heavy majesty of the blood-red swathed 'stone' set, before there you were, centre stage, gold crowning your magnificent shock of white hair, bearded and regal, every inch the King, commanding our silence in an instant, at once diminishing us from larky friends to humble servants and awestruck fans.

The next three and a half hours were, for me, nothing short of a revelation. For decades I have casually accepted that you are a good, solid actor (how else could I deign to call you Friend?!) but last Tuesday you made me redress the easiness of that qualification. Last Tuesday – at 13.00 hours – with the rain and wind howling without (and within!) – you didn't prove (for you had nothing to prove!) – you ripped open my eyes and mind to the simple fact that you are a GREAT ACTOR! No – a GREAT, GREAT, GREAT ACTOR!

"Some are born great, Some become great and Some have greatness thrust upon them." You were born great, you didn't have to become great, all you needed, was for this fickle industry to thrust greatness upon

you so that we might – at last – know it!

Your performance was so exquisitely measured – I have seen quite a few Lears, but never before have I 'felt' Lear! I raged with him, cried with him, howled with him and had my heart broken with him. You have given me a gift to carry with me for the rest of my life and it's YOUR Lear that I'll chatter about, around the idle dinner party tables. To meet the delicate balance of Majesty and Simple Man and have us find this Lear loveable is a phenomenal feat.

If there was a modicum of fairness in the world, you would unquestionably be up there with the Greats. I fervently pray that someone somewhere will have been as breathtaken as I was and will, at last, open that huge and heavy door. It's a travesty that this was called 'an understudy performance'! I challenge <u>any</u> of those who smugly tread those boards each night, safe in the conquest of 'having got the part', to meet the levels you reached under such inclement odds!

I am so proud of you, so proud of your extraordinary achievement and for retaining so sweet a heart, so honoured to know you and privileged to have been there on Tuesday 8ᵗʰ of January 2008. I'll not forget it.

With awe and admiration and love,
It's never too late…..!

Genevieve

Dear Genevieve – way, way, way over the top of course – but it's the nearest thing to a notice my now-defunct Lear will ever receive, and it brings a grateful tear to my eye.

PS: Chelsea reached the Final of the Carling Cup – and lost to 1-2 to Spurs!!

At least Melanie was happy…

About the Author

 David Weston was born in London and was educated at Alleyn's School Dulwich where he was taught by Michael Croft and helped to found the National Youth Theatre. After National Service, where he was commissioned in the Royal Artillery, he won a scholarship to RADA. After seasons of rep in Cheltenham and Manchester he spent most of the sixties making films, including leading roles in such classics as *Becket, Heroes of Telemark, Masque of the Red Death* and the leading role in Walt Disney's *Legend of Young Dick Turpin.* Although he has appeared in countless television series and plays, from *Dixon of Dock Green* and *Z Cars,* via *Minder, Lovejoy, Doctor Who* to *East Enders* and *The Bill,* his main career has been in the theatre where he has appeared in 27 of Shakespeare's plays, many of them several times.

He is married and has two sons and four grandchildren, and has supported Chelsea FC since 1957.